PAINT SHOP PRO 8
ZERO TO HERO

Sally Beacham
Ron Lacey

friendsof

DESIGNER TO DESIGNER™

an Apress® company

PAINT SHOP PRO 8: ZERO TO HERO

At friends of ED our mission is to unleash your digital creativity, providing technical know-how and inspiration in equal measure.

With our Zero to Hero series we've gone one better—we'll take you further, faster.

Zero to Hero is more than just a catchy slogan and an endless opportunity for gimmicks, puns, and graphical representations of phone booths, tights, and capes. It's a style of learning designed by friends of ED to reach beyond dry technical explanations and dusty old authors who wouldn't know good design if it slapped them round the face with a wet fish.

You can either first learn everything you need about Paint Shop Pro 8 or dive straight into the inspirational "Hero" chapters and refer back if you get stuck. When you're done, you'll be ready to wear your underwear outside of your pants, metaphorically speaking of course.

We'll not only unlock the toolset for you, we'll also feed your imagination—that's a promise.

So, what are you waiting for?

About the Authors

Sally Beacham is an instructor at LVS Online (www.lvsonline.com), specializing in Paint Shop Pro and Photoshop-compatible plug-in filters, Xara X, and FrontPage. She's been a private tester for Jasc Software, Corel, Alien Skin, Auto FX, The Plugin Site, and many other software companies. She also teaches Paint Shop Pro, graphics, and web design at community education programs in southern Maine.

Sally writes a column for for PSP Power (www.psppower.com) or, more accurately, she takes dictation for the FilterMunky, who tests and reviews plug-in filters specifically for use in Paint Shop Pro.

Sally's husband, John, many children (Wade, Emilie, Brittanie, Peter, George, Nina, and Dominic), and two cats (Moussie and Einstein) are grateful she occasionally looks away from the computer to acknowledge them.

You can visit Sally's web site, which features Paint Shop Pro resources and tutorials as well as resources for Photoshop-compatible plug-in filters, at www.dizteq.com.

Ron Lacey is an active member of the Paint Shop Pro community, where he is known as the vector guy. As well as running his own web sites, Ron has written tutorials for the Jasc web site and contributes a regular column to the PSP Power Newsletter (www.psppower.com). Being an avid amateur photographer and darkroom enthusiast for over 25 years sparked his interest in computer graphics in general and Paint Shop Pro in particular. As a private beta tester for Paint Shop Pro 6, 7, and 8, Ron has been able to stay on top of the Paint Shop Pro learning curve. He teaches Adobe Illustrator, Digital Photography, Digital Darkroom and, alongside Sally, several other Paint Shop Pro classes at LVS Online (www.lvsonline.com).

Ron makes his home with his wife of 30 years, Claire, and an Alaskan husky named Bijou in the country just north of Thunder Bay, Ontario. Semiretired from the heavy construction industry, he has plenty of time to spend working with computer graphics and pursuing his other interests, including sailing, scuba diving, photography, and during the very long northwestern Ontario winters, downhill skiing.

Angela Cable has been using Paint Shop Pro since version 3 and also was a beta tester for Jasc Software. She develops numerous resources for Paint Shop Pro and runs the resource and tutorial site www.psplinks.com.

Peggy Taranenko teaches beginner level classes in Paint Shop Pro at LVS Online (www.lvsonline.com), has been a Paint Shop Pro fanatic since version 6, and was a private beta tester for Paint Shop Pro 8 and other software. What began as a hobby, along with a 10 year fascination with computers and graphics, has evolved into a web design business. Peggy actually does have other interests, but those who know her can't fathom what they could possibly be.

Chapter Zero   1

Learn the Paint Shop Pro basics, and get started with material selection and the paint brush tools.

Chapter Zero

Selections and Text   27

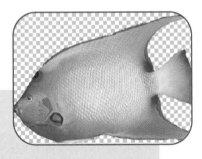

Make accurate selections with a variety of tools and learn how to add text to your images.

Chapter One

Layers and Masks   57

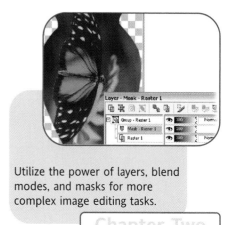

Utilize the power of layers, blend modes, and masks for more complex image editing tasks.

Chapter Two

The Digital Darkroom   83

High-quality photo editing and restoration techniques.

Chapter Three

Filter Effects 109

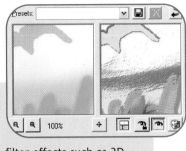

Use filter effects such as 3D, bevels, and art media to add extra dimensions to your images and text.

Chapter Four

Drawing with Vectors 133

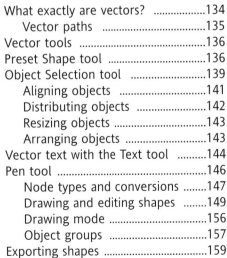

Create artwork for your graphic design projects using the vector drawing tools.

Chapter Five

Special Image Effects 161

Add fun elements and
special effects using prebuilt
Picture Tubes and
the deformation tools.

Chapter Six

Web Graphics 181

Optimize and export
graphics for the Web.

Chapter Seven

Paint Shop Pro 8: Have It Your Way 207

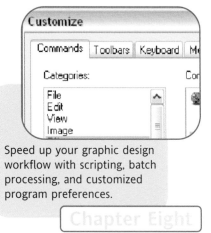

Speed up your graphic design workflow with scripting, batch processing, and customized program preferences.

Chapter Eight

Digital Divorce 223

Remove and replace unwanted sections of your photos.

Hero 1

Creating Logos with Vector Graphics 237

Combine vector graphics, text, and layout templates to create professional artwork and logos for print.

Hero 2

Web Page Interface 249

Build stylish navigation buttons and web site graphics.

Hero 3

Appendix: Paint Shop Pro 8: Resources on the Web 267

Index 271

Chapter Zero

Is that a Paint Shop Pro 8 CD-ROM sitting next to your computer? Perhaps you got it as a gift, or maybe you're interested in digital photography and someone recommended Paint Shop Pro to you. Or maybe you want to design web graphics, or images for a brochure, newsletter, or card-creator program.

Many computer books on the shelves these days perceive their readers as "dummies" or "idiots." But we know you're not a fool. Sure, your computer might reduce you to feeling like a "zero" from time to time, but that's another matter. We're here to turn you into a Paint Shop Pro "hero." By the time you finish this book, you'll be able to do just about anything you want with a digital image.

In this chapter, we look at the stuff you need to know about Paint Shop Pro 8 in order to make sense of this book. A couple of concepts might be a bit unfamiliar, but they'll soon be behind you so you can skip ahead and jump in anywhere throughout the book.

How to use this book

This book is broken down into three distinct sections to help get you working right away:

★ Chapter Zero: In this chapter (which you're currently reading), we cover all the basic concepts that you need to get the most out of Paint Shop Pro.

★ Chapters One through Eight: In these chapters, we've grouped everything you'll actually want to do in Paint Shop Pro. Although the chapters are arranged in order of ascending difficulty, they're also broken down into steps and examples that you can apply to your own work, dipping in wherever you choose.

★ Hero chapters: It's all very well being able to use the software, but we've added some chapters to really get you thinking and working like the hero you undoubtedly are.

And all the way through the book, you'll find every step clearly illustrated so you can see exactly what's going on.

Styles

To make things a little clearer, we use a few special typefaces in the book:

★ If we have any specific files to mention, we'll write them like this: `thisphoto.jpg`.

★ Menu commands are written out using little greater-than marks, for example: Selections > Modify > Expand.

★ If we're mentioning an important point for the first time, we'll make it **obvious**.

★ Finally, really important points and special tips will appear in boxes like the one on the right.

> *Yes, this one!*

Download files

Although all the examples in the book are designed so that you can apply the techniques and effects to your own images, we've also provided a chapter-by-chapter set of files available for download from www.friendsofed.com. This set of files will allow you to work along with the images you see in the book should you prefer to.

Support

We at friends of ED pride ourselves on our book support. Although we're confident that everything within these pages is easy to follow and error-free, don't hesitate to get in touch with us on the message boards at www.friendsofed.com/forums.

Getting started

Assuming you've installed Paint Shop Pro 8 according to the instructions that came with your software, fire up the program so you can start learning how to use it!

File format associations

If this is the first time you've opened Paint Shop Pro, you'll be presented with a dialog box that asks you to choose file associations. The default setting associates only the Paint Shop Pro proprietary image formats with the application, which are `.PspImage`, `.Psp`, `.PspFrame`, `.PspShape`, and `.PspTube`. However, you can choose to associate any of a mile-long list of image formats with Paint Shop Pro, which allows you to click directly on a file of that type in Windows Explorer and have Paint Shop Pro automatically open. Simply check the box to the left of any file format you would like associated, and then click OK.

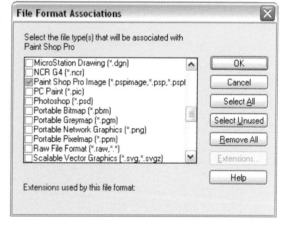

We strongly suggest that you *don't* associate the `.gif` format with Paint Shop Pro, as some GIFs contain animation that can't be viewed in Paint Shop Pro itself and could be damaged if you attempt to do so. You might choose to associate the `.jpg`, `.bmp`, `.tif`, and `.png` file formats with Paint Shop Pro, as these are the most common image file formats you're likely to encounter. However, even if you don't associate these formats with Paint Shop Pro, you can still open them from within the application and, as you'll discover in Chapter Eight, you can change just about any preference you designate at any time from within the application itself, so don't worry about having to live forever with the consequences of your actions (unlike in real life!).

Paint Shop Pro 8 interface

Once you've chosen your file associations, you're confronted with the Paint Shop Pro interface. Let's take a little tour:

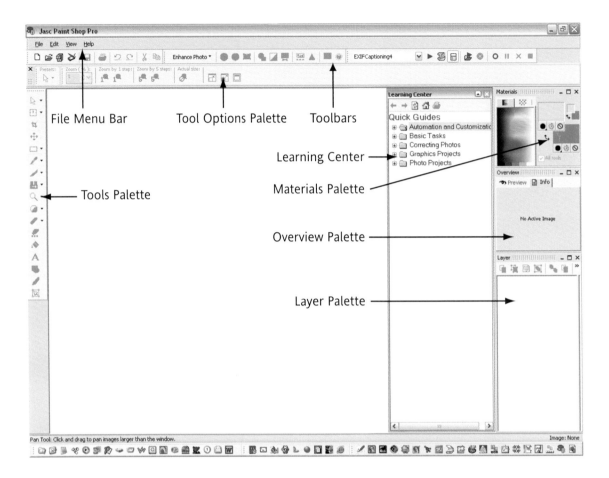

If you've already been using Paint Shop Pro and your workspace doesn't look like this, you may want to rearrange the furniture for ease in locating the tools and features we discuss. If you're comfortable roaming around the workspace in your current layout, don't touch it. Otherwise, follow these steps:

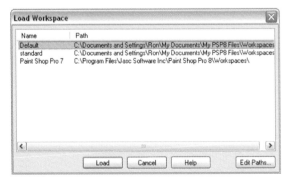

1. Go to File > Workspace > Load.

2. Highlight the Default entry and click Load.

Your workspace should now look similar to ours.

Across the top of the workspace is the File Menu bar. This area contains menus grouped in the familiar Windows-style sequence to help you find features within Paint Shop Pro. Let's use one of those commands now.

Starting a new image file

1. Go to File > New. The New Image dialog box opens.

Let's begin with the Image Dimensions area. Here you define the width and height of the image you want to construct, as well as the units of measurement and image resolution. The default setting for Units is **pixels**. Pixels are the basic building blocks of digital images, as displayed on a monitor, and they're the common unit of measurement when constructing a web graphic. In this book, we normally work on images measured in pixels.

2. Set the units of measurement type to pixels (if it isn't set to pixels already) by selecting Pixels from the Units drop-down menu.

3. Set both the Width and Height to 500. You can type 500 directly in the field (don't worry about the red highlight that shows up when you erase all the digits—that's a signal that the current value is "out of range," and it disappears when you type a number in).

The default image resolution is set when you install Paint Shop Pro as 200 pixels per inch. You can change this if you like, but normally, a setting of 200 pixels per inch is adequate for printing and doesn't affect a web graphic.

Let's move along to the Image Characteristics section.

4. By default, Paint Shop Pro chooses a raster background for images. For now, leave this set (we explain vectors in greater detail in Chapter Five).

5. As for Color depth, choose 16 Million Colors (24 bit). You can choose anywhere from 2 colors (1-bit) up to 16 million colors (24-bit), but in most cases the 16 million colors option gives you the flexibility to do anything you want, whereas the other options don't. You can always

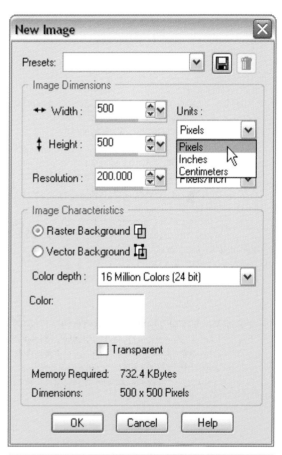

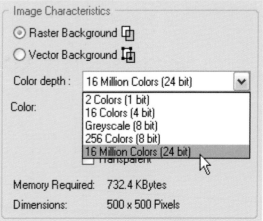

decrease the color depth later in the image construction process, if required.

6. You can choose any color you like for your image background by unchecking Transparent and then clicking the Color swatch.

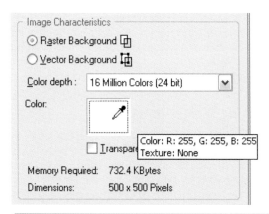

The Material Picker opens. You'll see this dialog box time and time again in Paint Shop Pro 8.

7. On the Color tab, click the red square in the upper-left corner of the color blocks (sometimes described as **swatches**).

We cover this dialog box in more detail in a bit, but for now, all you need is a solid red background. When you click the red chip, the Current color swatch at the right side of the dialog box changes to red.

8. Make sure that the Current color is red and then click OK.

9. You should now be looking at the New Image dialog box once again, with red set as the Color. Now that your image characteristics are confirmed, click OK to open your new image file.

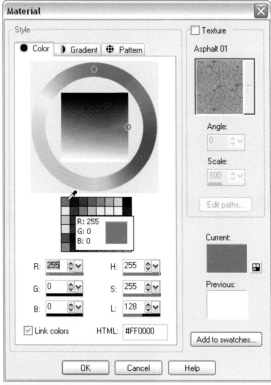

Would you look at that? An active 500x500 pixel image, with a red background color—success!

Now that you have an image open, take a look at the File Menu bar. You'll notice that it's expanded quite a lot, with more options than before.

Let's move on and take a look around the work-space now.

Working with toolbars

Now that you have a little more space to work with, look at the various toolbars under the File Menu bar. You'll see the **Standard** toolbar, which contains icons for common operations, many of which are found in the File and Edit menus.

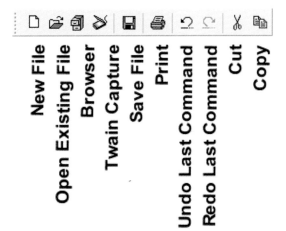

You'll also see the **Enhance Photo** toolbar next to the Standard toolbar. This toolbar contains icons and its own flyout menu for quick access to many of the photo enhancement tools. Click the down arrow next to Enhance Photo to open the flyout.

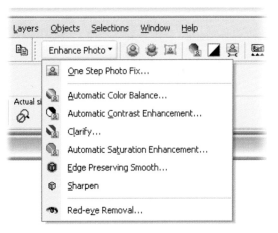

You can open a couple other toolbars that aren't turned on by default using the View > Toolbars menu option. See the little square box around the other toolbar icons in the menu? When the icon is surrounded by that square, the toolbar should be visible in the workspace. To turn it on, just click the menu item. Clicking the square again toggles the toolbar off.

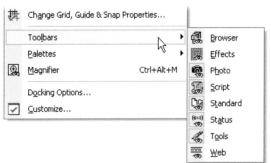

7

✫ Zero

You can drag a toolbar away from its **docked** position (when it's attached to a side of the workspace), which is called **floating**. To float a toolbar, just click the hatched line at the left side of the toolbar and drag it away from the side of the workspace.

We detail customizing the workspace in Chapter Eight, but if you should happen to inadvertently lose a palette or toolbar, try pressing SHIFT+CTRL+T to turn on any invisible palettes and center all undocked palettes and toolbars in the workspace. Alternatively, you can go to View > Workspace > Load and reload the default workspace.

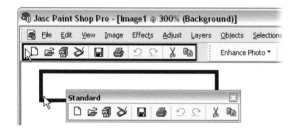

Tools palette

At the left side of the workspace is the Tools palette. These tools are the most frequently used features in Paint Shop Pro.

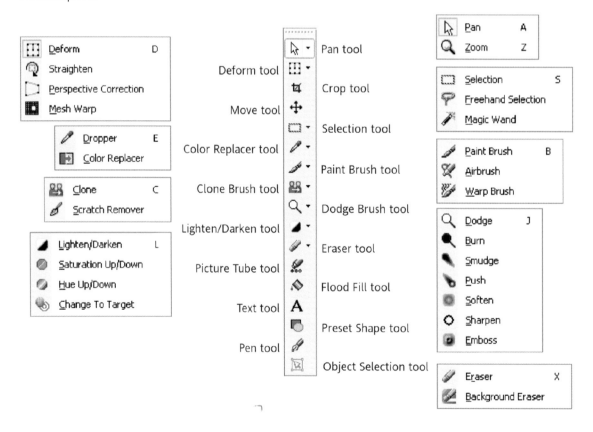

So many tools are available that they don't all comfortably fit on a toolbar sized for 800x600 monitor resolution (a common size), so some of the related tools are **nested**. Any tool with a tiny triangle to the right of it has a flyout menu containing similar tools. You click the tiny triangle to open the flyout. For example, there are different tools for creating selections, which are all stored with the main Selection tool button, as shown in the illustration opposite.

When you select a tool, it becomes the **active** tool in the Tools palette, which is indicated by the box highlight surrounding the icon. Also, if you hover your mouse over a tool icon for a second, the name of the tool is displayed in a tool tip.

Using the Materials palette

1. First, click the Flood Fill tool to make it active. Your cursor changes to match the Flood Fill tool icon.

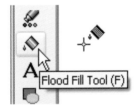

To the right of the workspace is the Materials palette. This allows you to define two different "materials" for use at the same time in Paint Shop Pro. A material can be a color, gradient, or a pattern, each of which can have additional texture applied to it.

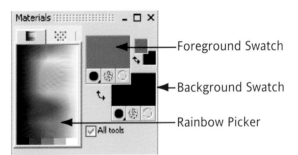

2. Make sure your Flood Fill tool is still active in the Tools palette, and then click directly on the **Background and Fill Properties** color chip in the bottom-right corner of the Materials palette (more commonly referred to as the **background color**).

When you click this chip, the Material Picker opens. Look familiar? You used this when you chose the red background color for a new image.

3. This time, choose a shade of blue by clicking a color swatch or by clicking a blue shade in the rainbow circle.

4. The hue range of the blue shade is represented in the box within the rainbow circle. If you would like a different shade within that range, just click the area in the box where the shade is located. The new color is represented in the Current color chip at the right side of the dialog box. Click OK when you're happy with the shade.

Look at the background color chip in the Materials palette—voila, blue! Now do the same thing with the other chip, the **Foreground and Stroke Properties** (or **foreground color** for short).

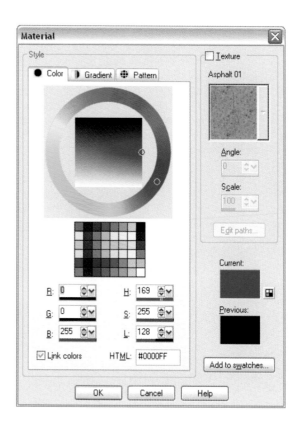

> *The terms "foreground" and "background" are arbitrary. Jasc could have easily used "Color 1" and "Color 2," or "Top" and "Bottom." In certain circumstances, the background color will automatically be used by Paint Shop Pro to complete an action.*

5. Click the foreground color chip in the Materials palette and set a new color in the Material Picker, just as you did in the last step. How about yellow?

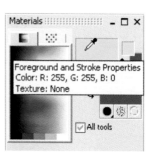

Now you have a red 500-pixel square image sitting on your workspace, the Flood Fill tool is active, and you have a yellow foreground color and blue background color in the Materials palette. All aboard?

6. Move your cursor over the red image and your cursor icon changes to a small fill bucket with a plus sign. Click anywhere in the image to fill it with yellow.

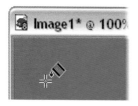

7. Don't like yellow and want to see blue? This time, right-click your image with the Flood Fill tool.

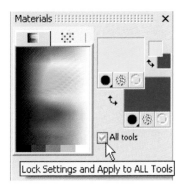

This is an important timesaving feature in Paint Shop Pro. As with many of the tools, left-click applies the foreground material and right-click applies the background material. If you check All tools in the Materials palette, any settings for foreground and background materials will be used by any tool in the Tools palette that uses materials. If you leave the option unchecked, you can assign different materials to different tools, which may or may not be desirable.

Painting with gradients

1. Now let's try a different kind of material. Click the little arrow at the corner of the color icon under the foreground chip to expand the flyout.

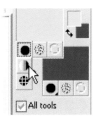

2. Choose the second icon in the flyout: the **gradient** icon.

Now you'll see a gradient (colors fading from one to another within a single swatch). If this is the first time you've used a gradient, you're probably seeing a blue-to-yellow gradient that runs vertically. This is called a **foreground-background gradient**, which uses the foreground and background colors as the start and end points of the gradient.

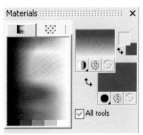

3. Click the foreground color chip to open the Material Picker. This time the Gradient tab is presented, on which you can make modifications to the gradient or pick a new one.

4. If the selected gradient is not a blue-to-yellow foreground-background gradient, click the Foreground-background drop-down arrow and select it from the gradient catalog (the gradients are listed in alphabetical order). It should now appear in the larger gradient swatch at the top of the Material Picker.

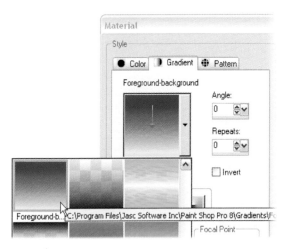

5. Turn the gradient Angle to 90 degrees either by typing 90 in the Angle field or by dragging the handle in the gradient preview. The cursor changes to a four-headed arrow when you do so.

6. Set the Repeats to 0. This controls how many times the gradient is repeated in the image. A setting of 0 repeats means that the gradient starts with one color on one side of the image and finishes with the second color on the opposite side (in the case of linear gradients).

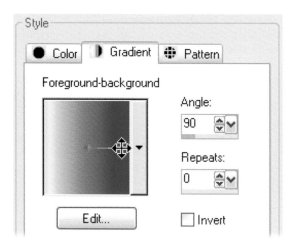

The Style section controls what type of gradient is produced:

★ **Linear gradients** are straight lines, graduating either top to bottom or left to right in an image.

★ **Rectangular** and **sunburst gradients** are similar. Both start at the outside perimeter of an image and fade to the second color in the center of the image.

★ **Radial gradients** are circular in nature, but the colors radiate like the hands on a clock.

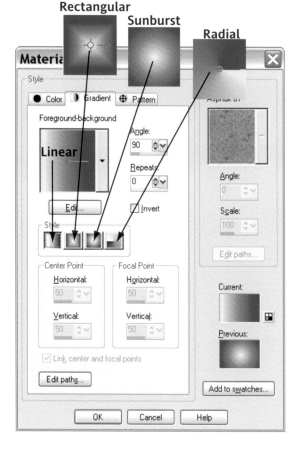

7. Click the sunburst style icon. You can also play with checking Invert. This reverses where the colors fall in the gradient.

8. You can move the center point of a sunburst, rectangular, or radial gradient by clicking directly on the large gradient swatch and dragging it, or by entering values between 0 and 100 in the Center Point controls (50,50 is the exact center). You can see these values take effect in the Current swatch preview.

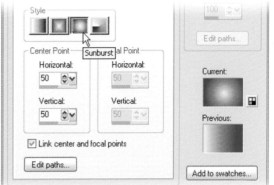

9. Click OK to set the gradient in the foreground color swatch of the Materials palette. Now use the Flood Fill tool to fill your image with this gradient by clicking anywhere within the image.

Now try setting a material using just the Rainbow Picker at the left of the foreground/background color chips in the Materials palette.

10. Hover your cursor over the rainbow spectrum area and you'll see a tool tip with information about the color under the cursor (which now looks like an eyedropper). Select a shade of green and right-click it to set that green shade as the background color.

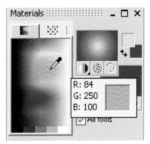

Easy, isn't it? Notice that the green color is set to the background, and the yellow color is *still* assigned to the foreground, but because you have a foreground-background gradient set as the property in the foreground color chip, that gradient is now yellow to green.

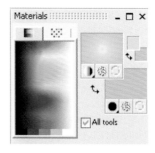

11. Now grab that Flood Fill tool again and right-click to fill the existing image with your green color.

Didn't fill the whole image? Don't worry, this is meant to happen—you control how the Flood Fill tool (and indeed any other tool) works using the Tool Options palette.

Tool Options palette

The Tool Options palette is located at the top of the workspace, under the main toolbars. This palette contains the controls and settings, and is **context sensitive** for any tool: when you change tools, the Tool Options palette automatically switches to show the options appropriate for that particular tool.

Take a look at the Match Mode control. The default setting RGB Value means that for the Flood Fill tool to fill pixels, those pixels must match the red/green/blue (RGB) values of the target pixel (the actual pixel you place your cursor over). Tolerance defines how closely these values must match. A Tolerance of 0 means the surrounding pixels must match the target pixel exactly.

So why did it work in the previous examples? Because *all* the pixels were the same solid red, blue, or yellow background color. But, with a gradient fill, you have subtle color shifts from one pixel to the next.

You may now be asking why the RGB Match Mode only allowed a ring of color to be filled. This is because the Tolerance is set to 20 by default, which allows a small variance in RGB values. Turn the Tolerance all the way up to 200 and watch what happens when you right-click your image.

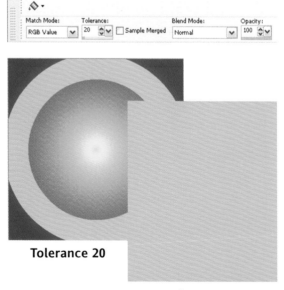

Tolerance 20

Tolerance 200

You don't have to fiddle with the Tolerance to get the Flood Fill tool to fill an entire image; all you do is set the Match Mode to None, so there are no matching criteria for the Flood Fill tool, and therefore all pixels in the image will be filled with the same material.

If your image is currently filled with a yellow-to-blue sunburst gradient with a green ring in it, you can reverse the action of adding the green ring with Edit > Undo Fill (CTRL+Z). You can also undo commands using the Undo button on the main toolbar.

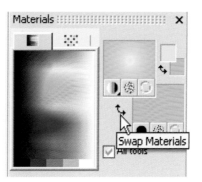

If you would like to flip-flop the foreground and background colors (which can be pretty useful at times), just click the little curved arrow between the two material chips.

Creating patterns with the Materials palette

There are many preexisting patterns in the Pattern catalog with which to fill your image.

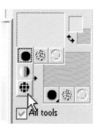

1. Click the pattern icon in the foreground color flyout to activate the patterns.

2. Click the foreground color chip itself to open the Material Picker again. The Pattern tab is similar to the Gradients tab, in that you can choose a pattern from the catalog by clicking the arrow to the right of the larger pattern preview pane.

3. Have a look around inside the drop-down pattern catalog and choose a pattern you like. Try the Autumn leaves pattern.

4. Change Angle to 45, change Scale to 150, and click OK.

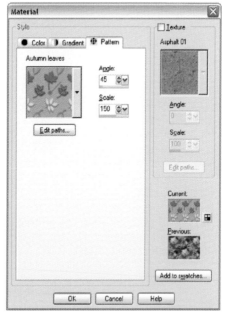

5. Now click in your image with the Flood Fill tool to see the pattern applied.

6. For an interesting quick trick, go into the Tool Options palette and set Match Mode to RGB Value, set Tolerance to 20, and right-click anywhere on the orange background. This should fill the background only with the background material assigned in the Materials palette (green, in this case).

You can also flood fill with a lowered **opacity** (transparency). All the flood filling you've done so far has completely covered up any pixels you've filled. But if you lower the Opacity setting in the Flood Fill Tool Options palette, you can add subtle variation without completely covering the existing pixels.

7. Click the background materials chip in the Materials palette and then select the Pattern tab in the Material Picker. Browse to the Marble pattern in the catalog.

8. Leave Angle set to 0 and set Scale to 200. Click OK.

9. In the Tool Options palette, set Opacity to 25 and return Match Mode to None. Now right-click in the image to apply the marble pattern at a lowered opacity.

You can click several times to see the pattern build up. If you continued clicking, the pattern would eventually cover the original, but two or three clicks will give you a subtle hint of the marble pattern without completely covering the leaves. If you feel you've added too much of the marble pattern, use Undo (CTRL+Z) until you're back to a point you like, and then experiment some more.

Creating custom patterns

Sometimes you'll want to add your own pattern to an image, or flood fill one image with another. It's a simple enough process.

1. Decide on the second image you want to use and open it (File > Open). Here you're going to use a photograph. Browse to your photo on your hard drive. You can choose to leave the Open dialog box set to display All Files or limit the view to a certain file type.

2. Once you find a photo you want to use, highlight it in the Open dialog box and click Open to open the file in Paint Shop Pro.

You now have two images open on the workspace: the original 500x500 image that you've been experimenting with and the new photograph. If the photograph you've chosen is very large, it's not going to make a good pattern fill unless you resize it. So how do you see how big an image really is?

3. Click the title bar of the photo in the workspace to make it the active image (the lettering on the title bar of the selected image is darker than the lettering on the other image, which is now grayed out).

4. Go to Image > Image Information (CTRL+I). A dialog box opens that gives you mounds of information about any image, whether created by yourself or from any other source.

On the Image Information tab is the name and type of file listed, and a section detailing the image dimensions. This is the information you need right now. If your image is larger than 500x500 pixels, it's already larger than the original 500x500 pixel image you've been flood filling, so you may need to resize your photo to make a good pattern fill.

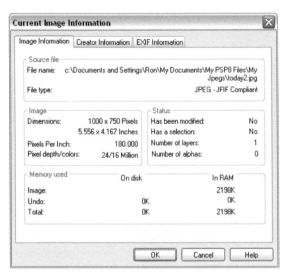

Another source of this image information is the Overview palette, which is docked to the right side of the workspace by default. If you can't see it, try toggling F9 to make it visible.

5. Click the Info tab in the Overview palette. The image dimensions are here, as is the color mode (this was defined when you started a new image).

It's important to be aware that *increasing* the size of an image significantly will result in the loss of image quality, whereas decreasing the size of an image is okay.

6. Go to Image > Resize (SHIFT+S) to open the Resize dialog box.

This dialog box allows you to resize an image by either a specific pixel value or a relative pixel value, or by a print size should you want to print out your image. The original image dimensions are at the top. Right now, you're only concerned with resizing the pixel dimensions. You'll set your photograph to be 240 pixels wide.

7. Make sure that Lock aspect ratio is checked, and then choose Pixels from the Pixel Dimensions drop-down menu.

8. Type 240 in the Width field, and the Height setting automatically updates because you told Paint Shop Pro to keep the aspect ratio constant in the last step. Click OK to resize the photo.

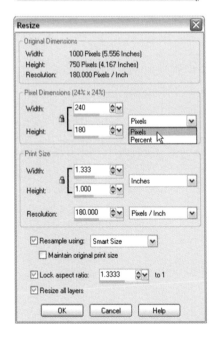

Now that your photograph is an appropriate size, you'll use it to fill another image. This time, though, it's time to give another tool a workout.

9. First, minimize the 500x500 pattern image you've been using. It's still available to be used in the workspace, but it's minimized to its title bar at the bottom of the workspace. This leaves you with only your photo open on the workspace.

Let's begin another new image.

10. Go to File > New and, in the New Image dialog box, use the following settings:

* Width and Height: Both 500 pixels
* Color depth: 16 million colors
* Raster background: Selected
* Image background color: Transparent

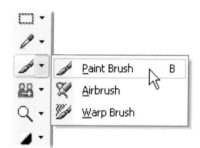

Now you have a 500x500 pixel image with a checkerboard background, which indicates that the image background is transparent.

Paint Brush tool

1. Activate the Paint Brush tool now (B). It's on the same flyout as the Airbrush and Warp Brush tools.

You can use the Materials palette with the Paint Brush tool exactly as you did with the Flood Fill tool. You can set foreground and background materials, which you can then apply to your image. Right now, you're going to set your resized photo as your foreground material.

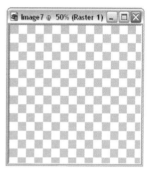

2. Click the foreground color swatch in the Materials palette to open the Material Picker. Click the Pattern tab, and then open the Pattern catalog.

At the very top of the catalog are thumbnails of any open images on the workspace, including those that are minimized (which is your marble/fur/leaf pattern).

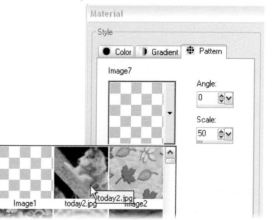

3. Click the thumbnail of your photo to make it the active pattern and set the Scale and Angle options for that photo/pattern too, if you wish.

Flood Fill tool

Paint Brush tool

Look at the Tool Options palette now that the Paint Brush tool is active. See how the options have changed with this now tool?

The basic brush tool can be shaped into either a circle or a square, and then modified further. Let's examine the various brush options:

Size: The size can range from 1 to 500 pixels. This option determines the size of area you cover with each brush stroke. When you're painting with a pattern, the size increases the area covered by a single impression of the brush, not the scale of the pattern.

Hardness: A brush may have very hard edges (a setting of 100), which means that brush impressions leave clearly defined edges. A hardness setting of 0 would result in a brush with very faded edges, and soft-edged brushes are very good for painting and photo repair work.

Step: This refers to the space between one brush impression and the next. If you click and hold down the mouse button while dragging the brush across your image, and you have a low step setting, the impressions will be very close to each other, resembling a solid stroke of color. With a very high step setting, the impressions look more separated from each other.

Density: A brush with high density values transfers all the pixels from the foreground (or background) material setting within the size and hardness parameters already set. So, a brush with a high hardness setting, a low step value, and a high density value appears to paint a very solid stroke. Hardness affects the edges of the brush stroke, but density affects the entire brush impression.

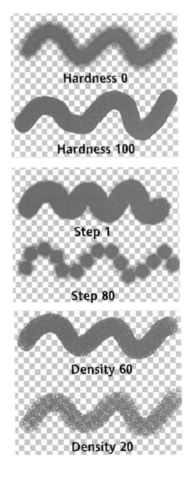

Thickness: This determines the shape of either a circular or square brush. Thickness settings of 100 leave the brush at the original basic shape, whereas lower settings change a circle shape to an ellipse and a square shape to a rectangle.

Rotation: This determines the angle the brush is "held" at. A circular brush shows no change, even if the rotation is changed, but a square brush rotated by 45 degrees becomes a diamond.

Opacity: Lower this setting to paint with a more transparent version of your material.

4. Okay! Now that you know what all those settings do, set them up for your pattern. Use the settings as shown in the following Tool Options palette (you can press TAB to advance quickly from one control to the next):

5. Once you've set the options, click once in the middle of your image. You should see a diamond-shaped impression filled with your photograph pattern.

You can use single clicks to place brush strokes randomly around the image, or you can hold down the mouse button and drag the brush around to simulate painting.

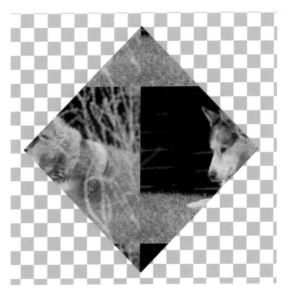

Here we've changed the scale of the pattern to 50 and painted the entire image. We've used a grass green foreground color and a black background.

6. Try alternate left- and right-clicking around the perimeter of your own image with the diamond-shaped brush to produce a border effect.

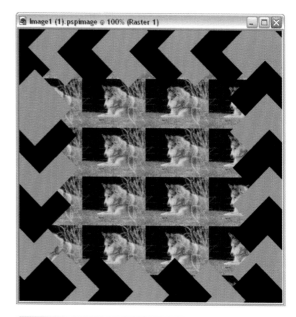

Saving images

Let's clear a few images off the workspace.

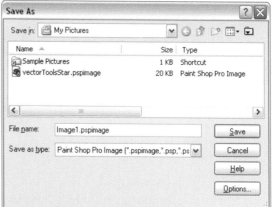

1. To save any of the masterpieces you've been working on, click the title bar of the image you would like to save and go to File > Save As (F12).

2. Browse to the folder where you would like to save your image and, in the Save as type field, choose to save your file as a Paint Shop Pro Image. This will save any Paint Shop Pro–specific information in your images. You'll see later in the book how to save images so that others can view them.

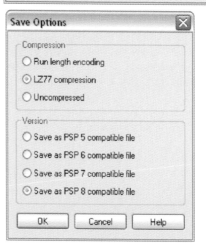

3. Finally, give your image file a descriptive name and click Save.

You can also save your Paint Shop Pro 8 images in a file format that is compatible with previous versions of Paint Shop Pro. This might be important if you've used previous versions yourself, or if you share files with other users.

To do this, click the Options button in the Save As dialog box.

You can save with compatibility as far back as version 5 of Paint Shop Pro. Be aware, however, that if you've used a feature in your image that wasn't available in the previous version, it won't show up in the saved version. This particularly affects any vector information, and gradients or text in certain cases.

You can use the Window > Close All command to close all images open on the workspace.

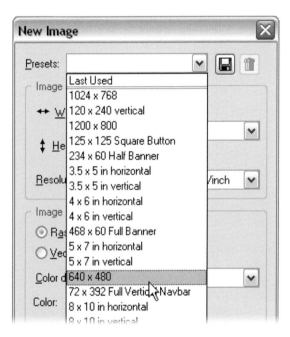

Painting with the Airbrush tool

1. Open another image (CTRL+N), and this time choose the 640x480 preset image size from the Presets drop-down menu in the New Image dialog box. Check the Transparent background color and click OK.

> *This* Presets *list contains some common and useful paper sizes, such as a postcard or business card. The image resolution has been set for the tasks the paper sizes are designed for.*

2. Activate the Airbrush tool (it's on the same flyout as the Paint Brush tool).

The Airbrush tool is very similar to the Paint Brush tool, except that the Paint Brush tool makes only a single impression when you hold the mouse button down; no more paint is applied. With the Airbrush, as long as you hold down the mouse button in the same spot, more and more paint is applied (known as **build-up**) until you release the mouse.

3. The Airbrush tool options behave similarly to the Paint Brush tool options. Set the Airbrush Tool Options palette as shown here:

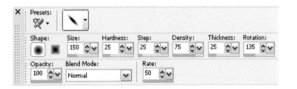

The Rate is peculiar to the Airbrush tool. A high setting applies more paint if the brush is dragged slowly or pauses in one place. A low setting applies the amount of paint consistently, no matter what the speed of the mouse is. Set the Rate to 50.

4. Click the foreground materials chip on the Materials palette and go to the Gradient tab.

5. Select the Rainbow gradient from the gradient catalog. Choose the Linear gradient style and check Invert.

6. At the top right of the dialog box, check the Texture box and scroll through the texture drop-down catalog to the Pinwheel texture.

> Textures and patterns are very similar in Paint Shop Pro. The major difference is that patterns are generally thought of as color and textures in shades of gray.

You might be wondering what the Add to swatches button does. A **swatch** is the Paint Shop Pro term for a "favorite material." You can save your favorites as a swatch, whether they're a particular color, gradient, or pattern.

7. If you want to save the rainbow gradient with the pinwheel texture as a swatch, click the Add to swatches button in the Material Picker and name the swatch something descriptive, such as Hero Rainbow Swatch. Now your material is saved for future use.

8. Click OK to set the foreground material.

9. Click the right tab in the Materials palette. Your new swatch is highlighted here. Also, notice that the texture icon (the center of the three icons beneath the foreground color chip) is depressed. This indicates a texture is currently applied to the material, which can be toggled on and off with this button.

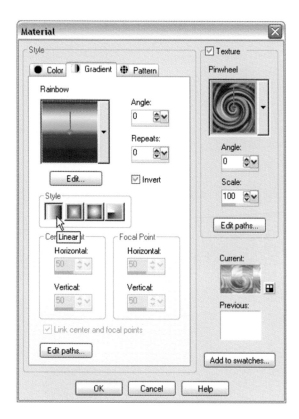

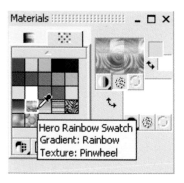

10. Choose a background material now. Click the background material chip and click the Pattern tab in the Material Picker.

11. Browse to the Gumballs pattern, and leave Angle set to 0 and Scale set to 200. Click OK.

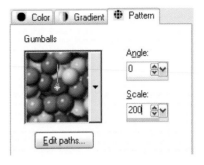

12. Now that you've set the Airbrush, foreground, and background materials, begin by right-clicking the image with the Airbrush tool and, holding down the right mouse button to build up the paint, brush diagonally across the image several times.

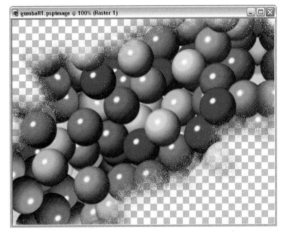

13. Now add the foreground material (left-click and drag), building up the paint so that it completely covers the top-left corner of the image. Repeat the action in the bottom-right corner, only this time don't build it up as much.

If you don't like the position of the gradient with the blue color at the bottom of the image, you can return to the Material Picker and invert the gradient, and then apply red pinwheels to the bottom area of the image and blue to the top.

But what happens if you build up too much paint, or you wish to remove paint from certain areas of the image?

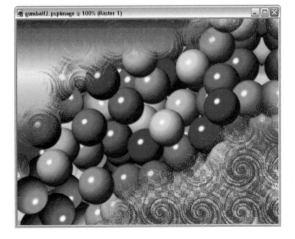

Eraser tool

The Eraser tool can clean up many mistakes and perform image tricks of its own. It's located on the same flyout as the Background Eraser tool in the Tools palette. The icons look similar, so make sure you've selected the regular Eraser tool!

1. The options for the Eraser tool are very similar to those for the Airbrush tool. Set the tool for a circular shape, Size 100, Hardness 25, Step 25, Density 100, Thickness 100, Rotation 0, and Opacity 100.

2. Click and drag the Eraser tool all around the perimeter of your image. Don't worry about making it neat and exact.

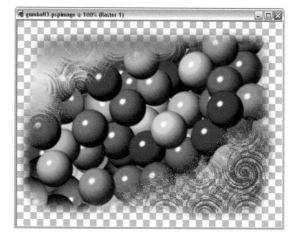

3. Return to the Airbrush tool. Click and drag all around the border to apply the rainbow pinwheel material. If you want to build the color up in certain areas, just go over it with the Airbrush tool again, or hold down the mouse button and let the Airbrush tool build up color in that spot.

4. Go to File > Save As and save this image as a `.PspImage`.

What's next?

In this chapter, we started with the necessary information, such as where to find the download files (www.friendsofed.com). Then we moved on to show you how to open new files, choose materials for your tools, and use several tools to create or paint images. It might not feel like much, but you've already mastered many basic Paint Shop Pro skills. Hero status is just around the corner. . . .

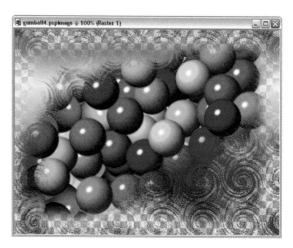

Selections and Text

In this chapter

In Chapter Zero, you learned how to navigate the Paint Shop Pro workspace, open new and existing files, save files, and use basic features such as the Paint Brush tools and Materials palette. In this chapter, we show you how to use the Paint Shop Pro selection tools to create images exactly the way you imagine them. In addition, we show you how to create and add text in a variety of ways to your images. We cover the following topics:

★ Basic and complex shape selection

★ The Freehand Selection tool

★ The Magic Wand tool

★ Text effects

★ Vector, floating, and selection text

One

Selecting basic shapes

You can think of a selection as the fence that keeps the flock of sheep in one area on the ranch—and that also keeps the wolf out of the sheep pen. If you select an area or object within an image, you can restrict or confine any actions you perform solely to that area. Without first selecting an area, any action you perform will be applied to the entire image.

If there is a selection on an image, it's indicated by a blinking **marquee** (sometimes referred to as **marching ants**). You can use selections to define an area for different purposes:

★ To protect it from further image manipulations while you work on other parts of the image

★ To perform actions solely on the defined area

Selections can be either **floating** or **defloated**. Think of a floating selection as creating a duplicate area that "hovers" over the surface of the image. You can move or modify this selection without actually changing the image below it, but this is a temporary condition. Once you defloat a selection, it becomes part of the image below it and any action you apply to that selection will alter the whole image.

Another important concept to understand when working with selections is **aliasing**. This refers to the characteristic "stair-step" look of pixels against a lighter background. If the object is made up of vertical or horizontal straight lines, aliasing is needed to keep them looking crisp and clear. However, due to the nature of pixel representation, if curved edges and angled lines are aliased, their edges can look jagged.

Anti-Aliasing softens the edges by blending the pixel colors along the edges of the object with the background color to minimize the stair-step effect. In many circumstances, an anti-aliased selection can produce a better-looking object, but it can also produce messy or blurred edges. We experiment with anti-aliasing on images in the following examples.

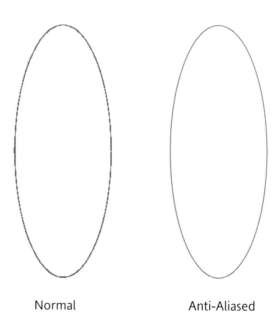

Normal   Anti-Aliased

Selection tool

1. Open a new 24-bit color image (CTRL+N) with a white background.

2. Click the flyout for the selection tools menu in the Tools palette, and choose the Selection tool.

3. Go to the Tool Options palette (if you can't see it, try toggling F4), which now displays the options for the Selection tool.

4. The Selection Type drop-down menu contains a number of different selection shapes. Choose a simple rectangle first.

5. To draw the selection, click at the top left of your planned selection and drag the mouse across and down. Release the mouse when you're happy with the selection, and you'll see the marching ants.

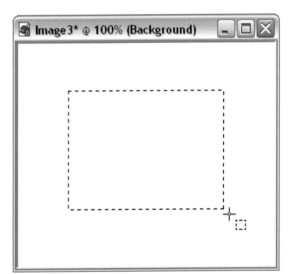

6. You can also position your cursor precisely when you begin drawing the rectangle. Turn on the Overview window (View > Palettes > Overview or F9), click the Info tab and, as you move your cursor over the image, the cursor's current coordinates are updated in the Cursor Pos field.

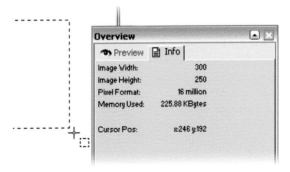

7. If you already know the dimensions of the selection you want to make, it's often helpful to turn on the grid with View > Grid (CTRL+ALT+G). You can set the size of the grid in View > Change Grid, Guide & Snap Properties.

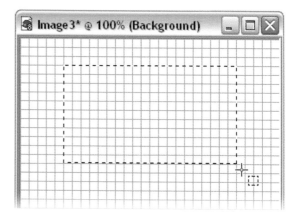

Let's see what happens when you attempt to do something to your image.

8. Set different foreground and background colors in the Materials palette.

9. Choose the Flood Fill tool (F) and click in the middle of the rectangular selection. Only the selected rectangle should fill with your new foreground color.

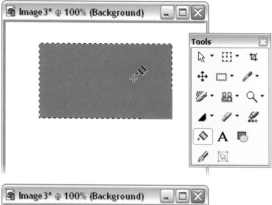

10. Now right-click outside of the rectangle selection. Nothing happened? This is because you're attempting to perform an image action *outside* of the selected area, and Paint Shop Pro ignores you.

11. If you right-click *inside* the selected rectangle, your rectangle should fill with the background color set in the Materials palette.

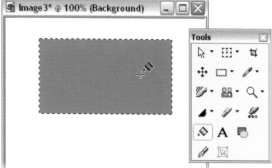

Deselecting selections

It's just as important to know how to deselect a selection as it is to select it in the first place. You do this with Selections > Select None (CTRL+D). Once there are no active selections on an image, any action you perform will affect the whole image. If you press CTRL+D and choose the Flood Fill tool again, left-clicking anywhere inside the image will fill the image with the current foreground color.

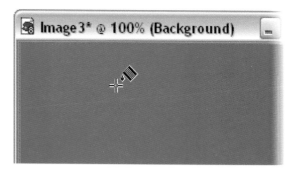

Selecting complex shapes

Paint Shop Pro comes with many preset selection shapes. Use the rounded rectangle to help produce a more complex selection shape.

1. Open a new 400x400 image and activate the Selection tool.

2. Choose Rounded Rectangle from the Selection Type drop-down menu in the Selection Tool Options palette and, this time, set the selection Mode to Add.

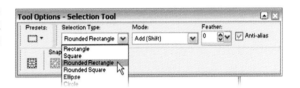
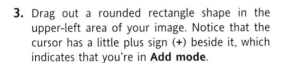

3. Drag out a rounded rectangle shape in the upper-left area of your image. Notice that the cursor has a little plus sign (+) beside it, which indicates that you're in **Add mode**.

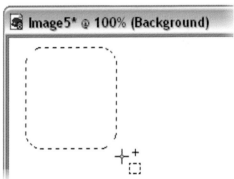

4. Make sure you're still in Add mode and drag out a second rounded rectangle that overlaps the lower-right corner of the first selection. When you release the mouse, you have a single selection combined from the two.

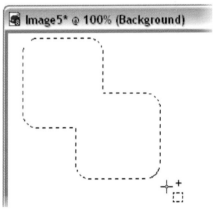

You can use the **Remove mode** of the Selection tool to further refine selection shapes. Whereas Add mode adds to the current selection, Remove mode deletes any portion of the selection you're applying that overlaps the existing selection. You can tell when you're in Remove mode because the cursor also modifies itself, this time with a minus sign (–).

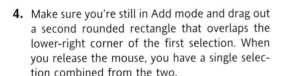
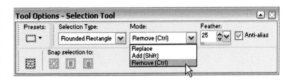

You can apply these modes without changing the setting in the Tool Options palette by using the keyboard:

★ Hold down the S<small>HIFT</small> key while dragging to **add** to a selection

★ Hold down the C<small>TRL</small> key to **subtract** from an existing selection

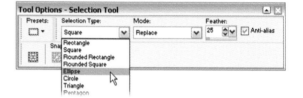

Feathering a selection

1. Open a photograph that has an element you would like to use for a vignette.

2. Choose the Selection tool in the Tools palette.

3. Open the Selection Type drop-down menu in the Tool Options palette and choose a shape for your vignette. Here we've chosen the Ellipse shape, which we'll use to select an elliptical area on the photo.

4. In the Feather field, insert a value of 25. The amount of feathering applied determines how smooth the transition is between the unselected and selected areas. Higher feather settings create softer edges, and lower values produce harsher edges. Leave the Mode setting at Replace and keep Anti-alias checked.

5. Click with your mouse cursor at the center point of your planned vignette and drag outward. Dragging horizontally increases the width of the ellipse, and dragging vertically makes it thinner.

6. Don't release the mouse until the ellipse is the size and shape you want. While you're drawing the selection, you'll see the ellipse represented by solid lines and, when you release the mouse, you'll see the marching ants indicating an active selection.

7. Go to Selections > Invert (CTRL+SHIFT+I). This reverses your selection, deselecting the ellipse and selecting the rest of the image instead.

8. Now set the background swatch on the Materials palette to a color you'd like the vignette background to be. White or a soft pastel may be a good choice.

9. Use Edit > Clear or just press the DELETE key. This will remove the selected area of the image and replace it with the background color in the Materials palette.

10. Press CTRL+D to deselect everything.

11. Save your file (File > Save As).

Freehand Selection tool

The shape Selection tool is handy, but life and nature don't present you with images or objects that neatly fit into the preset selection shapes. In such cases, you need a selection tool that allows you to draw your own precise selections: the **Freehand Selection tool**.

In the Freehand Selection Tool Options palette, the Mode and Feather options function identically to those of the shape Selection tool and are common to all freehand selection types. Smoothing enables you to round out sharp angles or curves as you draw the selection. You can enter a value between 0 and 40. The higher the value, the smoother your selection will be.

The Freehand Selection tool has four different selection modes that are appropriate for use on different images. Let's try them out!

Edge Seeker mode

The Edge Seeker mode does what its name implies: it tries to seek out edges and select them.

1. Open queenangel.jpg (included in the download files).

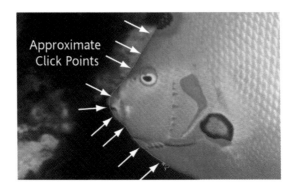

2. Activate the Freehand Selection tool and set the following options in the Tool Options palette:

   * Selection type: Edge Seeker
   * Mode: Replace
   * Feather: 0
   * Range: 10
   * Smoothing: 10
   * Anti-alias: Checked

In this mode, you click along the edge where you would like a selection created. The Range setting lets you define how far away from the edge a selection point will be made yet still "snap" to that edge. The Edge Seeker will look for an edge within a range of 0 to 15 pixels from the point you click. Smoothing smoothes out any jagged edges and sharp curves, although you may not want to apply smoothing if you need a precise selection.

3. Click along the edges of the fish, adding a new click wherever there is a curve or change in direction. Keep the selection marquee on the outside edge of the fish, rather than inside the blue edge.

Approximate Click Points

4. You may want to zoom in to around 150% to 250%. If you miss the edge and want to undo a click, press the DELETE key and the previous click will be deleted, allowing you to redo that section.

5. Once you've finished clicking all the way around the fish, right-click or double-click and the selection marquee becomes active.

6. You can now copy your fish with Edit > Copy (CTRL+C) and paste it as a new image with Edit > Paste > Paste as New Image (CTRL+V). It's a fish out of water!

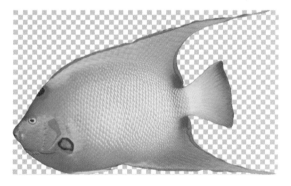

Freehand mode

This mode allows you to draw precise selections by hand.

1. Open ducks.jpg. This male mallard looks a little outnumbered with all those female ducks chasing him. Let's give him somebody on his own team to even the odds.

2. Activate the Freehand Selection tool and choose Freehand from the Selection type drop-down menu. Set Mode to Replace, Feather to 10, and Smoothing to 10, and check Anti-alias.

3. Click and drag around the male mallard in a roughly elliptical shape, avoiding all the female ducks. This action is similar to a paintbrush action—you don't need to click to make a direction change.

4. When you release the mouse the selection marquee will close, completing the selection.

5. Copy the selection with CTRL+C.

6. Go to Edit > Paste > Paste as New Selection (CTRL+E). A second mallard will appear on your existing image but with no marquee visibly active. However, if you move the mouse cursor at all, you'll see that the selection is "stuck" to the cursor.

7. Drag the second duck to position it and click once to drop it in position. At this point, you'll see the selection marquee active around the second duck, and the cursor turns to the four-headed Move tool. You can now position this selection precisely in your image.

Eureka, there's a new duck in town!

Point to Point mode

Point to Point is a straight-line selection between mouse clicks. The first click is the start of a selection, then a straight-line segment will join it to the next click, and so on. When you finish, a right-click joins the two ends and closes the selection marquee.

1. Open `sanfran.jpg` and `washington.jpg`. Here you are going to use the Point to Point selection mode to trace the roofline in `sanfran.jpg`.

2. Activate the Freehand Selection tool and then set the following tool options:

- ★ Selection type: Point to point
- ★ Mode: Replace
- ★ Feather: 0
- ★ Smoothing: 0
- ★ Anti-alias: Checked

3. Starting at the left edge, click and follow the roofline, adding a click wherever there is a direction change. You may need to zoom in to get in close to the chimney area and the eaves.

4. When you reach the right edge of the roofline in the image, click and drag straight down to the bottom-right corner of the image.

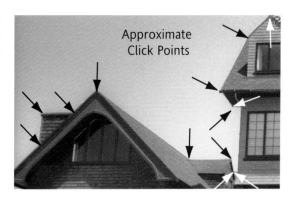

Approximate Click Points

5. Now click and drag to the bottom-left corner. Click again and drag straight up to meet the original starting point of your selection. Double-click or right-click to make the selection ends join up and become active.

6. Copy the selection with CTRL+C.

7. Activate the `washington.jpg` image by clicking its title bar, and go to Edit > Paste > Paste as New Selection (CTRL+E) to paste the San Francisco houses on the `washington.jpg` image.

8. Click the image to drop the selection, and position the houses with the Move tool if necessary.

Smart Edge mode

The Smart Edge selection mode is similar to the Edge Seeker mode in that it finds well-defined edges, but here you don't set a range. Use the Edge Seeker mode to select areas with subtle differences in color or lightness, and use the Smart Edge mode when there are strong differences. In this case, you'll use this image of a stargazer lily on a stark, contrasting green background.

1. Open `lily.jpg` from the download files.

2. Activate the Freehand Selection tool and set the tool options as follows:

- ★ Selection type: Smart Edge
- ★ Mode: Replace
- ★ Feather: 10
- ★ Smoothing: 0
- ★ Anti-alias: Checked

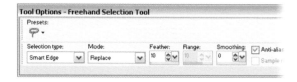

3. As you move the mouse, a perimeter box will follow. To make an accurate selection, you need to make sure that the edge you're selecting remains within that box. Click at each direction change and curve in the lily, working all the way around it. If you make a mistake, press DELETE to remove the previous point and redo it, always keeping the edge of the lily within the selector tool perimeter.

4. Once you've finished clicking all the way around the lily, right-click or double-click to complete the selection. Now invert this selection with Selections > Invert (CTRL+SHIFT+I).

5. Set the background color to white in the Materials palette.

6. Press DELETE and the green foliage area is replaced with your white background color.

Selections with the Magic Wand tool

All the selection tools you've used so far use physical drawing methods to produce the selection. The Magic Wand tool, however, can select areas based on color, hue, or brightness—and these areas don't even need to be touching each other or even all that similar in color.

1. Open the `sailboat.jpg` and `sky.jpg` images from the download files.

2. Make the sailboat image active and choose the Magic Wand tool.

3. Set the following options in the Tool Options palette:

   ★ Match mode: RGB Value
   ★ Tolerance: 10
   ★ Feather: 0
   ★ Anti-alias: Checked and set to Outside mode

Tolerance refers to the color variance that the Magic Wand will allow when picking pixels of a certain color. If Tolerance is set to 0, the Magic Wand will select only pixels of an exact color that are touching. As Tolerance is increased, Paint Shop Pro allows a greater variation from the initially selected color, so that pixels of closely related colors may be selected simultaneously. Here you're choosing a Tolerance setting of 10, which allows the Magic Wand to pick closely related colors, as well as the individual pixel you initially select.

4. Click in the middle of the sky area with the Magic Wand tool. You'll see that much of the sky area is now selected, but not all of it.

5. Hold down the SHIFT key and click in an area of the sky that isn't selected. An alternative to holding down the SHIFT key is to change Mode in the Tool Options palette to Add (Shift) and then click in any areas of the sky you want added to the selection, such as close to the shoreline and between the sails.

You've selected most of the sky, but there are still a few little holes in the sky selection.

6. Go to Selections > Modify > Remove Specks and Holes. When the dialog box opens, you'll need to zoom out using the Zoom Out icon to 12% (if you're using the example sailboat image). To preview the selected area without the unselected area, click the Toggle Selection icon.

7. Use the settings shown here in the Remove Specks and Holes dialog box to select the remaining small holes in the sky selection.

8. Click OK to apply the selection modification.

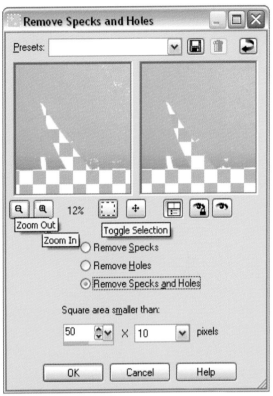

9. Now the sky area should be entirely selected. Go to Selections > Invert (CTRL+SHIFT+I) to select everything *but* the sky.

10. Press CTRL+D to deselect the marquee, and then save the image.

11. Go to Edit > Copy (CTRL+C).

12. Now activate the other image, sky.jpg, by clicking its title bar, and then go to Edit > Paste > Paste as New Selection.

13. Position the selected water/boat area on the new image so that only the new sky area is showing (none of the farmland should be showing).

14. When you have positioned it correctly, click once to drop it in place. There you go—the original dreary sky now becomes interesting!

Using the Magic Wand tool to select areas by color and then using the Selections > Modify menu to modify the selection can help you make complex selections easily. A couple of other selection modifiers that come in handy are as follows:

★ Selections > Modify > Expand expands the existing selection by a defined number of pixels.

★ Selections > Modify > Contract contracts the selection by a defined number of pixels.

These two features used in conjunction with the selection tools can be very handy when combined with layers (see Chapter Two) or many of the filter effects (see Chapter Four).

Editing selections

One of Paint Shop Pro's new features is the ability to edit a selection. By making use of this feature, you can create extremely detailed selections.

1. Begin by opening a new 500x500 image that's 24-bit color with a white background.

2. Using the Selection tool set to the Octagon shape, drag out a large octagon.

3. Go to Selections > Edit Selection to toggle on the Edit Selection mode. Your selection is now covered by a ruby overlay. Many of the normal selection modifier tools are now available to you.

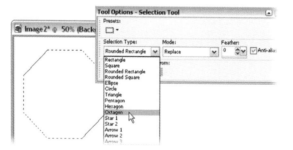

4. Click the Paint Brush tool and set the brush settings as follows:

   ★ Shape: Square
   ★ Size: 100
   ★ Hardness: 100
   ★ Density: 100
   ★ Rotation: 135

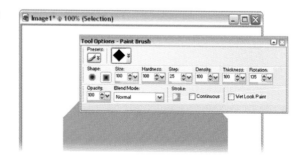

If you look at the Materials palette now, you'll notice that there are only black, white, and shades of gray in the palette. This is because the Edit Selection mode is a special mode that is a variation of the Mask mode you'll learn about in Chapter Three. If you use white (background or right-click drag) to paint on your selection edges, it *adds* to the selection. If you use black (foreground or left-click drag), it *subtracts* from the selection.

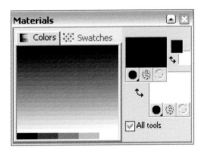

5. With your foreground color set to black in the Materials palette, use the Paint Brush tool to "dab" some diamond shapes in the interior of the octagon. Use the grid lines to help you align them in a pattern. You'll notice that wherever you click with the Paint Brush, the red overlay disappears and you can see the original background color.

6. Set your foreground color to white and add more diamond shapes outside the original octagon selection on your image. When white is the foreground color, you'll see the red overlay wherever you click with the Paint Brush.

7. Continue to paint with black and white to add and subtract diamond-shaped areas from your selection.

8. Choose Selections > Edit Selection to toggle the edit mode off again. Your new selection marquee should show on your image. Fill this new selection with a pattern using the Flood Fill tool and the foreground color in the Materials palette set to Pattern.

9. Go to Image > Crop to Selection. Paint Shop Pro crops the image canvas to a rectangle that "bounds" the outer perimeter of your selected areas.

10. Press CTRL+D to deselect any selection that is still present on the image.

The Edit Selection feature is very powerful. You can use many tools and effects to edit selections in interesting ways—the Brush, Eraser, and Warp Brush tools, and a number of the effects that you'll learn about in Chapter Four. Feel free to play with this feature!

Text

You can use text in a variety of ways, from adding a caption to a digital photo through to designing a business logo or brochure. You can control the font (the type design), size and style (**bold**, *italic*, ~~strikethrough~~, <u>underlined</u>), color (solid, gradient, pattern, or filled with nearly anything you can imagine), and the type characteristics such as leading and kerning.

You can create text in Paint Shop Pro in several modes: **Selection**, **Floating**, and **Vector**:

* Selection text creates a selection (familiar to you by now) on your image.
* Floating text creates a selection and also fills this selection with the attributes you select in the Text Tool Options palette.
* Vector text is the most flexible form of text that you can create in Paint Shop Pro. You can edit it after you've applied it to the image.

You must choose the type of text you want to apply in the Text Tool Options palette before you can place it. Let's start by using the Text tool to add some text to an image.

Using the Text tool

1. Open a new 500x500 image that's 24-bit color with a white background.

2. Activate the Text tool. Hover your mouse cursor over your image and a special text cursor appears.

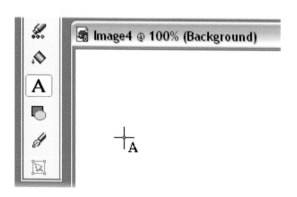

Take a look at the Text Tool Options palette. Many of the options for controlling text are similar to those of a word processor—but some may not be quite so familiar.

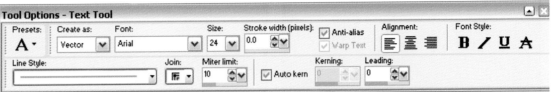

3. Select Floating from the Create as drop-down menu.

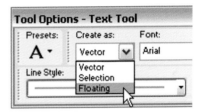

4. Click your image where you would like to place some text. The Text Entry dialog box opens. You should see a blinking cursor at the beginning of the entry field. Type some text into this field (don't worry about font styles or color for the moment—we cover that in a bit), but *don't* click the Apply button at this point.

The Text tool is a little different from many of the other tools in Paint Shop Pro. You can still change settings in the Materials palette, even if the Text Entry dialog box is open. You'll need to highlight the text you want to change, just like you highlight text in a word processor.

5. Set the foreground/stroke color to black in the Materials palette, and also set a contrasting background color to fill the text.

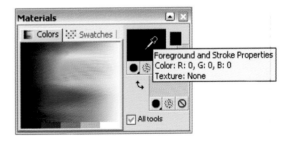

6. In the Text Tool Options palette, set the Stroke width field to 2 and the font size to 48. Still *don't* click Apply in the Text Entry dialog box. You'll see your text style updated on your image.

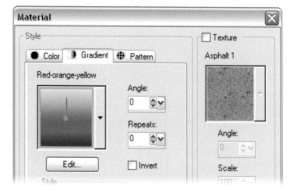

7. You can also use gradients, textures, and patterns as both your stroke and fill colors for text. To do this, make sure that the text is highlighted in the Text Entry dialog box and then set the stroke and fill properties in the Materials palette. Here, we've set an orange stroke and a red-orange-yellow gradient.

Now let's change the text's font.

8. First, make sure that your text is highlighted in the Text Entry dialog box and choose a font you like from the Font drop-down menu in the Text Tool Options palette. This drop-down list displays lists all the fonts installed on your computer and previews the actual font style.

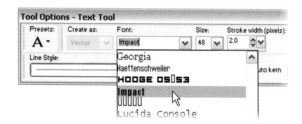

As long as the text is highlighted in the Text Entry dialog box, you should see the text update on your image as you change the tool options.

9. Adjust the size of your text now. Either pick a fixed number between 8 and 72 points from the font Size drop-down menu (the height of the highest character in your text string is determined by the font size you set) or type whole numbers into the numeric field, up to a maximum of 999 points.

10. To edit your text's stroke size, use the Stroke width field in the Text Tool Options palette. Either click the arrows to increase or decrease the width (in pixels) or use the slider, which you activate by clicking the large arrow and dragging it to quickly resize the stroke width.

A stroke width of 0 means that no stroke will be applied, even if you have a foreground color or pattern defined in the Materials palette.

11. If you check the Remember text box in the Text Entry dialog box before you apply the settings in the Text Tool Options palette, your text string will be retained for the next time you open the Text tool. If you're happy with the adjustments you've made to the text, click Apply.

You should see your text applied to your image, with the selection marquee active around it. This is known as a **floating selection**.

12. If you want to reposition your floating text, hover your mouse over the text until you see the cursor turn to the four-headed Move tool. Next, click directly on the selected text and drag it to the desired position.

13. To fix the text to your document once you're happy with its location, press CTRL+D.

We'll now move on to examine a couple of important text attributes: **kerning**, **leading**, and **font styles**.

Kerning

Some fonts are **fixed pitch**, meaning that the width of any character in the set is constant—the width of "V" fills just as much space in a text string as does an "I". Other fonts (also known as **proportional-pitch** fonts) such as Impact (shown here) have built-in **kerning**, which adjusts the space between letters to make them look more natural when placed alongside other letters (such as the letters "AV").

Fixed pitch
Font: Courier New

Proportional pitch
Font: Impact

You can manually adjust the space between characters by first highlighting the text string or groups of letters in the Text Entry dialog box and then turning off Auto kern and using the Kerning slider in the Text Tool Options palette. Negative values move the letters closer together; positive values increase the distance between them.

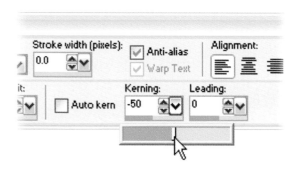

Paint Shop Pro Zero to Hero   0 Kerning

Paint Shop Pro Zero to Hero   -60 Kerning

Paint Shop Pro Zero to Hero   60 Kerning

Leading

Leading adjusts the vertical spacing between lines of text. If you have several lines of text highlighted in the Text Entry dialog box, adjusting the Leading value in the Text Tool Options palette controls the level of spacing. Negative values move the lines closer together; positive values increase the distance between lines.

PSP Zero To Hero is the book to read for all your graphics needs.

0 Leading

PSP Zero To Hero is the book to read for all your graphics needs.

-400 Leading

PSP Zero To Hero

is the book to read

for all your graphics

needs.

400 Leading

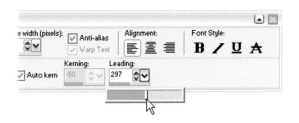

Font styles

Many fonts have entire **font families**, meaning that when you install them you get variations on the font style such as bold or narrow. Though many fonts don't actually come in these variations, Paint Shop Pro allows you to simulate these font style attributes with the **bold**, *italic*, ~~strikethrough~~, and underline options in the Text Tool Options palette. Even if a bold version of the font already exists, such as Arial Black, applying the bold option will make the font even bolder.

Creating effects with text

Let's try a fun text effect and create some multicolored text.

1. Open a new 500x500 image that's 24-bit color with a white background.

2. Set your foreground color to red and your background to blue by right-clicking directly on the foreground color swatch to bring up the Recent Materials dialog box. This contains the primary colors, black, white, and shades of gray, as well as some of the colors and patterns you've recently used.

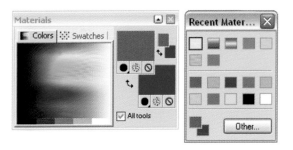

3. Select the Text tool and choose Floating from the Create as drop-down menu in the Text Tool Options palette. Choose a fat font type (here we've used Boink LET Plain), with a font size of 48 and a stroke width of 3. Add any other font styles you like by clicking the appropriate icon in the Font Style area.

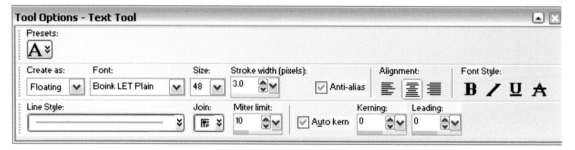

4. Click on the canvas and type some text in the Text Entry dialog box. If you'd like to make a sentence-length text string, you can put it all on a single line, or you can insert line breaks by pressing the ENTER key where you want the line to break. There's no word wrap in Paint Shop Pro.

5. You can also stipulate paragraph alignment while formatting the text string. Click the Alignment icons to align text to the left or right sides, or to center it. You can change any of these attributes at any time by highlighting the text string and changing the particular text attribute in the Tool Options palette.

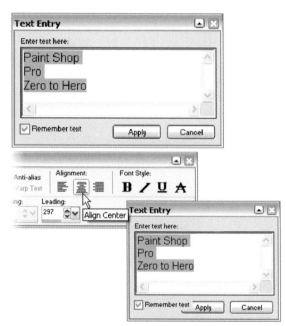

You should see the text string previewed on your image.

6. Now highlight a letter or word in your text string, right-click the background color in the Materials palette, and choose a yellow color. Your highlighted letter or word should change to a yellow fill.

7. Highlight the next letter or word, right-click the background swatch, and choose another color from the Recent Materials color palette. Continue highlighting text in turn, changing the color fill until each letter or word is a different color of the rainbow.

8. Click Apply and your text appears with a floating selection marquee. Again, if you want to reposition the text, hover the mouse cursor over the text until the four-headed Move tool appears, and then reposition it.

9. Set the background color in the Materials palette to a solid color of your choice. This color will replace the existing background color when you perform the next step.

10. Go to Selections > Defloat (CTRL+SHIFT+F) and then use Image > Crop to Selection (Shift+R). Your text image is now cropped large enough to contain your text.

Phew! You put the Text tool and the selections features through a workout! Let's move on to another type of text.

Text backgrounds from photos

This text feature applies a selection *only* to your image, using the text attributes of size and type. No stroke or fill color will be applied, even if you have these set in your Materials palette. This can be very handy to produce text from an existing image.

1. Open a photo of your choice. We've gone for a bright red chrysanthemum.

2. Activate the Text tool. Set the mode to Selection text and choose a font style that's fairly wide, set with a large font size.

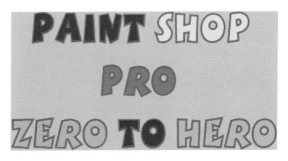

3. Type in some text and click Apply in the Text Entry dialog box. You should see a selection marquee in the style and size of the font you chose, but with no fill or stroke.

4. Use Edit > Copy (CTRL+C) to copy the selected portion of the photo to the Windows clipboard.

5. Open a new image (CTRL+N) with the same dimensions as your original photo (you can check the size of your current image using Image > Canvas Size). Choose a background color that will complement your selected text.

6. Make this second image active and go to Edit > Paste > Paste as New Selection. When the selected text appears in the second image, it will "stick" to your cursor. Position it where you like and click the canvas once to drop the text, at which point the selection marquee will appear.

7. Deselect the selection with CTRL+D. The photo contents that were beneath the text selection in the original photo are now the text fill in your new image.

Defloating text

Using a function of a defloated selection can create another interesting text effect.

1. Open a photo of your choice.

2. In the Materials palette set the background color to black and the foreground to white.

3. Select the Text tool and set the mode to Selection text. Choose a font style and make the font size quite large.

4. Type a text string into the Text Entry dialog box and click Apply. You should see the familiar selection marquee on your photo.

5. Hover the mouse cursor over the text selection until you see the four-headed Move tool. Click and drag the selection slightly up and to the right. A black shadow area appears behind the text selection. When you move a selection, Paint Shop Pro floats it and replaces the area beneath the selection with the background color currently set in the Materials palette.

6. Now go to Selections > Defloat (CTRL+SHIFT+F) and click the swap colors arrow in the Materials palette to reverse the foreground/background colors, making white the background color.

7. Place your cursor over the selection and this time click and drag it slightly to the left and down. This creates a white highlight area on your text selection.

8. Use CTRL+D to turn off the selection marquee and admire your handiwork.

You can use any of the brush tools, including the Flood Fill, Airbrush, and Picture Tube tools, to fill text selections. You'll try some airbrushed text next.

Filling text with the Airbrush tool

1. Open a new 500x500 image that's 24-bit color with a white background.

2. Go into the Materials palette and set the foreground/background colors as you like.

3. Activate the Text tool. Set the mode to Selection text; choose a wide, blocky font type; and set the font size to 80 points.

4. Type in a text string and click Apply in the Text Entry dialog box.

5. Activate the Airbrush tool and, in the Tool Options palette, set Shape to Round, Size to 90, Hardness to 50, Density to 50, and Opacity to 100.

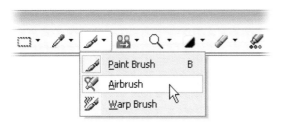

6. Right-click to apply the background color to the text selection with the Airbrush tool and, using a broad, sweeping stroke, fill your text selection with paint by dragging the Airbrush tool across it.

You can keep filling the areas not covered with the first application. Don't worry about being too neat and precise.

7. Deselect your text with CTRL+D and save your image.

Vector text

Vector text is the most flexible form of text that you can create in Paint Shop Pro. You can edit it after it's been applied to the image, and you can use it to add even more variety to your installed fonts. We cover vector graphics and text more thoroughly in Chapter Five.

1. Open a new 500x500 image that's 24-bit color with a white background. Set the foreground color to black and the background color to null.

2. Activate the Text tool and choose Vector from the Create as drop-down menu. Choose a large font such as Elephant, set Size to 36 points, set Stroke width to 1, and check the Anti-alias option. Click the image to open the Text Entry dialog box and enter your text.

The text is applied to your image and surrounded by a bounding box selection. This indicates that the text is vector and is also selected.

3. Go to Edit > Copy (CTRL+C) to copy this text object to the Windows clipboard.

4. Now use Edit > Paste > Paste as New Vector Selection (CTRL+G) to paste a copy of the vector text on the image. Drag it to a position you like, and click to release it.

5. You can now resize this text. Activate the Object Selection tool. Use this tool to resize, transform, or reposition vector text by dragging the corner handles (we cover editing vector shapes like these in detail in Chapter Five).

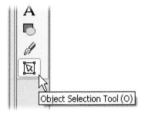

You can continue to paste more copies of the vector selection and use the handles to resize them or position them anywhere you like.

Two

Layers and Masks

In this chapter

Layers are an important feature of professional image-editing applications. Paint Shop Pro's layers are powerful, flexible, and easy to use. When you combine layers with the more advanced features of masking tools, you can create some superb and complex imagery. In this chapter, we cover the following topics:

★ The Layer palette

★ Layer groups

★ Blend modes

★ Mask features

Layers: The basics

Think of an image with layers as a sort of a gelatin salad, where a layer of gelatin is transparent but might contain some nontransparent goodies such as cherries or marshmallows. Then you might put another layer on top of that layer, which is also transparent gelatin with some walnuts in it. When you look down into the bowl of gelatin, you can see the cherries, marshmallows, and walnuts (if the walnuts aren't aligned with the cherries!). If you add a layer of cream cheese over those layers, you won't be able to see any of the goodies under it, because cream cheese isn't transparent. If you scrape some of the cream cheese away from the edges, you'll be able to see some of the cherries again.

Certainly, this is pretty simplistic, but layers in Paint Shop Pro work in much the same way. A layer can be transparent but contain some opaque objects that can be seen if another transparent layer is added on top. If an opaque layer is added, layers beneath it are not visible. If parts of the opaque layer are removed, you can see any layer material under the top layer. Let's make it work!

1. Open a new 24-bit color, 500x500 image with a transparent background.

2. Make sure the Layer palette is visible by choosing View > Palettes > Layers (F8). For the purposes of this exercise, you may find it easier to undock the Layer palette and keep it handy in the workspace. There's currently one layer in your palette called Raster 1.

3. Go to Layers > New Raster Layer to open the New Raster Layer dialog box. Rename this layer red by typing in the Name field.

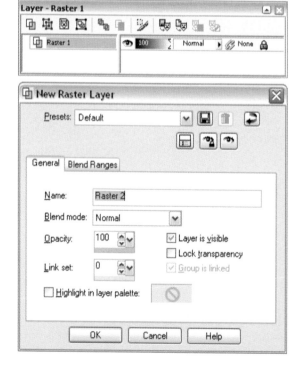

As you'll soon discover, the ability to rename layers is very useful when you're working with lots of layers, as it helps you keep track of the location of each element in your image.

Digital imaging applications can produce either **raster** or **vector** images. Raster images are pixel-based and are sometimes referred to as **bitmapped** images. You'll learn more about vector images in Chapter Five, but for now it's important to know that raster layers contain raster image information and vector layers contain vector image information.

Raster layers can contain information in 24-bit color mode or less, but vector layers can contain only 8-bit color information.

Well, the image looks exactly like it did before you started. However, look at the Layer palette itself. There are now two layers: Raster 1, your original image layer, and a second layer above it called red.

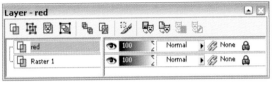

4. Click the layer titled red directly in the Layer palette to make the layer **active** (this is indicated by the gray highlight). Many actions in Paint Shop Pro affect only the active layer.

5. Now select the Flood Fill tool (F) and fill this layer with—you guessed it—red.

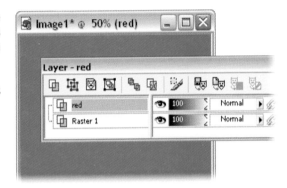

Let's add another layer.

6. An alternative way to add a new layer is to right-click directly on the red layer title in the Layer palette and choose New Raster Layer from the context menu. The New Layer dialog box opens as normal. This time, name the layer blue.

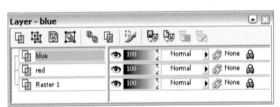

7. Activate the Text tool (T) and apply some text to this new layer—make it blue. Set your background color to blue and your foreground color to null. Set the Text tool options as follows:

   ★ Create as: Floating text
   ★ Font Size: 72 points
   ★ Font Style: Your choice

8. Apply the text and use the Move tool to move the text to the center of the image, if necessary.

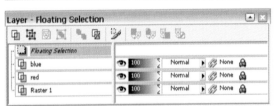

Look at the Layer palette. You'll see a Floating Selection layer above the blue layer. You can **defloat** this selection so that it drops down to the layer beneath.

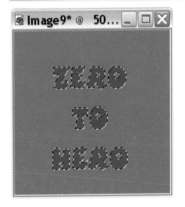

9. To defloat the selection, right-click the layer named Floating Selection in the Layer palette and choose Defloat (CTRL+SHIFT+F) from the context menu.

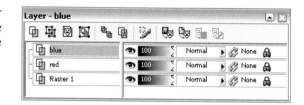

10. Your image should now show blue text on a red background. The text is still selected so, to finish off, go to Selections > Select None (CTRL+D).

11. Now add yet another layer. Click the New Raster Layer icon at the top-left corner of the Layer palette. The new layer is added directly above any layer currently highlighted in the Layer palette.

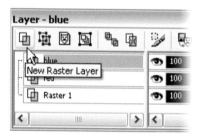

12. Name the layer yellow in the New Raster Layer dialog box.

13. Set the foreground color to black and the background color to yellow.

14. Activate the Preset Shape tool (P). In the tool options, uncheck Retain style and Create as vector. Set line Width to 2 and choose Rounded Rectangle from the Shapes drop-down catalog.

15. Click and drag to draw out a rectangle on the new yellow layer, so that it completely hides the blue text. This layer should be at the top of your Layer palette.

Notice the black-and-white slider in the Layer palette, with the 100 on it? This adjusts the opacity for each individual layer.

16. With the yellow layer activated, drag the opacity slider to the left to decrease the layer's opacity and set it to 50. The yellow gradually turns to orange (because the lowered yellow opacity allows the red layer beneath to show through), and the blue text underneath becomes visible, appearing gray in color.

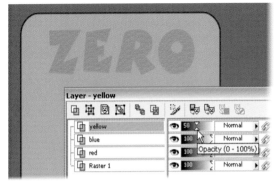

17. Select the Move tool (M) and try to move the text to the top of the image by clicking and dragging it. What, it won't move? The yellow rectangle keeps moving? Check which layer is active in the Layer palette—it's the yellow layer again.

To successfully grab the text, you need to turn the yellow layer's visibility off.

18. Click the eye icon on the Layer palette to the right of the yellow layer title. You can use this toggle to switch the layer visibility on or off. When layer visibility is switched off, you can't see any of the layer's contents. They're still there, just invisible. This is denoted by the red X through the eye icon.

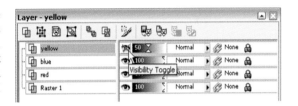

Now you can see only your blue text on top of the red background.

19. Activate the blue layer and try to move the text again. If you click directly on the text, you should now be able to move it freely. Paint Shop Pro "grabs" image information across a transparent area and, because the yellow rectangle originally covered all of the text, it was hard to "hit" a nontransparent area of text to grab. By turning off the layer visibility, you eliminated that problem.

Say you want to position the blue text directly on top of the yellow rectangle. In its current position, the color is affected by the yellow rectangle over it. The solution is to move the layer itself.

20. Make the blue layer active and drag it directly above the yellow layer in the Layer palette.

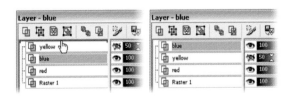

21. Now use the Move tool to move the blue text back into position and toggle the yellow layer visibility back on. It's much easier this time to grab the blue text if it's on top of the rectangle.

Did you at any time miss when you were moving the text or the yellow rectangle, and accidentally move the red background? It's a good habit to check which layer you're actually on before you move, delete, or otherwise make a change to a layer's contents. Nothing is more frustrating than being on the wrong layer and making changes, only to discover your error later.

Layer groups

You know that the blue text and yellow rectangle were created on separate layers, but what if you want to treat them as if they were on the same layer, and move them at the same time?

1. Right-click the blue layer and choose New Layer Group from the context menu.

2. The New Layer Group dialog box opens. Name this group Text Group. Check Highlight in layer palette and you'll see the color swatch become active. The default highlight color is yellow, but you can change this in exactly the same way as you would change any other color swatch in Paint Shop Pro. Accept yellow for the color and click OK.

The Text Group layer group is active in the Layer palette, with its icon highlighted in yellow and the blue layer as a sublayer of the group.

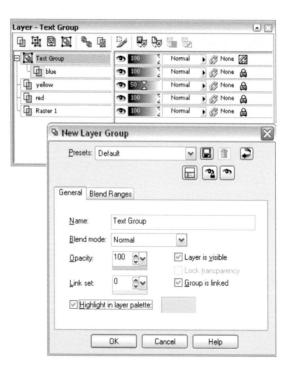

3. You want to add the yellow layer to this group too, so drag it up the layer stack until it's directly under the Text Group title and release it. You *must* release it directly under the title Text Group or you may have difficulty getting it to join the group.

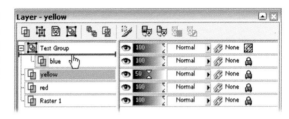

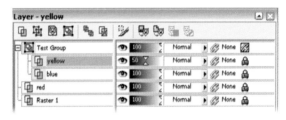

4. Now move the blue layer to the top of this group. Click and drag it above the yellow layer. Don't move it out of the group, as it will snap into place elsewhere in the Layer palette.

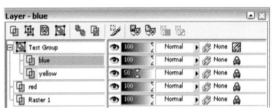

These two layers are now grouped. By using the layer group, if you move one layer, you'll move the other. Even if you turn off the layer visibility, you'll still move them together. You can turn them off simultaneously by switching off the layer visibility on the Text Group layer.

5. Let's turn things upside down a bit. Make sure the Text Group layer is active and go to Image > Rotate > Free Rotate. Set the rotation direction to Right. Click Free and set the degrees to 45. Uncheck All layers to apply the rotation effect to just the active layer or, in this case, the layer group. Click OK.

6. Now make the blue layer active and return to Image > Rotate > Free Rotate. Click the Left direction button. Only the blue text rotates back to the original position.

So, it *is* possible to perform an action on a layer that's part of the layer group, as long as that layer alone is active and not the layer group.

If you want to delete a layer group, just right-click its title and press DELETE. However, this action also deletes all the layers that are part of the group. You may want to just "ungroup" the group. In this case, click the layer you would like to disassociate from the group and drag it above or below the layer group. It breaks free from the layer group. If you drag the last remaining layer out of a layer group, the layer group itself disappears too.

It's possible to collapse a layer group's structure to make it easier to view the Layer palette when it contains many layers. Click the minus sign (–) to the left of the layer group title and the group collapses. The minus sign will change to a plus sign (+). To expand a collapsed layer group again, click the plus sign.

Working with layers

Although Paint Shop Pro's native file format .PspImage supports the layers feature and file formats from previous versions of Paint Shop Pro (5 through 7, .psp), most other image file formats do not support layers. Paint Shop Pro 8 can also read certain layer information in Adobe Photoshop's native file format, .psd, unless the .psd file contains unusable information (such as Photoshop's layer styles).

1. You're going to work on a photograph now (babysally.jpg in the download files). Open this photo and look in the Layer palette. Notice that the single layer is called Background.

This photo is a .jpg file, which does not support layers. When a .jpg image is viewed in the Layer palette, it has only one layer: the Background layer. You can, however, work on this image in Paint Shop Pro and use the layer features. But if you save the image as a .jpg file, the ability to use the layers in the future will be lost.

2. Right-click the Background layer and choose Duplicate. A second layer is added—an exact duplicate of the Background layer. Look at the Layer palette. The new layer is called Copy of Background.

3. Duplicate the layer again (you can also use the Duplicate Layer icon on the Layer palette to duplicate an active layer). This layer is named Copy (2) of Background. All three layers are exactly the same.

4. Hover your mouse over the Background title. See the thumbnail view of the layer pop up? Now hover your mouse over the Copy of Background layer—the thumbnail shows the layer is exactly like the first one. Hovering the mouse over the top layer should show the same view.

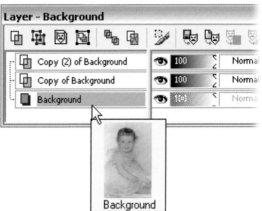

You can view layer contents quickly this way. It's most useful when you forget to give layers meaningful names, and you want to see the layer contents without actually making the other layers invisible.

5. Turn off the layer visibility on the top layer, and then make the middle layer active. Set the foreground color in the Materials palette to a beige-pink (R:234, G:176, B:152).

6. Now set the background color to an auburn-brown shade (R:111, G:87, B:61).

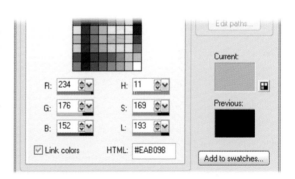

7. Activate the Paint Brush tool and set the following tool options:

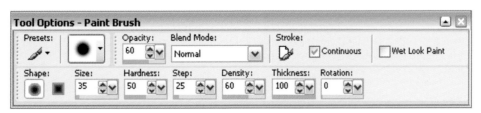

8. Make sure that the middle layer is still active and click to paint the baby's face, arms, and legs with the beige-pink foreground shade. Avoid the eyes, but don't worry if you cover over the other facial features.

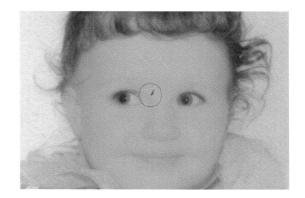

9. Choose the Change to Target brush from the Tools palette. Set the following options:

- ★ Size: As required
- ★ Density: 50
- ★ Hardness: 100
- ★ Opacity: 100
- ★ Mode: Color

10. Right-click to use the background color (or reverse the materials by clicking the Swap Materials icon in the Materials palette), and paint the baby's hair with the brown color. The Change to Target brush colors only the baby's hair; it doesn't color the surrounding areas.

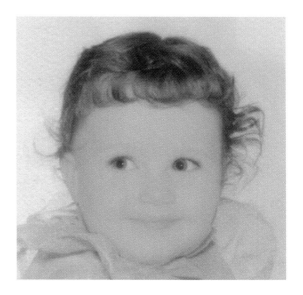

11. Next, add some rosy cheeks. Make sure the foreground color is pink, click the foreground swatch to activate the Material dialog box, and change the Hue to 3, leaving the other settings as they are.

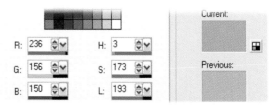

12. Activate the Paint Brush tool again, change the brush Size and Opacity to 40, set Hardness to 0, and uncheck Continuous. Click over the cheek area a couple times to add some color on the areas where a baby might naturally blush.

13. Return to the foreground color swatch and click it to open the Material dialog box again. This time, change Saturation to the maximum amount (255). This gives you an intense version of the shade you've been using for the cheek blush. Change the brush Size to 10, check Continuous, and paint the baby's lips with this new color.

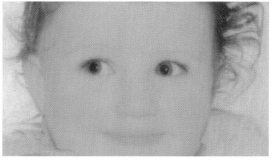

14. Change the foreground color to R:83, G:84, B:135. Choose the Change to Target brush again from the Tools palette, and set the following options:

- ★ Size: 17
- ★ Hardness, Density, and Opacity: 100
- ★ Mode: Hue

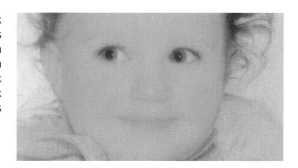

15. Click once in each pupil to color the eyes blue.

You might be thinking that this doesn't look very natural. Be patient and wait for the magic!

16. Open the Material dialog box for the foreground color and change the Lightness value of the blue color to 190.

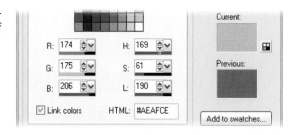

17. Return to the Paint Brush tool and set both the Density and Opacity to 50. Use a large brush size of 80 or so and paint the baby's dress with this lighter blue shade, taking care to keep the color away from the arms and legs.

18. Now for the magic. Slide the Copy of Background layer opacity down to 50. See how the color from the middle layer blends with the lower layer?

Let's not forget about that top layer. We're going to use it to introduce another feature of the Layer palette: **blend modes**.

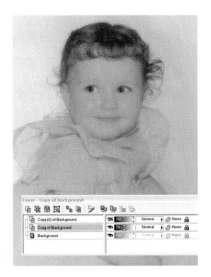

19. Make the top layer active by clicking its title bar and make it visible again. See how the old baby is back? Go to Adjust > Blur > Gaussian Blur and apply a blur of 3.00.

Well, now you have an out-of-focus baby. Not much of an improvement, would you say?

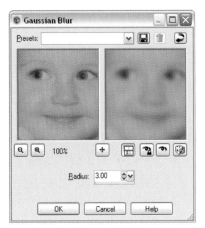

20. More magic coming up—click the arrow next to the word Normal in the top layer. Choose Multiply from this blend mode menu, and then set the layer opacity to 50.

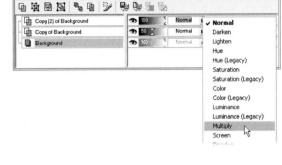

21. Return to the bottom layer, duplicate it one more time, and drag it to the top of the layer stack. Click the arrow next to the word Normal on the top layer's title bar and choose Burn from the blend mode menu.

22. Set this layer's opacity to 19. If you have a hard time with the slider, double-click the layer title to bring up the Layer Properties dialog box, and set the exact amount in the Opacity control (you can also change the blend mode here).

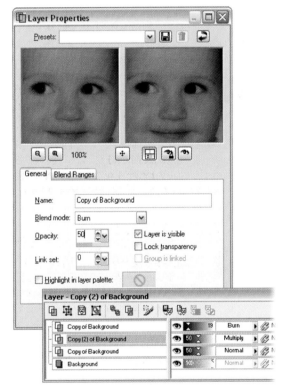

Voila! A subtly colored and enhanced smiling baby face! You still have four layers, though. You can save this image as a `.PspImage`, but if you want to show it to anyone else without Paint Shop Pro, you'll need to prepare it for saving in another file format. So, let's get rid of some of those layers.

Wait a minute, how can you delete the layers when there's information in them that you need to keep your baby happy? You can **merge** the layers, so that layer information from separate layers is combined on a single layer. Merging is useful if you've finished manipulating an area or object, and you want to "glue it" in place in the image. Sometimes you may want to merge certain layers in the image and not others.

23. Go to Layers > Merge > Merge Visible to merge all layers in the image. Look at the Layer palette now. There's now a single layer titled Merged.

24. You can save this completed image as a `.jpg` file so that you can send your creation for others to view.

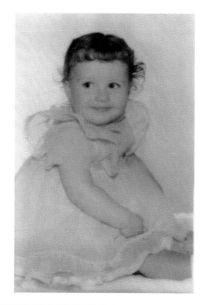

Feel free to try your hand at your own photos. If you'd like some samples of hair and skin colors to use with your own photos, check out the palettes at www.retouchpro.com/pages/colors.html. You can save the images and sample them for your own colors, or you can download `.pal` files at www.retouchpro.com/pages/ColorPals.zip. Extract the files to the Palettes folder in either My Documents > My PSP 8 Files or Program Files > Jasc Software Inc > Paint Shop Pro 8.

Once you've extracted the files, go into Paint Shop Pro and open the image you wish to colorize.

Next, go to Image > Palette > Load Palette and choose the palette of your choice from the Palette drop-down menu.

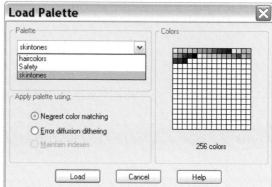

Layer blend modes

As you've already seen, you can make use of Paint Shop Pro's layer blend modes to modify the look of certain layers by adding new layers above them, manipulating the pixels with the blend modes, and then merging the layers. However, the concept of blend modes can be confusing. Let's work with them a little more.

1. Open a new 600x600 image, with a 24-bit color depth and raster background. For the background color, open the Materials dialog box and choose the Animal zebra pattern from the Pattern catalog. Set Angle to 0 and Scale to 100.

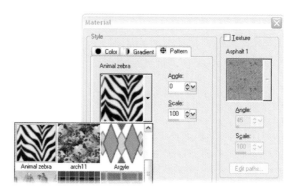

This zebra pattern has stripes that are not quite white. For this example, you'd like them to be much brighter and whiter. This is where you'll use layer blend modes.

2. Duplicate the Raster 1 layer. Set the layer blend mode on Copy of Raster 1 to Screen (remember that you can open the layer blend mode menu with the small arrow). This makes the white stripes brighter and lighter.

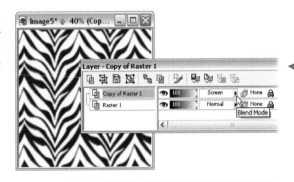

3. Let's merge these two layers. Right-click Copy of Raster 1 and choose Merge > Down. This merges all layers beneath the highlighted layer and results in a single new layer named Raster 1. In this case, as you had only two layers in the whole image, you could have also used Merge > Merge All (Flatten), which would have given you a single new layer titled Background.

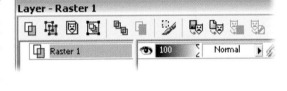

4. Now that you have your bright white and black zebra pattern, double-click the Raster 1 layer title and rename it zebra.

5. Add another raster layer to this image and name it gradient. Click the background color in the Materials palette and go to the Gradient tab. Choose the Landscape morning gradient with the following options:

   ★ Style: Linear
   ★ Angle: 0
   ★ Repeats: 0

6. Activate the Flood Fill tool and fill this new layer with the landscape gradient.

7. Open sphere.PspImage (from the download files). Now you get to learn to copy and paste layers! With the sphere image active, go to Edit > Copy (CTRL+C).

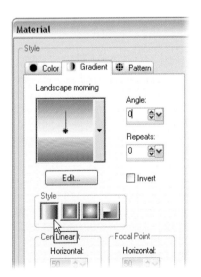

8. Return to the first image and, with the gradient layer active, go to Edit > Paste > Paste as New Layer (CTRL+L). This pastes the sphere image into your existing image as a new layer, on top of the gradient layer. Rename this new layer sphere.

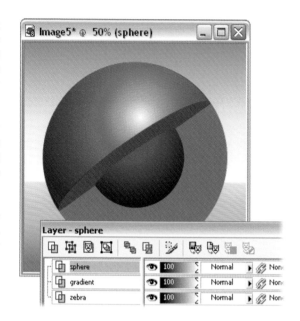

Pasting an existing image as a new layer will center the new image in the existing one. You can move this object with the Move tool by clicking and dragging it to any spot you desire. In this case, leave your sphere in the center.

Let's play with the blend modes again. You used the Burn and Multiply modes on your baby image earlier, and you saw how to use Screen mode to make your zebra stripes whiter in this current image.

As you may have noticed, you use a blend mode adjustment on a layer that's *above* another layer. This is because blend modes control how the pixels of a top layer combine with the pixels of a layer beneath it. Using a blend mode on a layer gives you a preview of how that layer will look when combined with the layers beneath it using that particular blend mode. The layers aren't actually combined until you merge them. Here's a quick explanation of what most of the blend modes do:

★ **Normal**: Well, it's normal. Isn't that nice?

★ **Darken**: The darker pixels in either the upper or lower layers are used in the resulting image. Lighter pixels disappear.

★ **Lighten**: The lightest pixels in either the upper or lower layers are used.

9. Return to your image. Turn off the layer visibility on the sphere layer, and set the blend mode on the gradient layer to Darken.

There are no pixels in the gradient layer that are darker than the black zebra stripes, so those pixels over the black stripes disappear. However, *all* the pixels on the gradient layer are darker than the white zebra stripes, so you see the gradient colors where the white stripes would be.

10. Change the blend mode to Lighten on the gradient layer. Now the white stripes from the zebra layer appear because they're the lightest pixels in those areas, and the formerly black stripes take on the gradient shades from the gradient layer, because all those pixels are lighter than the black stripes.

Many times you'll find that certain blend modes have little or no effect on your image. In this case, the Hue modes will show little effect, whereas the Saturation modes will only show any effect in the area of the black stripes that actually have gray pixels, as they blend into the white stripes. Let's move on to take a look at some of the other available blend modes.

> What's this "Legacy" stuff in the blend modes? The ways in which several blend modes work with Paint Shop Pro 8 has changed from previous versions, but the old modes are retained in case long-time users miss them. So the Color blend mode works as it's designed to now, and the Color (Legacy) mode works as it used to—which still might be handy!

Color blend modes

The Color blend modes apply the hue and saturation settings from the uppermost layer's pixels to the underlying layers.

1. Change the blend mode on the gradient layer to Color. There are areas of the white and black stripes that are already fully saturated, but the gray pixels between the two areas are not, so you'll see the gradient colors applied to those areas more or less vividly, depending upon the amount of gray in an area.

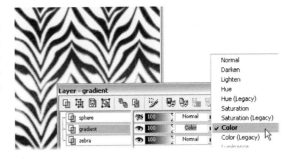

2. Now turn the visibility back on for the top sphere layer and set this layer's blend mode to Luminance. This applies the luminance values of the uppermost layer to the luminance values of the lower layers. In this case, you have two lower layers, so you can see the zebra stripes through the sphere, but they're colored by the gradient on the second layer.

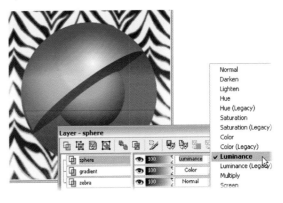

One of the most useful blend modes is **Multiply**. It combines the colors of the uppermost layer with the underlying layers to produce darker colors. Multiply a color with black and you get black; multiply a color with white and the color is unchanged.

3. Set the blend mode on the sphere layer to Multiply.

See how the black stripes from the bottommost layer are visible, but the white stripe area is filled in by the sphere from the top layer?

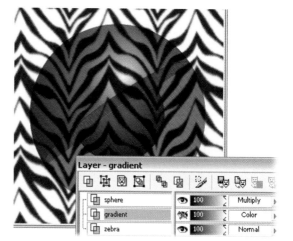

4. If you turn off the gradient layer's visibility now, you also lose the colored stripe edges around the outside of the sphere, as none of the gradient layer will be used.

Screen is another useful blend mode. It produces a lightened version of the underlying layers, but it uses quite a bit of complicated math to do it.

5. If you want to lighten or brighten an image, try the Screen blend mode. In this case, a lighter version of the sphere colors fills the black stripes of the zebra layer but not the white stripes.

Dissolve randomly mixes pixels from the underlying layers with the top layer to create a speckled effect.

6. Set the sphere layer's blend mode to Dissolve and lower the opacity down to around 50 to see this effect in action.

Overlay will generally preserve the colors on the uppermost layer, while keeping the shadows and highlights from underlying layers (which is very useful in photos). **Hard Light** and **Soft Light** also preserve and enhance shadows and highlights.

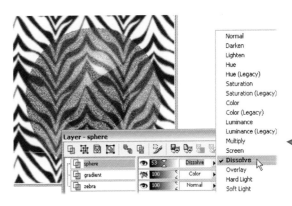

Difference and **Exclusion** are the blend modes' wacky twins. They have similar effects, but Exclusion is a softer version of Difference.

7. Change the sphere layer's blend mode to Difference, bump its opacity back up to 100%, and make the gradient layer invisible.

8. Make sure all your layers are visible now, and then set the gradient layer's blend mode to Luminance and its opacity to 65. Set the sphere layer's blend mode to Luminance (Legacy), with an opacity of 100.

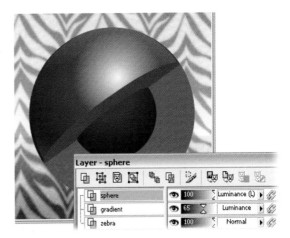

9. Go to Window > Duplicate (SHIFT+D) to make an exact copy of this image with all layers intact. On the first image, right-click the gradient layer and choose Merge > Down to merge the bottom two layers.

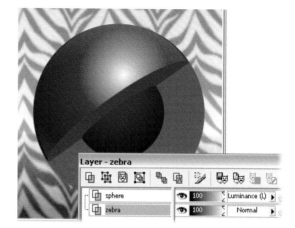

10. On the second image, turn off the layer visibility for the bottom zebra layer, and right-click the top sphere layer to make it active. This time choose Merge > Merge Visible. The top two layers will be merged. Now turn the visibility of the zebra layer back on to complete the image.

As you can see, merging different layers in the same image can give vastly different results. That's the power of layers and the beauty of blend modes.

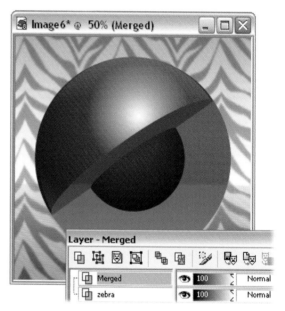

Masks

A **mask** is a grayscale image that's applied to a layer. Masks can hide parts of layers or fade areas, and they have much in common with selections, which you learned about in Chapter One. You use a mask to conceal parts of an image in much the same way that you use masking tape to cover the trim when you paint a wall.

Masks are actually 8-bit grayscale raster images. The gray value of a mask determines how much of the image is blocked or masked out. Where the mask is black, everything is covered, and where the mask is white, nothing is masked out. Shades of gray between these two extremes determine how much of the image is masked out, producing semitransparency.

1. Open `glassvase.tif` and `butterfly.tif` from the download files for this chapter.

2. The vase image contains a mask already on an alpha channel. Activate that mask by clicking the vase image, go to the Layer palette, and click the Load Mask From Alpha icon. You may be prompted by an autoaction to promote the background to a full layer—if so, click OK.

3. When the dialog box opens, choose `glass-vase.tif` from the Load from document drop-down list. Select Fit to canvas under Orientation, and also select Show all mask under Options. Make sure Invert transparency is not checked, and then click Load.

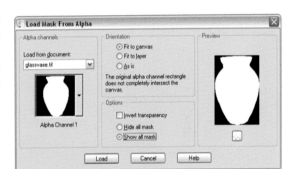

You should now see the checkerboard pattern around the vase, with the background masked away. If you look at the Layer palette now, a new layer group has been created, with a mask layer included. The mask layer is a special layer that holds the grayscale mask image. If you hover your mouse over the layer title, you can see the mask in the layer thumbnail.

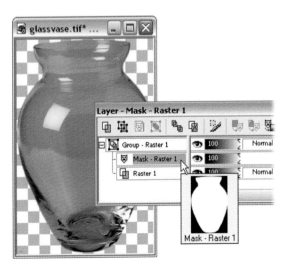

You need to now delete the mask to continue working with your image.

4. Right-click the Mask layer and choose Delete. A message asking if you would like to merge the layer with the mask below pops up. Click Yes, otherwise the mask will be deleted with no action.

Now you have a perfectly masked glass vase, which you could copy and paste into other images with no pesky background. However, we've got other plans for this vase. . . .

Turn your attention to the butterfly. The butterfly does *not* contain a mask on an alpha channel, but the vase still does. Just as with selections, any open image in the workspace that contains an alpha channel mask is available to any other image on the workspace.

5. Make the butterfly image active, and click the Load Mask From Alpha icon again in the Layer palette. You'll see the same `glassvase.tif` available in the Load from document area.

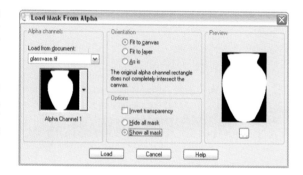

Fortunately, these two images are the same size, so the mask can be loaded in the same spot in each one. If you want to load a mask on a smaller or larger image, Paint Shop Pro gives you the following options to place the mask:

★ As is loads the mask at exactly its size.

★ Fit to canvas loads the mask and expands it to the height and width of the image itself.

★ Fit to layer expands the mask's height and width to the layer, if it was smaller than the image itself.

For this image, all three options result in the same thing.

6. Choose Fit to canvas, select Show all mask, and click Load. Your butterfly image now contains a vase-shaped area masked away from the background.

You can use this, too, as is or as part of an image composite. Delete the mask on this image so you can continue to use it.

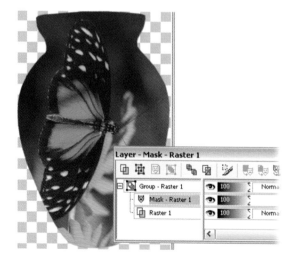

7. Ensure the mask is active in the Layer palette and, this time, go to Layers > Delete. The same message pops up asking if you want to merge the mask with the layer below. You do, so click Yes.

8. Now you'll use the knowledge you gained earlier in this chapter. Copy the butterfly image on the layer Raster 1 (not the whole Group – Raster1) to the clipboard (CTRL+C). Select the Raster 1 layer in the vase image and choose Edit > Paste as New Layer (CTRL+L). Your vase-shaped butterfly image should now be aligned over the glass vase. If it isn't quite aligned, grab the Move tool and align it in the image.

9. Now go to the Layer palette and click the Raster 2 layer. (When Paint Shop Pro pastes layers, it names them in sequence for you. You can rename them yourself, if you prefer.) Set the blend mode for the Raster 2 layer to Overlay.

Would you look at that? Butterfly under glass, complete with reflective highlights.

79

Creating photo borders with masks

1. Start by creating a new 800x600 image with a white background at 24-bit color. Set the foreground color to white and the background to black.

2. Open the Add Borders dialog box with Image > Add Borders and check Symmetric. This allows you to fill out one field that will be copied to the remaining three. Input a value of 25 in any one of the Size in pixels fields, and set the color swatch to black if it's not already set.

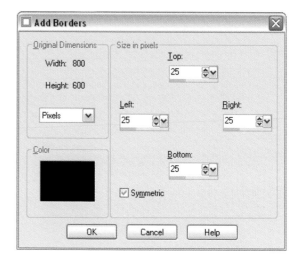

The border is added to the outside of the image, which has now been resized to 850x650 with the border.

3. For this next bit you can get creative. Select the Smudge brush from the Tools palette and set the tool options as follows:

4. Smudge the brush around the edge of the border randomly to get an effect you like.

5. Now you're going to make a mask out of the image you just created. Choose Layers > New Mask Layer > From Image and you'll see the Add Mask From Image dialog box. (Accept the autoaction to promote the background to a full layer if it pops up.)

The Source window is the current image. The three options in the Create mask from area determine the parameters that are used to create the mask:

★ Source luminance produces degrees of gray or partially-masking pixels according to the luminance value of each pixel.

★ Any non-zero value creates a mask of black and white values only, completely masked or completely transparent.

★ Source opacity uses the opacity of a pixel to determine the degree of masking.

You want the pixels either masked or not, so choose Source luminance.

6. Now you'll save the mask for use in other images. Click the Save Mask To Disk icon on the Layer palette. This image will be saved as a .PspMask file, which is the native file format Paint Shop Pro uses for mask images.

7. This will save your mask to either My Documents > My PSP 8 Files > Masks (by default) or the Paint Shop Pro program files, if configured as such. Give your mask a descriptive name and click Save.

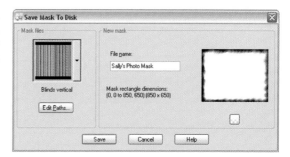

8. Now open a photograph of your choice. It can be any size, but choose one that doesn't contain important elements near the edges. In the Layer palette, click the Load Mask From Disk icon and navigate to where you just saved the mask.

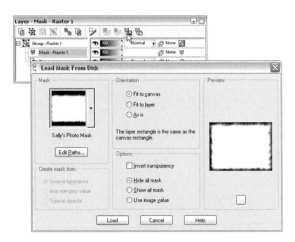

Now your photo has interesting torn edges!

9. Delete the mask layer, and you can use the photo image as is or copied and pasted over an interesting background.

Mask resources on the Web

If you'd like to try out a series of premade images that are perfect to turn into mask files, check out the Edge and Frame Galaxy at www.thepluginsite.com/products/efgcd/index.htm.

There's a free functional demo containing 50 image files that you can easily turn into mask files. You can also purchase the full download version, which contains 450 images, or the really full version on CD, which contains 1,600 images.

Phew! You've accomplished a lot. So far, you've learned how to choose your tools, pick your materials, make good selections, apply text in a variety of ways, and use layers, blend modes, and masks. Next, you'll learn about Paint Shop Pro's special tools and features that can help you put the finishing touches on your images.

The Digital Darkroom

In this chapter

At the turn of the twentieth century, George Eastman, the founder of Kodak, coined the phrase "You press the button, we do the rest" to promote his company and, for over a hundred years, most of us have had no alternative to turning our film over to a photo lab for our pictures to be developed. Now digital technology has liberated us. Digital cameras, scanners, PCs, and photo-editing software can give you complete control over the whole photographic process.

At the most basic level, you can simply download images from your camera to your computer and print them out on your inkjet printer. Some printers will even let you print photos without the use of a computer. Sharing photos with friends and family is also a snap with e-mail or photo web sites, but your computer is much more than a convenient 1-hour photo center. With the right software, you can do things with your images that even a skilled photo finisher with a well-equipped professional darkroom would find difficult, time consuming, and often impossible. In this chapter, we cover the following topics:

★ Scanning photographs, negatives, and slides

★ Controlling color balance, contrast, and saturation to enhance photographs

★ Removing red-eye from photographs

Image resolution

An important concept to grasp when editing photographs is **resolution**, as the resolution of an image directly affects the quality of your image and the size at which you can print it while still retaining quality.

Most digital cameras use a small, rectangular piece of silicon rather than a piece of film to receive incoming light. This silicon wafer has been manufactured and segmented into an array of individual light-sensitive cells called **photosites**. Each photosite is one element of the whole picture. Individually, they're called picture elements or **pixels**. It's the number of photosites on the silicon wafer that determines the resolution of an individual camera.

Camera resolutions are given in **megapixels** (or millions of pixels), which indicate the maximum number of pixels in any image produced by that camera. Although more may sound better, the real question you should ask yourself is "How many of these megapixels do I really need?" If all you want to do is post pictures to your web site, resolution isn't a particular concern, as you'll rarely need to post an image greater than 800x600 pixels.

However, if you plan to print your images, then the number of pixels in your image *is* an important factor. A rule of thumb to achieve quality prints on an inkjet printer is to print between 200 and 300 pixels per inch (ppi). This table indicates the approximate minimum camera resolutions needed to produce good prints.

Resolution	Print Size
1 megapixel	3x4 inch print
2 megapixels	5x7 inch print
3 megapixels	8x10 inch print
6 megapixels	11x14 inch print

Scanning photographs

You can scan conventional printed photographs using a flatbed scanner. When using a scanner, you have to decide on the resolution at which to scan your pictures. Resolution is described in most scanner software, somewhat erroneously, as dots per inch (dpi). What it really means is pixels per inch (ppi). This determines the size in pixels of the scan.

For instance, if you scanned a 4x5 inch print at 150 dpi, the resulting digital image would be 750x600 pixels.

The resolution you choose largely depends on what you want to use the picture for. The 750x600 file is an adequate size for displaying on a computer screen, but it might be too small to make a quality print. For quality printing, you need an image large enough to allow you to print it at 200 to 300 ppi. A print scanned at 300 dpi will print at the same size as the original 300 ppi. If you scanned the same print at 600 dpi, you could print it at twice the original dimensions at 300 ppi.

4x5 Inch Photo Scanned at 150 ppi

Scanning negatives and slides

If you scan 35mm negatives or slides, either on a flatbed scanner with a transparency adapter or a dedicated slide/film scanner, you need to use much higher scanning resolutions to achieve quality prints.

A 35mm film frame measures 24x36 mm, approximately 1x1.5 inches. As a result, scanning at 150 dpi gives you a file of only 225x150 pixels, which isn't much good for anything other than a thumbnail image. Typically, to make 8x10 inch prints, you need a dedicated slide scanner. Most of these scan up to at least 2400 dpi and some as high as 4000 dpi. Because negatives and slides pack a lot more detail into a much smaller area than photographic prints, it's a good rule of thumb to scan these at the highest possible resolution that your hardware is capable of. This ensures that you collect the most detail, leaving you with the most options for printing. You can always scale a large scan down into a high-quality smaller image, but not vice versa.

Nikon 35mm Slide/Film Scanner and a Hewlett-Packard Flatbed with Transparency Adapter

If you're already a serious photographer using single lens reflex (SLR) camera bodies and lenses, a dedicated slide/film scanner is a good alternative to buying an expensive digital SLR body. Typically, a good 35mm transparency scanner will cost four to ten times less than a digital SLR.

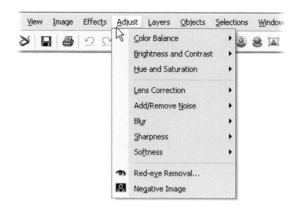

Three

Autoenhancing photographs

There are several automatic tools for basic photo editing and correction in Paint Shop Pro. These deal with color balance, brightness and contrast, and hue and saturation, and are located in the Adjust menu.

There is an optimal order to making basic photo adjustments, both in color and contrast, as well as sharpening. Any enhancement you make has an impact on previous adjustments, so you should apply them in a logical order to accumulate the effects properly:

1. **Automatic color balance** should be applied first because of its effect on saturation and contrast.

2. **Saturation** is the difference between a given color and gray. The act of adjusting the color balance has an affect on what is defined as gray and subsequently on saturation and contrast.

3. Apply **contrast** enhancements last of all.

Automatic color balance

Different types of light have different colors, and objects illuminated by them take on that color to a certain degree. You don't notice this in real life because your brain has a built-in white balance. The color of a light source is defined by its color **temperature**, measured on the Kelvin scale. This scale defines 6500° as normal daylight. Any higher than this and the light becomes blue or **cooler**, and lower values are orange or **warmer**. Incandescent or tungsten light bulbs are much warmer than regular sunlight.

You may have images that were taken under incandescent light and have an orange cast about them. These are good candidates for the auto color balance. Both digital and conventional photos taken on overcast days may have a bluish cast about them, whereas photos taken at dusk or dawn may appear overly yellow or orange. These are all candidates for color balance correction.

1. Find a photo that needs some color correction. Here, you're going to work through the three autoenhancement tools using the same photo.

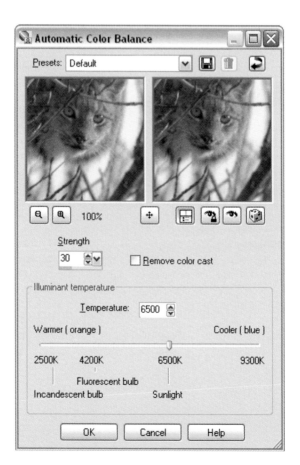

2. Go to Adjust > Color Balance > Automatic Color Balance. The default setting is 6500° Kelvin with a Strength of 30. If your Automatic Color Balance dialog box isn't set up like the preceding dialog box, click the Reset to Default button at the top right of the dialog box.

3. Determine what's wrong with the color balance to begin with. In most cases, your picture will be too cool (a bluish gray) or too warm (yellow/orange). To correct this, move the Illuminant temperature slider in the appropriate direction, keeping an eye on the preview pane.

4. Using the default Strength of 30 is a good starting point. If you find you have to drag the slider right to its limits to get near the desired result, increasing the strength can help you out here.

5. If your image has a **color cast** (a color that appears overlaid on the entire picture), check Remove color cast. Only use this when absolutely necessary, though, as it can result in loss of image information and color saturation.

6. Click OK once you're happy with your settings.

Original Photograph

After Automatic Color Balance

Automatic contrast enhancement

Contrast is the difference in lightness that corresponds to a black-and-white image and is the main reason we can see detail in an image. However, the saturation of a color is also dependent on its lightness—and therefore contrast can affect saturation—so we apply it prior to a saturation correction. A photograph should contain a complete range of intensities between light and dark, but there needs to be balance between the two; dark areas need to have detail, whereas light areas shouldn't appear washed out. It's contrast that helps give your photos depth.

1. Continue with your photo to work on its contrast.

2. Go to Adjust > Brightness and Contrast > Automatic Contrast Enhancement.

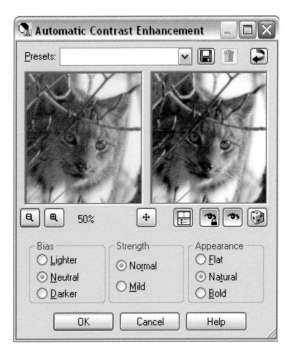

3. If your photo's density is reasonable (that is, if it's not too light or too dark), choose Neutral in the Bias options. Lighter is suitable for a dark photo, and Darker would be appropriate if the image is too light or washed out.

4. Choose between the two Strength options to determine the degree to which the contrast is enhanced. In most cases, Normal will work, but if your image already has a high contrast, set this to Mild.

5. Choosing Bold in the Appearance settings will accentuate the highlights and dark areas, and selecting Flat will tend to increase contrast in the midtones.

After Automatic Color Balance

After Automatic Contrast Enhancement

Automatic saturation enhancement

Next in the three-step autoenhancement process is automatic saturation enhancement. Good color saturation will make your photos seem more vibrant and alive, but you need to be careful that you don't overdo it. There's a fine line between a well-done and an overdone saturation.

1. Continuing with your photo, go to Adjust > Hue and Saturation > Automatic Saturation Enhancement.

2. Check Skintones present if you're working with a photo containing a significant area of skin tone.

3. In most situations, Bias and Strength should be set to Normal.

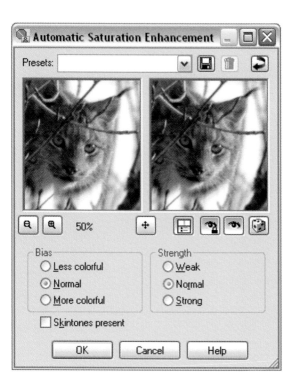

4. If you have a particularly washed-out image, you can use the More colorful bias and Strong strength settings or a combination of these. Less colorful won't make your image less colorful than it already is—it will still increase the saturation but to a more subtle extent than the other two Bias options. Use this option if an image is already quite vibrant or if you want a photo to be more muted but you still want to boost the color.

After Automatic Contrast Enhancement

After Saturation Enhancement

Sharpening

This method of photo enhancement may sound a little misleading; sharpening isn't going to fix a photograph that is out of focus. As wonderful as photo-editing software is, you can't always create something that wasn't there in the first place. Movies have you believe that you can sharpen a fuzzy video capture from a cheap surveillance camera to the extent that it can be blown up to read a minuscule license plate number half a mile away. This just ain't true.

So what's the point of sharpening, then? Well, it's possible to improve the appearance of a slightly blurry image. In our experience, almost any photograph, whether scanned in or imported from a digital camera, can be improved with some degree of sharpening. Paint Shop Pro provides three options when it comes to sharpening. Two are fast and easy, and the third is slightly more complex, giving a degree of user control.

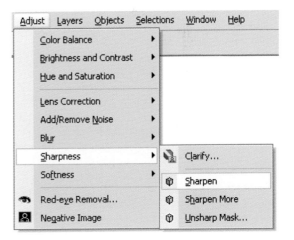

Sharpen and Sharpen More filters

We perceive an edge in a digital photograph when there is a difference in color or brightness between adjacent pixels. When this difference is abrupt across only two pixels, you get a very sharp edge, but if it's spread across several pixels, you get a softer edge.

The **Sharpen** and **Sharpen More** filters increase the contrast between pixels by lightening those above a certain threshold and darkening those below that threshold, making the edges crisper. The Sharpen and Sharpen More filters differ only in the degree of the contrast increase. There is no user input dialog box for these filters; simply clicking the menu item will apply them to the active image.

Original

Sharpen

Sharpen More

Unsharp Mask filter

The seemingly misnamed **Unsharp Mask** filter is indeed a tool for sharpening images. The term **unsharp masking** comes from a photographic darkroom technique that is used to create a positive mask sandwiched with the negative to mask out fuzzy or unsharp areas. Despite its name, the Unsharp Mask filter in Paint Shop Pro has nothing at all to do with layer masking.

Unlike the Sharpen and Sharpen More filters, Unsharp Mask allows for user input, so, in order to make informed choices, you need to know how it works. Although the Sharpen filters apply their effect to *all* pixels in an image, Unsharp Mask evaluates the contrast between adjacent pixels to seek out only the *edges*, rather than applying changes to the entire image. The idea is that a large contrast difference between adjacent pixels usually represents an edge. However, the filter doesn't really recognize edges, just pixel differences, so successful sharpening requires finding the settings that accentuate the edges in the image in a natural-looking way.

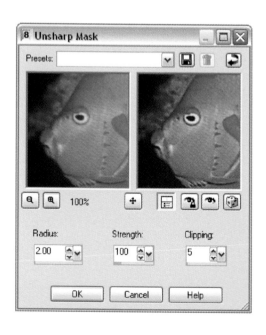

1. Open an image that you would like to sharpen.

2. Go to Adjust > Sharpness > Unsharp Mask. The Unsharp Mask dialog box gives you three user input fields.

3. Try experimenting with the Radius setting and see how the image changes in the preview pane.

When the Unsharp Mask filter finds an edge, the Radius setting determines how many pixels beyond the edge it will adjust the contrast. For a smaller web-sized image, the setting will tend toward the lower end and, for larger print-sized megapixel pictures, higher values work better. Lower values prevent the effect from bleeding over to other edges and compounding the effect. On large images, the radius may have to be increased to make any effect evident.

The proximity of edges also affects the desired Radius setting, as images with many edges close together work better with a smaller radius, whereas those with few edges that are far apart can tolerate a larger radius. Too large a radius will accentuate a halo effect often associated with sharpening. The Radius setting is the most important part of achieving the optimum sharpening effect.

4. The Strength setting determines the amount of contrast increase and dictates the amount of sharpening. A small radius needs a higher strength than a large radius to produce the same degree of visual sharpness.

5. Clipping is basically a noise-reduction setting, telling Paint Shop Pro to ignore a certain amount of difference between pixels when sharpening. Higher values avoid oversharpening lightly textured areas, such as skin tones, or accentuating noise or JPEG artifacts.

The Unsharp Mask filter, though complicated to use, is the preferred sharpening tool, particularly if you're planning to print larger images.

Before Unsharp Mask

After Unsharp Mask

Clarify filter

The Clarify filter is another contrast enhancement filter that you can use to restore detail in old or faded photographs, as well as those taken under misty or poor lighting conditions. Although automatic contrast enhancement adjusts the overall contrast of the image, Clarify is a unique filter that modifies local image contrast to make detail stand out in a natural way, without the halos associated with sharpening filters.

This filter also modifies the lightness or darkness of the image. It can have an effect on saturation too, usually decreasing it. For this reason, it should be used after the auto contrast enhancement but before saturation enhancement.

1. Open a faded photograph that requires clarifying. We've used this photo of a digger in the mist.

2. Select Adjust > Brightness and Contrast > Clarify. The Clarify dialog box contains a single Strength control. A setting of 3 is a good starting point, but adjust the strength to produce as much fine detail as possible without the effect becoming too obvious or intrusive.

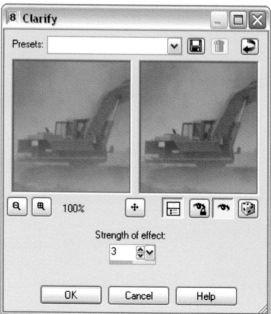

Histogram

The **histogram** (F7) represents the distribution of pixels on a graph according to various values: colors, grayscale, hue, saturation, and lightness. Its purpose is to aid you in analyzing an image.

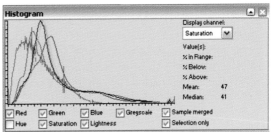

The most important histogram graph is the lightness or luminance graph. Ideally, the histogram should be spread evenly across the full range of the horizontal axis without any sharp spikes. If it has values throughout 0 to 255, it shows that the image is taking full advantage of the range of lightness available. If the graph begins at a value much higher than 0 and ends below the far-right 255 value, the range of the lightness is being limited and the image has less contrast and detail than it could. If the image spikes at the left or zero end of the graph, the image is too dark. If the spike is to the right, it's too light.

Manual histogram adjustment

1. Open up an image that's in need of some life (where the color seems to have drained out). The flower image we use in this example is in the download files.

2. Select Adjustment > Brightness and Contrast > Histogram Adjustment to bring up the Histogram Adjustment dialog box.

3. Choose whether you want to adjust the overall luminosity of the image or the individual red, green, and blue channels by clicking either of the two Edit radio buttons below the image preview area.

Although you can edit individual colors, it's easier and more effective to just work on the luminosity (though do try playing with individual colors to create some special effects in your images).

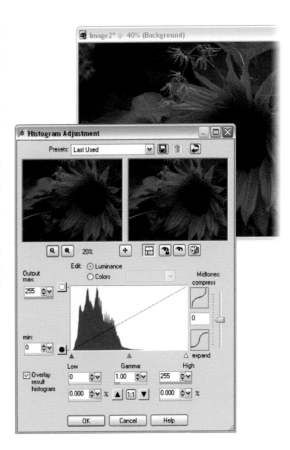

4. The first thing to look at is where the 0 pixel points at the high and low end of the graph are. If these are not right at 0 and 255, respectively, it means that there are no pixels in the image that are pure white or pure black. Therefore, the picture is not taking advantage of the full range of luminosity available to it. You can remedy this by moving the Low and High clip limit sliders to the point where the histogram starts to rise or by entering the values for those points in the Low and High fields.

As you move the sliders or change the values, the ruby overlay will update to reflect how the histogram would appear at those settings (you can toggle this feature in the Overlay results histogram checkbox).

5. Below the Low and High fields are percentage fields that indicate the percentage of pixels contained between 0 and the new Low value in the low limit, and 255 and the new High value. These pixels will be lost if you apply the new limits. If these percentages are too high, it will result in an unacceptable loss of detail. A good rule of thumb is to never allow either of these to exceed 0.01%. In fact, it's a good idea to input 0.01% in both the low and high clip limit percentage fields and save this as a preset so you can apply it to any image quickly.

6. Switch on the preview lock in the Histogram Adjustment dialog box to keep checking the effects of any adjustments you make.

7. If your image is still too dark or light, and the histogram graph peaks to one side or the other of the histogram, use the Gamma adjustment to compensate. If the peak is left of center, dragging the gamma slider to the right will increase the lightness value of all the pixels and move the peak toward the center.

The Midtones compress and expand slider helps you control the contrast. Expanding the midtones will widen the midtone range on the graph and increase the difference in lightness between pixels of similar values, accentuating detail and increasing contrast.

Compressing the midtones will do the opposite and *decrease* contrast. Usually, if you start with a dark picture and increase the gamma, you'll want to expand the midtones. If you start with a light picture and decrease the gamma, you'll need to compress the midtones. Excessive compression will result in lost detail, as pixels of similar values will be forced to take on the same value.

> *Remember your order: the histogram is a contrast adjustment and it may impact saturation, so always use it prior to any saturation adjustments and after any color balance adjustment.*

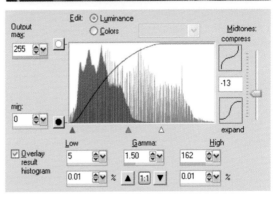

Adjustment layers

Another handy photographic tool in Paint Shop Pro is **adjustment layers**. Unlike regular layers, adjustment layers don't contain actual picture or image elements. Think of them as a set of filters that the photograph has to pass through before you can see it. You can't actually see an adjustment layer; you can only the effect it has on the layers below it in the Layer palette. The advantage of using adjustment layers is that they don't actually change the information in your original image, so you can experiment with contrast, brightness, and color as much as you like without ever affecting your original photograph. They are non-destructive—that is, nothing is actually changed on the image layer itself—so if you save them to the .PspImage format, you can revisit and edit adjustments or remove them altogether.

There are a couple of ways to create an adjustment layer.

You can select Layers > New Adjustment Layer or right-click the Background layer in the Layer palette and choose New Adjustment Layer from there. In either case, you're presented with the adjustment layer type submenu. For straight photo enhancement, your primary concern will be Color Balance, Brightness/Contrast, and Hue/Saturation/Lightness.

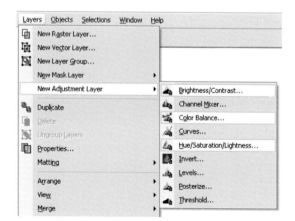

Let's see what you can do with adjustment layers. First, you're going to manipulate the color balance of the photograph.

Color balance

1. Open a photo from your own collection that you feel could use some fixing. Follow along with this example, but experiment with the user settings for your own particular photograph.

2. Now go to Layers > New Adjustment Layer > Color Balance to bring up the Color Balance dialog box. We'll focus on the Adjustment tab first.

The Tone balance controls allow you to choose which area of brightness to apply a particular adjustment to:

★ Checking Shadow applies the adjustments only to the dark areas of the photo.

★ Checking Midtones applies adjustments only to areas of medium brightness.

★ Checking Highlights applies the adjustments only to bright portions of the photo.

Poor color balance is most evident in the midtones, but you could apply a separate adjustment layer for each of the three tonal areas if necessary. Preserve luminosity maintains the brightness of the image as you increase or decrease the color levels.

A color balance problem usually manifests itself by making an image appear too cool or too warm. Our example was taken under tungsten or incandescent lighting with daylight film, so the image has an orange/yellow cast.

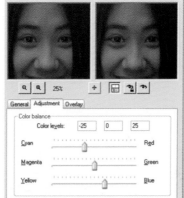

3. Too cool an image like this down, move the Cyan/Red slider toward the cyan end and the Blue/Yellow slider toward the blue end. If the image is too cool, you would adjust the same sliders but in the opposite direction.

As you move the slider, the adjustments appear as plus or minus values in the Color levels fields above the sliders (these are values for red, green, and blue working from left to right).

Other color balance problems may involve different combinations. For instance, if you took a photo that was illuminated by light reflecting off foliage, it might have a greenish cast, in which case adjusting the Magenta/Green slider toward the magenta side would help balance the image.

4. Click OK when you're finished and your new color balance adjustment layer will appear in the Layer palette. Also, like any other layer, you can adjust its opacity, which gives you the opportunity to soften the effect, or you can turn off its visibility by clicking the eye icon. Quick access to the Color Balance dialog box is available by double-clicking it in the Layer palette.

Brightness/Contrast

1. Continue with the photo from the previous color balance example (or open a new image if you prefer).

2. Select Layers > New Adjustment Layer > Brightness/Contrast to bring up the Brightness/Contrast dialog box.

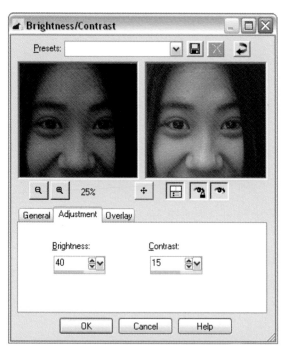

There are two aptly-named adjustment sliders on the Adjustment tab for contrast and brightness. The default is 0 for both fields. A plus value increases the brightness or contrast, whereas a minus value decreases it. As a general rule, when you increase the brightness, boost the level of contrast too.

3. Once you're happy with the brightness and contrast settings, click OK. The new adjustment layer appears in the Layer palette.

Hue/Saturation/Lightness

Now let's deal with hue/saturation/lightness (**HSL**). Go to Layers > New Adjustment Layer > Hue/Saturation/Lightness to create a new HSL adjustment layer and bring up the HSL dialog box.

In most cases of basic photo editing, you won't want to touch the Hue slider and you'll deal with lightness issues in a separate Brightness/Contrast adjustment layer. Here, we just address **saturation** with a simple plus/minus slider to increase or decrease the saturation.

Be cautious with saturation adjustments. There's a temptation to increase saturation to bring out bright colors, but this can often result in a very unnatural-looking photograph. Unless you have a particular color cast that you wish to address, select Master from the Edit drop-down menu. In our example here, the original was too saturated and didn't exhibit the natural skin tones of the subject, so we chose to tone down the saturation.

Editing adjustment layers

Once you've laid down an adjustment layer, you can revisit and change any setting you made simply by selecting and double-clicking the adjustment layer in the Layer palette. This brings up the appropriate dialog box with the current settings for that adjustment layer. You can edit these settings in the dialog box and click OK to apply them. This is useful if you find that after making one type of adjustment layer, you don't like what it does in combination with a previous one. Perhaps changing the saturation makes you want to change your color balance choices—and this is the great advantage of adjustment layers: they don't affect the original photo and nothing is carved in stone.

Another way to edit an adjustment layer is to work on it directly on the canvas.

An adjustment layer is, in reality, an 8-bit grayscale layer. If you select any adjustment layer in the Layer palette, notice that your Materials palette changes to grayscale. On an adjustment layer, white is opaque and black is totally transparent, with the shades of gray in between representing varying degrees of transparency. The lighter the shade, the more opaque the layer. The opacity of the layer determines the degree of effect it has on the underlying image layer.

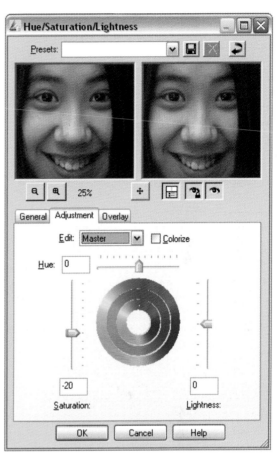

⭐ Three

One of the best reasons for editing an adjustment layer is to make selective adjustments to a photo by bringing out detail in dark shadow areas or toning down bright, blown-out areas.

For this example, we'll use a photograph of people looking over the brink of Niagara Falls. We like the way the Falls dwarfs the tourists but, although the people have a good exposure, the Falls itself is over-exposed and washed out.

What we need to do is bring out more detail in the water, but leave the foreground untouched.

1. Create a new Contrast/Brightness adjustment layer (Layers > New Adjustment Layer > Brightness/Contrast).

2. Insert some pretty extreme settings in the Brightness/Contrast dialog box to help bring out the detail and texture in the white water flowing over the falls—something in the neighborhood of –70 Brightness and +40 Contrast.

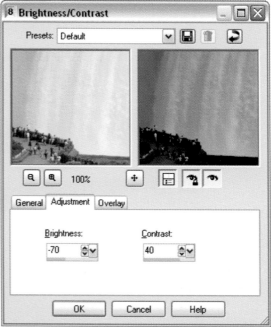

The Falls looks pretty awesome now, but the foreground is way too dark. What you have to do is remove the effect of the adjustment layer from the foreground area.

3. If you look in the Layer palette, there's a mask icon to the extreme right of the adjustment layer. This is the **View Overlay** icon, and it works the same way with an adjustment layer as it does with a mask: it creates a ruby overlay to represent the mask.

4. If you bring up the adjustment layer's properties dialog box, you can adjust the color and opacity of the overlay using the Overlay tab. The overlay will assist you in editing by making the changes you make on the adjustment layer more apparent. Initially, it will simply be a uniform red over the entire image.

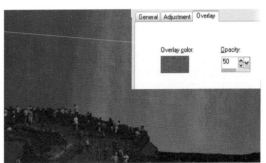

5. Now select the Paint Brush tool. In the Tool Options palette, make the Shape round and set its Size to 100 pixels, though this depends on the size of the image you're working on. In many cases, it may be necessary to vary the size as you work on it. As you don't want the transition to appear too abrupt, set the brush Hardness to 50 to introduce some feathering on the edges.

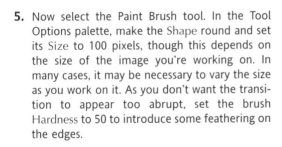

In the Materials palette, the foreground color is black and the background is white. This way, if you paint on too much, you can touch it up by right-click painting white.

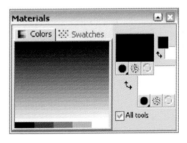

6. Now it's simply a matter of painting on the area where you want to remove the effect from. Zoom in to be more precise and right-click paint to replace those places where you go over the line.

7. You should try and be as precise as you can, but you don't need too be too picky, particularly if the adjustment layer isn't too extreme. Turn off the ruby overlay every now and then while you're working, using the mask icon in the Layer palette, to see how you're doing and note whether or not tiny corrections warrant the trouble. Use a large brush size for big areas, and then work a smaller one along the edges.

In some cases, you may want to mute the effect of an adjustment layer over selective portions of a photo. You can use the same method but, rather than painting with white, use a shade of gray, keeping in mind that the darker the shade of gray, the more of the effect it will remove. When you're painting with gray, the ruby overlay will only partially fade, depending on the darkness of the gray shade you're using.

Removing noise

Noise can be a problem with digital cameras and, with scanned negatives or slides, its analog cousin **grain** can manifest itself. Paint Shop Pro has a very handy tool for removing noise or grain from photographs: the **Edge Preserving Smooth** filter.

1. If you have an image that needs noise or grain removing, choose Adjust > Add/Remove Noise > Edge Preserving Smooth.

2. The Edge Preserving Smooth dialog box has only one field. For straight photo enhancement and removing noise or grain, the Amount of smoothing should not exceed 10 or you run the risk of losing too much sharpness.

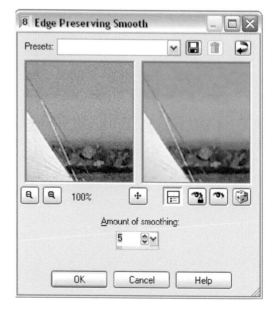

3. Click OK and your image should now look much smoother and more natural.

Removing red-eye

Red-eye is familiar to many of us who take photos using an electronic flash, particularly with cameras that have a built-in flash. It occurs when the light from the flash travels through the subject's pupil and reflects off the retina straight back into the camera lens. The reason it's more likely to happen with built-in flashes is because of the proximity of the flash to the lens, which makes for a narrow angle of reflection. This allows the light to enter and exit the narrow iris opening right into the lens.

Red-eye can be avoided by using bounce flash (the technique of aiming the flash at the ceiling, a wall, or a reflector rather than directly at the subject) or changing the location of the flash unit by moving it further away from the camera. Although these methods are fine for cameras using an external flash unit, they're not options for those with built in-flashes. Fortunately, our digital darkroom has the tool to correct red-eye.

1. With an image open that needs red-eye removing, select Adjust > Red-eye Removal.

2. Select Auto Human Eye from the Method drop-down menu, click the center of the eye, and drag out a round selection to encompass the entire eyeball. Size handles will appear to allow you to resize and change the size of your selection.

3. If you want to start the selection over, click the Delete Eye button. This will replace the entire pupil and iris with a preset one whose attributes you set in the other fields.

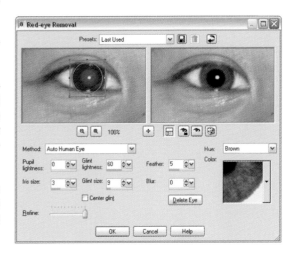

4. Pick the Hue that most closely matches your subject's natural eye color. The hue will apply a color to the iris.

5. Once you have chosen a hue, check the variations on the iris in the Color drop-down menu.

6. Once you're happy that you have the most realistic eye possible in the preview pane, change your view to the subject's other eye and make another selection. The same selected options will apply to that eye, too.

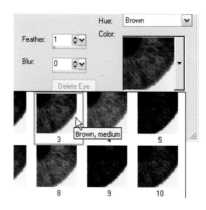

If you have a group picture, you can change the eyes for one person and then move on to the next person and choose different settings appropriate to that individual. Any setting changes you make will apply only to the current selection.

7. You can also choose the Freehand Pupil Outline or Point-to-Point Pupil Outline options from the Method drop-down menu to define the pupil area. These methods may be necessary if you have an eye partially obscured by an eyelid or you have an odd-shaped animal eye. When using the freehand method, you only trace the pupil or the area that is red. Because you use the real iris, there are no options for color, hue, or iris size.

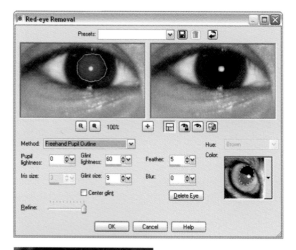

8. Once you've worked through all the eyes in an image, click OK to apply the filter:

Straighten tool

When taking photographs, we often don't pay enough attention to detail. One common area where this becomes obvious is the quick snapshot (often from a moving vehicle) that presents us with a crooked horizon.

1. Choose an image where the horizon is crooked (this is `straighten_boats_start.tif` in the download files) or, say, a building that doesn't appear to be vertical.

2. Choose the Straighten tool from the Deform tool flyout.

There are some caveats involved with using the Straighten tool:

★ Any rotation of a pixel-based image other than a multiple of 90° results in some image degradation. You can't rotate a square pixel several degrees without **resampling** it (when the software interpolates an intermediate new pixel based on information from the original and adjacent pixels).

★ You'll lose some of the image area because it has to be cropped back to a rectangular shape after it's been rotated.

3. Once you've chosen the Straighten tool, a line with handles on each end appears on the active image.

4. Click and drag this line to any position on the canvas by placing the mouse cursor over it anywhere except the end handles. Move the line close to what should be a either horizontal or vertical element in the photo, such as the coastline. You can then drag the end handles to align the line in Paint Shop Pro with the (coast)line in the image.

5. The Tool Options palette gives you several choices. In the Mode drop-down menu you can set Auto, which will align the line and image to either the horizontal or vertical (whichever you set the line closest to).

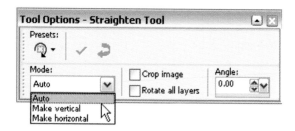

6. Because you're going to rotate the image, it will need to be cropped when you're done. You can do this yourself with the Crop tool (which we look at in a moment), or you can check Crop image in the Tool Options palette.

7. If you're using a multilayered image, check Rotate all layers. Leave this option unchecked if you want to rotate only the current layer.

8. Once you've set the straightening line and tool options, click the Apply check mark in the tool options or simply double-click the canvas.

Crop tool

If you didn't check the Crop image option when using the Straighten tool, you'll have to use the Crop tool to get a proper image.

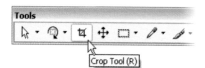

1. Here's the quick way to crop an image. First, select the Crop tool.

2. Now drag out a crop perimeter on top of your image. You can change the perimeter size by dragging any of the handles on the sides or at the corners.

3. When you're happy with the perimeter, double-click inside the crop perimeter to apply the crop.

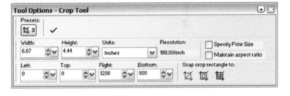

You can also directly input values in the Crop Tool Options palette to make more precise crops.

4. Open a new image and enter a size value in the Width and Height fields, depending on the Units selected (inches, centimeters or pixels).

In the Left, Top, Right, and Bottom fields, you can define the boundaries of the crop in pixels relative to the entire image. Once you've defined a crop in either of these areas, the crop perimeter box will appear on the canvas.

You can drag or resize it using the size and corner resize handles. Checking Maintain aspect ratio is useful in keeping the aspect ratio constant while you resize.

If Specify Print Size is checked, resizing the crop perimeter will automatically change the print resolution in pixels per inch to maintain the print size specified in the Width and Height fields. The resolution field updates this in real time.

The Snap crop rectangle to icons, when clicked, will (from left to right)

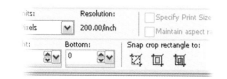

* ★ Snap the crop tight against an active selection.

* ★ Snap to any opaque area on the active layer.

* ★ Snap to the opaque areas on all the layers.

5. Once you've made your crop settings, and you've located and sized the perimeter box on the image, double-click to apply it.

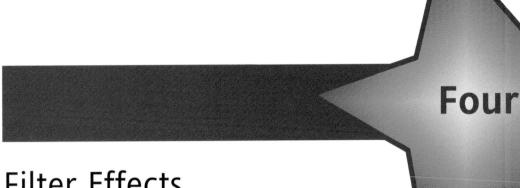

Filter Effects

In this chapter

Paint Shop Pro includes a number of features called **effects**. You can use many of these effects to produce image enhancements that mimic the effects produced by photographic filters over a camera lens. For this reason, effects are sometimes referred to in image manipulation programs as **filters**. However, digital filters can produce effects that could never be produced by a mechanical filter, sometimes beyond the most vivid imagination! (Have you ever wanted to warp the in-laws? Now you can.)

Earlier versions of Paint Shop Pro included many different effects, most of which can be found in Paint Shop Pro 8. In addition, there are some brand-new effects. This chapter covers the following topics:

★ The Effect Browser

★ 3D effects

★ Artistic effects

★ Preset filter effects

Filter effects

Effects and filters (we use the terms interchangeably) often require an image in 16-million color mode (24-bit) in order to work correctly. So, your first step whenever you want to apply an effect should be to make sure that you're in 24-bit mode. If you try to apply an effect but it's unavailable in the Effects menu (i.e., it's grayed out), check out the color mode of your image with Image > Image Information (SHIFT+I). The color mode is listed under Pixel depth/colors in the Current Image Information dialog box.

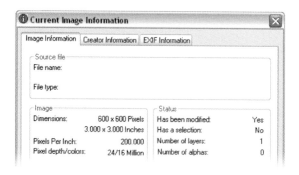

If the mode isn't 24-bit, 16-million color, you'll need to change it. You can do this by selecting Image > Increase Color Depth > 16 Million Colors (24-bit) or using the shortcut CTRL+SHIFT+0.

Effect Browser

The Effect Browser lets you quickly preview any native effect contained in Paint Shop Pro, as long as at least one preset exists in your Presets folder (Program Files/Jasc Software Inc/Paint Shop Pro 8/Presets on your hard drive) for that effect. It works a little like the Image Browser, which in turn functions like Windows Explorer.

When you open the Effect Browser (Effects > Effect Browser), it builds a quickly rendered thumbnail of your open image with all possible presets for all effects that can be applied to it. This is obviously very handy to preview how a certain effect will look or get ideas for image enhancements. However, if you have a lot of presets, the Effect Browser can take a long time to build its catalog.

Click the Presets folder in the left pane to expand it, and then click the individual effects folders to see the presets for that particular filter applied to a thumbnail of your image in the right pane. (If you don't select the Presets folder, you'll see the entire effects preset catalog applied in the right pane, which may take a little time if you've got lots of presets.)

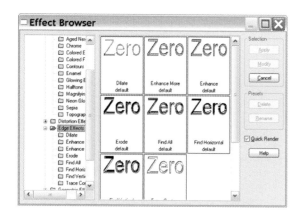

It's possible to rename and delete presets from within the Effect Browser. Note that if you delete a preset from within the Effect Browser, you're permanently deleting it, not just removing it from the Effect Browser view.

Paint Shop Pro also saves any user-created presets to the My Documents/My PSP 8 Files/Presets folder, unless otherwise configured upon installation or changed in the program with File > Preferences > File Locations.

The Effects dialog box

When you choose an effect, either from the Effects Browser or from the menus, a dialog box will open. What options you have will depend on what effect you've chosen, but the top portion of the dialog box is always the same.

The **Reset** button will return any dialog box to the default factory settings. This can be very handy if you've used the filter for some wacky effects, as the dialog boxes retain any settings that were used last. The View buttons act as **Zoom** tools for the preview panes (very useful when the dialog box is maximized). You can proof the effect directly on the image by clicking the **Proof** icon, and you can also automatically update any new settings by clicking the **Auto Proof** icon. Two things to note here are

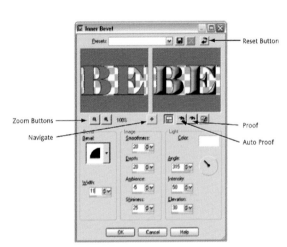

* Auto Proof may slow down some systems considerably.

* Using Auto Proof doesn't apply the effect to the image—the effect is only applied when you click the OK button.

Presets

Presets are setting configurations that you can save and reload in an instant, re-creating the exact effects you applied on another image. You can also save your own presets and exchange them with other Paint Shop Pro 8 users. Presets from previous versions of Paint Shop Pro won't work in Paint Shop Pro 8, and Paint Shop Pro 8's presets won't work in previous versions.

1. To save a preset, click the Save Preset icon near the top of the filter dialog box. Here, we're continuing with our Inner Bevel from the last example. Click OK to save your preset.

2. You can browse to your preset in the Presets drop-down menu at the top of the dialog box. Click it to load these settings into the effect controls.

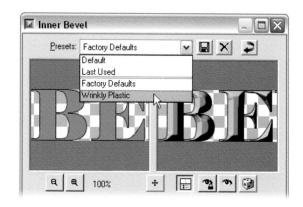

If you have a lot of saved presets, the list may become long and unwieldy to use. The presets for every filter are stored in Program Files/Jasc Software Inc/Paint Shop Pro 8/Presets on your hard drive or in the My Documents/My PSP 8 Files/Presets folder as previously noted.

The presets are actually part of Paint Shop Pro 8's new scripting features (for more information on these, see Chapter Eight). Because they're scripts, they can be traded with other users—just drop the file in the Presets folder described previously and the presets will automatically appear in the Presets drop-down menu for that particular filter.

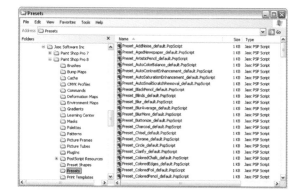

Groups of effects

Paint Shop Pro groups its effects in various subcategories. We show some examples of the different types here; the principles of controlling all effects are similar. Effects that are usually used for manipulating photographs are covered in Chapter Three.

3D effects

Look in Effects > 3D Effects. These effects can make a two-dimensional (2D) image take on a 3D look, and they can be very useful when combined with other effects. (As with many things in life, a little can go a long way. And here's another great truism: just because you *can* do something doesn't mean you necessarily *should* do it!)

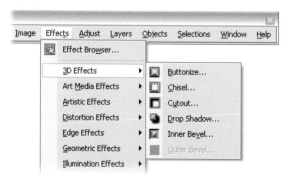

Drop Shadow effect

The first thing to know about the **Drop Shadow** effect is that it needs a selection or an object on a transparent layer to show any effect. Also, you can't select the entire image and see the effect, because the Drop Shadow actually needs some *image space* to create its magic. In the case of the Drop Shadow, a selection defines the area to be shadowed and the actual shadow appears *outside* the selection.

1. Open a new 500x500, 24-bit color image with a white background. We're going use text to show off the effect, although you can add a shadow to any selection.

2. Select the Text tool and choose a blocky font style. Set the foreground/stroke and background/fill colors to your liking. In the Text Tool Options palette, select Floating text from the Create as drop-down menu and make the font size 72 points. Set Stroke width (pixels) to 1 and check Anti-alias.

3. Click the canvas, type in your text, and click Apply. Use the Move tool to position the text where you'd like it on your image.

4. Choose Effects > 3D Effects > Drop Shadow to open the Drop Shadow dialog box. Set the Vertical and Horizontal offsets to 10, Opacity to 80, Blur to 10, and Color to black, and check Shadow on new layer.

By inputting numerical values in the Offset fields, you can place the shadow relative to the object that is casting the shadow. Negative Vertical offset values move the shadow above the object, whereas positive values move it below, as if a light source was shining down from above.

Negative Horizontal offset values place the shadow to the left of the object (your left as you look at it), and positive values place it to the right.

You can interactively place the shadow and see it immediately updated in the preview pane.

5. In the placement pane, you'll see a small "target." Place your mouse cursor over the target, and you should see your cursor turn to a four-headed arrow. Click at this spot and drag the target in the direction you would like your shadow to appear.

6. You can set the shadow color by clicking the color swatch in the Drop Shadow dialog box and selecting any color from it, just as you would any color in Paint Shop Pro. You can also hover over any open image on the workspace and select a color using the eyedropper that appears.

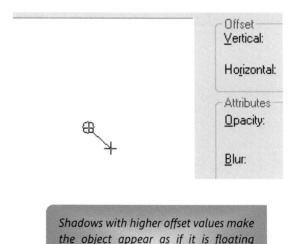

Shadows with higher offset values make the object appear as if it is floating above the background of the image.

7. You can adjust the shadow's opacity and blur using the Opacity and Blur sliders. The higher the blur settings, the softer the edges of the shadow. Shadows with higher blur settings make the object appear as if light is cast on it from a distant light source, as opposed to a very close source, which would cast a harder-edged, more defined shadow.

We've checked the option to add the drop shadow on its own layer in our image. You'll often find that creating a drop shadow on a selection on a layer with a background color creates an unattractive "halo" of color. These are pixels that have been drawn from the background and intermixed with the shadow color. By allowing Paint Shop Pro to create a shadow on a new layer, there will be no background pixels to create the haloing effect. If you defloat the selection, the Drop Shadow effect will be placed on the same layer as the selection it's shadowing.

8. Click OK to apply a shadow to your object. Voila! Instant depth and dimension added to your object. You can add multiple shadows, either with the same offsets to gradually build up a realistic shadow, or you can use different offsets, colors, and opacities to create special effects.

Bevel effects

Let's now look at a group of other useful 3D effects: the **Bevel** filters. The Inner and Outer Bevel filters share some common features and, in fact, the only real difference between them is the way in which the effect is applied to a selection. As shown here, in the Outer Bevel (the blue cross) filter, the 3D effect is applied to the *outside* of the selection, so that the bevel is actually formed from the background of the selected object. In the Inner Bevel filter, the bevel is formed *inside* the selection, so the raised edge begins at the edge of the selection and is constructed using pixel information from the selected object itself.

1. Open a new 24-bit color image that's 500x500 with a white background. We're going to demonstrate with some text.

2. Select the Text tool and choose a blocky font in the Text Tool Options palette. Set the foreground/stroke and background/fill colors to your liking, set Create as to Floating, set the font size to 72 points, give it a 1-pixel stroke, and check Anti-alias.

3. Go to Effects > 3D Effects > Inner Bevel to bring up the Inner Bevel dialog box.

4. Choose an edge design from the Bevel drop-down menu that appeals to you by clicking directly on it in the catalog.

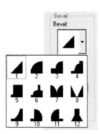

5. Move the Width slider in the Bevel settings and preview the effect in the preview pane. Higher Width settings make the beveled edge more pronounced.

The set of Image sliders controls how the edge appears:

- ★ Higher Smoothness settings create smooth edges and can smooth the interior of the object too.
- ★ Depth controls how deeply the bevel is cut into the interior of the object.
- ★ Ambience and Shininess control how light appears to be reflected on the object.

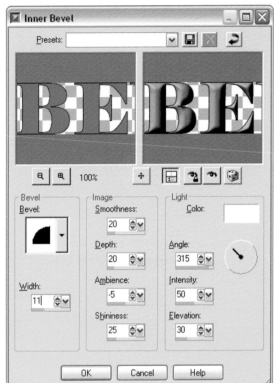

This 3D bevel look is created by the interplay of light and shadow on an object, and it uses colors and light intensities to simulate the actual object. Higher settings here can make an object seem glassy or metallic, by adding more highlights to the edges of the bevel. Lower settings make the surface appear matte.

The light color is set in the Light settings' Color swatch, as normal. You'll often use white here, because it simulates natural light. Bright colors may recolor your entire object, whereas an "opposite" color on a color chart (such as a red light on a green object) may produce completely unexpected results. Natural sunlight is often portrayed as coming from the top-left corner of an image, so a light Angle of about 315° is realistic here. Intensity refers to how bright the light source seems to be, and Elevation denotes how far from the light source the object appears.

6. Once you're happy with the settings, apply them to your selection by clicking OK.

Depending on your settings, you can achieve a variety of effects. This particular wrinkly plastic look was produced on this image with the settings as shown.

7. If you add a Drop Shadow effect right now, you'll really make your 3D effect pop! Your object should still be selected, so you can immediately access the Drop Shadow effect and apply it.

You may want to contract your selection a pixel or two (Selections > Modify > Contract) before applying the Drop Shadow effect, as bevel filters tend to add a bit of jaggedness to edges in the filtering process.

Buttonize effect

The **Buttonize** effect is similar to Inner Bevel filter, as it allows you to add beveled edges to a rectangular selection or object, which makes quick work of web page buttons (hence the name "Buttonize"). Although it's not nearly as flexible as the Bevel effects and will function correctly only on square or rectangular shapes, the Buttonize effect is quick to use. Go to Effects > 3D Effects > Buttonize to open the Buttonize dialog box.

You can set the Height and Width of the button's edge, as well as the color and opacity of the edge effect. You can also choose between a Solid Edge and a Transparent Edge effect by clicking the appropriate radio button in the dialog box. This effect can be applied to a separate layer, or to a background or merged layer.

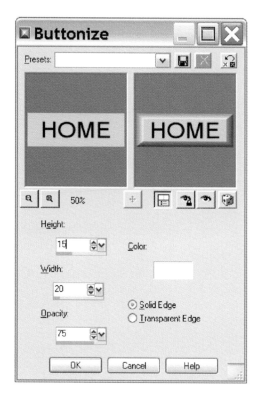

As you can see on the right here, a transparent edge gives the button a softer, more rounded edge.

Solid Edge   Transparent Edge

Chisel effect

The **Chisel** effect makes the edges of a selection appear as if they're carved out of the image background.

1. Open a new image and use the Text tool to write some text on the canvas.

2. Select all the text (the Chisel effect will be unavailable if you don't first select the content to apply it to).

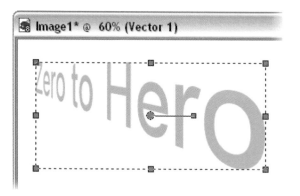

3. Go to Effects > 3D Effects > Chisel.

4. The Chisel effect isn't as flexible as the Bevel effects, but you can set the width of the effect and the chiseled edge colors using the dialog box and the usual Rainbow Picker. Like the Bevel effects, you have the option to set transparent or solid colored edges.

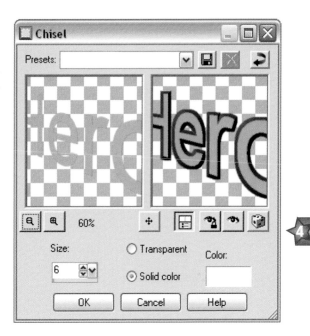

5. Click OK when you're happy with your settings to apply the Chisel effect.

Art Media effects

The **Art Media** effects menu contains effects that simulate real art materials, such as pencil sketches, charcoal drawings, and paintbrush strokes.

Brush Strokes effect

1. Create a 500x500 image that's 24-bit color with a white background. Choose a sky blue shade (R:155, G:170, B:200) for your foreground color and a medium green (R:5, G:220, B:15) for your background color, as shown here on the right.

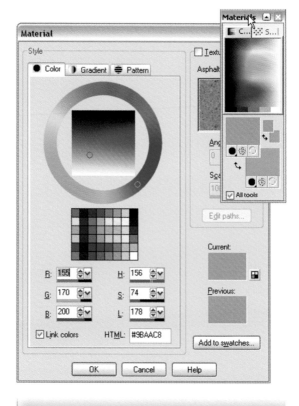

2. Select the Paint Brush tool and, in the tool options, set a Round brush shape with a size of at least 150 pixels. Set Hardness to 20 and Opacity to 100. Check Wet Look Paint and paint the upper part of the image in broad strokes, filling in the sky area. Don't worry about filling every bit in.

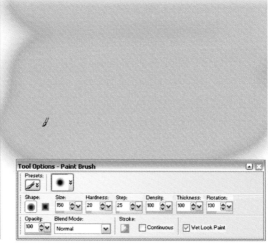

3. Change your brush size to 20 and uncheck Wet Look Paint in the tool options. Right-click and drag to paint with the background color (green), and make some jagged strokes (to simulate grass) along the bottom third of your image.

4. Click the background color swatch to open the Rainbow Picker. The Lightness (L) setting on the original green shade was 113, but change it now to 70, creating a darker shade of green.

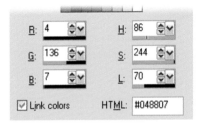

5. Back in the Paint Brush tool options, check Wet Look Paint, set your brush size to 70, and continue to paint in the green grass area, adding strokes with the darker green. Again, don't worry about filling it all in. The Wet Look Paint option will leave the look of wet edges and also build up the color in areas that you paint over a second time.

6. Next, set the foreground color to white, the brush size to 100, and the brush opacity to 50, and uncheck Wet Look Paint. Click randomly in the sky area to add some puffy white clouds.

7. Set the foreground color to yellow (R:255, G:255, B:0) and click where you'd like to add a sun. Click several more times in the same spot to build up a soft sun shape.

8. Set your foreground color to a dark gray/blue (R:78, G:82, B:88). Change the brush shape to Square, and set Size to 30, Thickness to 25, and Rotation to 130. Uncheck Wet Look Paint and draw some random V-shapes to represent birds in the sky.

Now we know what you may be thinking: "This looks a lot like my 7-year-old's refrigerator art." This might well be the case, so let's make some magic.

9. Duplicate this image several times with Window > Duplicate (SHIFT+D) to create new copies of the image. You'll need some extra unfiltered copies as a base for the effects you'll use next.

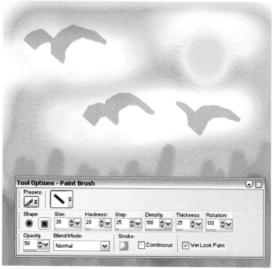

10. Go to Effects > Art Media Effects > Brush Strokes. Apply these settings and watch your finger-painting assume the look of painted strokes on canvas.

You can play with the Brush, Strokes, and Lighting settings to achieve different painted effects. You can also apply one Brush Strokes effect, and then reapply the filter with different settings for interesting effects.

> *Setting the Color to black gives the brush strokes a flat appearance. Lighter colors will result in a more raised look.*

It now looks like your 7-year-old's refrigerator art but with real brush strokes.

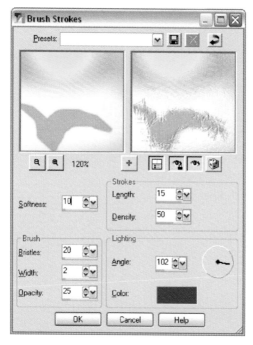

Black Pencil effect

1. Return to one of your unfiltered duplicate copies of the painting that you made in the previous example.

2. Go to Effects > Art Media Effects > Black Pencil.

To get a good noticeable effect, you'll want to set a very high level of Detail, perhaps all the way to 100. This will give you a sort of pencil hatch effect on the lighter edges of your image and darker, thicker lines on the edges of higher contrast. Experiment with the opacity; it determines how much of the original image shows through the effect. A very high setting will give you a grayscale image covering up the original color.

Colored Pencil effect

The Colored Pencil effect (Effects > Art Media Effects > Colored Pencil) can create a realistic colored sketch effect. Again, a high Detail setting works best here. The Opacity setting has the same effect as it does with the Black Pencil filter.

The Colored Pencil effect also has an interesting little quirk that you can use to make a diamond tile pattern, but first you'll prepare an image to use this effect on and investigate the Kaleidoscope effect.

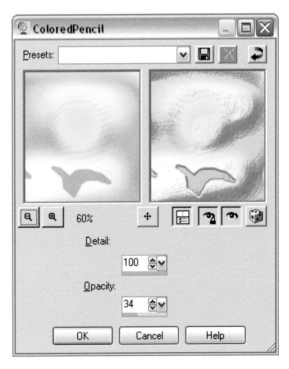

Kaleidoscope and Pencil effects

1. Open a new 500x500 image that's 24-bit color with a white background. Select the Brush tool and lay down a few broad strokes using two or three different colors.

2. Go to Effects > Reflection Effects > Kaleidoscope. Here's our opportunity to introduce you to one of our favorite new features of Paint Shop Pro 8: the **Randomize** button.

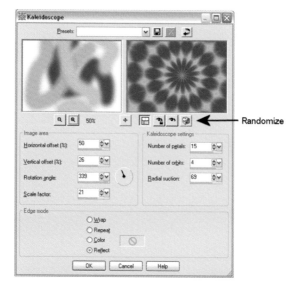

The little die icon symbolizes "throwing the dice." When you click the Randomize button, Paint Shop Pro generates random parameters for the effect. For some effects, you'd rarely use such random parameters (it's unlikely you'd ever want a random drop shadow, for example). However, for other effects, Randomize is not only useful, but also downright fun, producing effects you'd never come up with intentionally!

3. Once you're happy with your settings, click OK to apply the Kaleidoscope effect to your image.

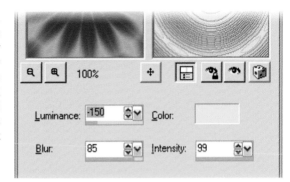

4. Now go to Effects > Art Media Effects > Pencil. Slide the Luminance value to a low negative number, at least −150. Choose a light color for your color swatch, and set the Intensity between 50 and 100. You can fiddle with the Blur setting to your taste—low Blur settings will show quite a bit of your original image, and higher values will blur out the interior details and leave pencil-sketch lines around the object outlines.

5. Click OK to apply the effect, and look at the right and bottom edges of your image. See that thin black border along the edge? It's created when you have very low Luminance values in this filter, which might be unsightly for certain purposes, but you're going to take advantage of those borders. You're going to turn this into a pattern for your Flood Fill tool.

6. Go to File > Save As, give the image a descriptive title, and navigate to the Patterns folder (this should be Program Files/Jasc Software Inc/Paint Shop Pro 8/Patterns). Save your image as a .PspImage file.

7. This image should now be available to you as a pattern. Select Pattern for your foreground in the Materials palette and double-click the swatch to choose a pattern style.

8. Click the Pattern tab, and you can now access the Pattern catalog directly from the drop-down menu. Go find your pattern!

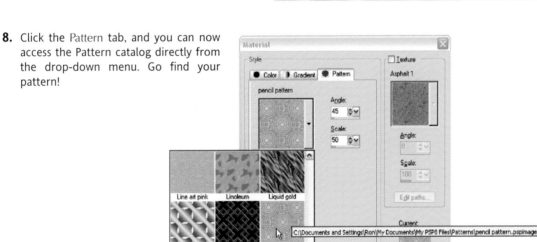

9. Click the pattern to set it as the current pattern. You can also set the Scale and Angle of the pattern here, which makes it very versatile.

10. To make an interesting ceramic tile effect, set Angle to 45 and Scale to 50. Open a new 500x500 image and use the Flood Fill tool to fill it with your new pattern.

Artistic effects

The next category of effects we'll look at is the **Artistic** effects—some wild, some wacky, some slightly subtler. The one we concentrate on is **Balls and Bubbles**.

Balls and Bubbles effect

1. Open a new 500x500 image, 24-bit color, with a gradient background. We've used a black-to-white inverted circular gradient as our background.

2. Add a new raster layer to your image (Layers > New Raster Layer). Add some floating text and position it in the middle of the canvas.

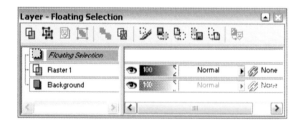

3. When the text is positioned correctly on the canvas, defloat it to the new layer (CTRL+SHIFT+F) and then deselect it (CTRL+D). Here we've added text in red and centered it in our image.

4. Duplicate this image so you have a second copy to use later in the exercise (Window > Duplicate or SHIFT+D).

5. Go to Effects > Artistic Effects > Balls and Bubbles.

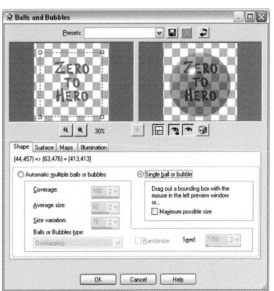

You'll see the original image and a preview pane with the current settings applied as usual, but there are also four tabs on this filter. You have the option to create multiple or single spheres in your image.

In the left pane, you should see a "bounding box" selection tool. You can grab the corners of this box to resize the parameters of your bubble shape and also use it to position your bubble in your image. If you check Maximum possible size, your bubble will be centered in the image and sized to the height or width parameter of your image, whichever is smaller (only circular bubble shapes can be produced).

If you choose the Automatic multiple balls or bubbles option, there are Coverage, Average size, and Size variation options for you to play with, as well as Balls or Bubbles type.

★ Intersecting kind of resembles those molecular chains we were forced to study in high school!

★ Non-intersecting is where the balls don't touch.

★ Overlapping is where the balls touch but don't lose their spherical shape as they do with the Intersecting type.

You're going to choose Single ball or bubble here and use the bounding box in the left pane to drag out a square with the text centered in it.

6. Click the Surface tab. Set Opacity to 75, Shininess to 50, and Gloss to 20. Try modifying the basic surface properties of your bubble by editing these settings.

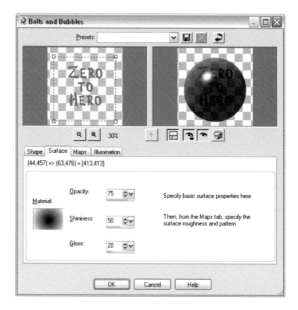

7. Click the Material swatch on the Surface tab to bring up the Material Picker, where you can choose a color, gradient, pattern, or texture for your bubble's surface. Use the same circular gradient you used for the image background (black to white), only this time don't check Invert.

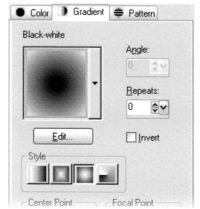

8. Once you're happy with your surface settings, click the Maps tab. This allows for use of **bump maps** (usually grayscale images that give the bubble a 3D texture) and **environment maps** (usually 24-bit images that provide surface reflections). Check both Environment map and Current Image. This uses the text you placed on the layer as the environment map for this bubble. Also set Opacity to 75.

The default path to these maps is Program Files/Jasc Software Inc/Paint Shop Pro 8/Bump Maps and Environment Maps. As with nearly everything else in Paint Shop Pro, you can add additional folders using File > Preferences > File Locations (this process is covered in detail in Chapter Eight).

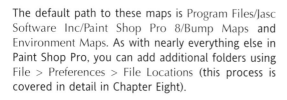

9. Take a look in the Illumination tab. The settings here affect the way light appears to shine on the bubble. Set the Ambience Maximum to 90 and the Ambience Minimum to 0. The light color swatch lets you use the Rainbow Picker or eyedropper in the usual manner. Set Color to white and Highlight size to 15.

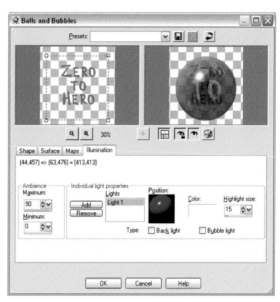

The Highlight size setting is the actual bright spot that connotes reflected light on a sphere. You can add more than one light source by clicking the Add button in Individual light properties area.

You can position each light source by clicking its name in the Lights box, and then click-dragging the highlight in the Position box.

Each light source can have its own color and other illumination attributes. Let's add a second light now.

10. Click Add in the Individual light properties area and make the following settings:

- ★ Color: Yellow
- ★ Maximum Ambience: 75
- ★ Minimum Ambience: 11
- ★ Highlight size: 8

11. Position the light toward the lower-right corner by dragging it in the Position window. You can reset the properties on any light by highlighting it in the Lights field and making adjustments, but the adjustments will apply only to the highlighted light. You can remove highlighted lights by clicking the Remove button.

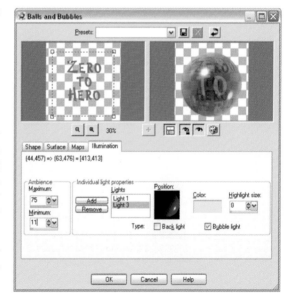

Checking Back light makes the selected light appear to come from behind the bubble. Checking Bubble light adds a fainter highlight opposite the main one to imitate the internal reflection and lighting of a highlight.

12. Click OK to apply the effect.

13. If you'd like to try the same effect with multiple bubbles, use the copy of the original image you made and open the Balls and Bubble filter again (Effects > Artistic Effects > Balls and Bubbles).

14. Your last used settings should be active, so click Automatic multiple balls or bubbles on the Shape tab.

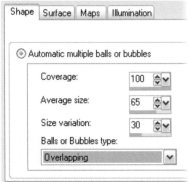

15. Set Coverage to 100, Average size to 65, and Size variation to 30. Choose Overlapping from the Balls or Bubbles type drop-down menu and click OK. Now your image is filled with many, many Heroic bubbles!

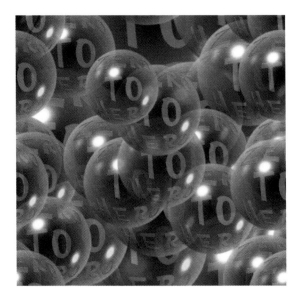

Image effects: Seamless Tiling

Want to create patterns that tile seamlessly when you're filling images or selections, or for web page backgrounds? If so, then this is the filter for you. You can turn parts of your favorite photos, or nearly any other image, into seamless patterns with the **Seamless Tiling** effect.

1. Open an image of your liking and crop or resize it to 250x250. (You can try different sizes; we're just going for a square pattern at the moment.) This cropped area will form the tile for your background.

2. Go to Effects > Image Effects > Seamless Tiling.

In the left preview pane, you'll see an offset target that you can pull around the preview image. The same settings are controlled by the Horizontal offset and Vertical offset controls on the right side of the dialog box. These control what portion of the original image becomes the start of the tile effect.

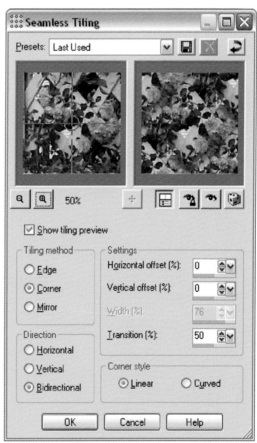

There are several tiling methods: Edge, Corner, and Mirror. You can easily see the differences among these methods if you check Show tiling preview.

Edge tiling creates a seamless "transition" area around the rectangular edge of the selection or image. Mirror tiling creates a mirror image of the center of the selection. Corner tiling creates an offset effect, with the image divided into four quadrants that are then offset so that the central part of the image repeats on the diagonal. We've chosen Corner tiling here because it will repeat the diagonal lattice effect in the photo. We've also chosen Bidirectional as the tiling direction, because we want the tile to be used over a large area.

The Transition (%) setting refers to the amount of edge area on the original image that will be used to create the seamless effect. We've used 50% here, which creates a smooth transition between repeats of the pattern but still looks natural.

You can also change the Horizontal offset and Vertical offset, which place the center of the tiled effect. The crosshairs on the preview pane show where the tiled effect originates. You can either use the numeric entry controls or click-drag the crosshairs themselves to change the center of the effect.

3. Check Show tiling preview. A separate panel opens, showing you the image tiled. You may need to zoom out to see the pattern repeated, just as if it were on a large image.

4. Once you're happy with your settings, click OK to apply the effect.

5. Now you can save this image as a pattern in your Paint Shop Pro files. Click File > Save As, browse to the pattern files on your computer, and save the image as a .PspImage file.

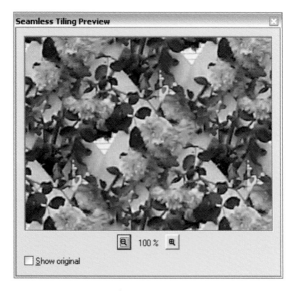

6. If you set this pattern as your foreground or background material in the Materials palette, you can use it with the Flood Fill tool to fill a larger image. Here we've used it on an 800x600 image as a background fill.

Drawing with Vectors

In this chapter

Sometimes the mere mention of the word "vectors" can strike fear into the heart of even a seasoned computer graphics user. If you're one of these people, sit back and relax. Vector graphics are nothing to be afraid of and can be a very powerful tool. In this chapter, we cover the following topics:

★ Using the Preset Shape tool

★ Aligning and positioning objects

★ Working with vector text

★ Using the Pen tool

★ Drawing cartoon characters with vectors

What exactly are vectors?

Computers render graphics in one of two ways: **vector** or **raster**. Although there are many graphic file formats, they basically represent data as either vector or raster (though some formats can contain both types of information).

Raster graphics are made up of tiny individual squares called **pixels** (short for picture elements). The number of pixels in an image determines the resolution of that image and, when displayed on a computer monitor, the size of the image. A 640x480 graphic measures 640 pixels tall and 480 pixels wide. If you displayed this image on a computer monitor set to a resolution of 640x480, it would fill the entire screen. This file would have to contain information on the color, lightness, and position for each and every one of the 307,200 pixels (640 multiplied by 480).

On the other hand, a vector file contains no pixel information whatsoever. Instead of detailed information on individual pixels, a vector file contains a set of mathematical instructions that tell the computer how to draw the image. At the most basic level, vector instructions describe the path a line takes: where it starts, where it ends, and the route it takes to get there via coordinates. It contains information on

* **Stroke**: The outline edge of the shape

* **Fill**: The interior of the shape surrounded by the stroke

Other basic information may also be included in a vector file:

* Does the path have a stroke or not?

* If so, what's the color of the stroke?

* How thick is the stroke?

* Is the interior of the path filled with a particular color, gradient, or texture?

* Is the path **closed** (does it start and end at the same place)?

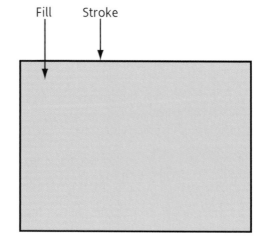

Consider a simple vector graphic image of a stroked square that's 72x72 pixels. The file contains instructions telling the computer to start at a given coordinate and draw a straight line to another point, turn right, move on to another coordinate, and so on until the four sides of the square are complete. Add a little fill and line information and you have your picture; it's much more compact than the 5,184 (72x72) pixels a raster file would have to keep track of.

Another advantage of vectors is that they're easy to scale up yet keep crisp. Say you wanted a really big rectangle. The instructions would simply change to describe how long the four lines should be, with no pesky pixels to resize and get all thick and fuzzy. The image remains crisp and clear.

So, if vector graphics are so great, why don't we use them for all our images? Although vector graphics are getting more and more sophisticated and can render pretty realistic-looking objects when used skillfully, they are not up to photographic work. Nonetheless, vector graphics are finding their way to the Web through plug-ins such as Macromedia's Flash Player. The Scalable Vector Graphics (SVG) format is also in the process of becoming a web standard.

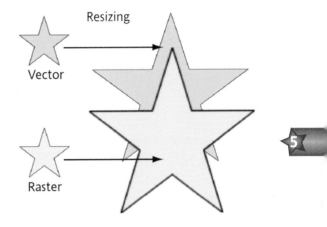

Vector paths

A vector path or object is made up of one or more **contours**, which is basically just a line that has a start and end point. If the start and end points are in different locations, the path is **open**. A **closed** path is **contiguous**—it starts and ends at the same place. All paths have a direction that is defined by the start and end points.

You don't actually see a path or contour; rather, you see its rendered attributes or properties. These properties define the appearance of the stroke and fill.

The properties of the stroke are defined by the settings in the Materials palette at the time the path is laid down and can have any of the following attributes: solid color, gradient, and pattern, as well as texture. In effect, when you work with vectors, these swatches become the stroke and fill swatches.

Although a single path may contain any number of contours, it can have only one set of properties for the stroke and one set for the fill. All the contours contained in a single object will share common stroke and fill styles.

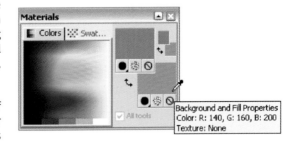

Vector tools

To create and edit vector paths or objects, you need to use one of the four vector tools at the right of the Tools palette:

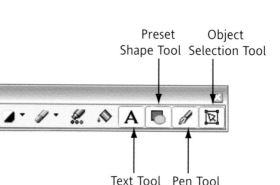

The Text and Preset Shape tools are used to create paths. The Pen tool works as both a path creation tool and a path editor, and the Object Selection tool is used to make a path available for editing.

Preset Shape tool

Paint Shop Pro comes complete with a selection of predefined vector shapes that you can easily lay down with the Preset Shape tool. Let's take this tool out for a test-drive.

1. Open a new image with a transparent raster background. Choose your own dimensions and resolution.

2. Click the Preset Shape tool (P) and look at the Preset Shape tool options:

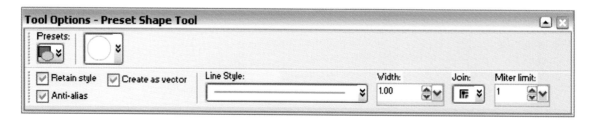

3. Open the shape drop-down menu to preview the preset shapes available. Some are complex; others are plain and simple. You'll begin with one of the basic shapes: the ellipse.

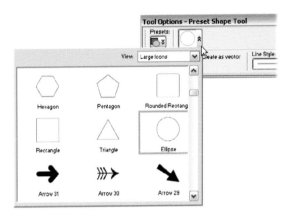

At the bottom left of the tool options are three check boxes:

★ Retain style causes the shape to be laid down with any stroke and fill characteristics it was originally created with and, if checked, it will appear similar to the preview.

★ Create as vector ensures that the shape is laid down as a vector. If this option is not checked, Paint Shop Pro will turn the shape into a raster graphic when you lay it down.

★ Anti-alias applies anti-aliasing to the object, which will alleviate the dreaded jagged edges.

4. Make sure that all three of these options are checked, and lay out a flattened ellipse that's slightly smaller than your canvas by dragging from upper left to lower right.

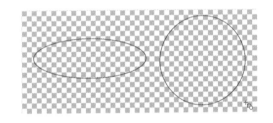

5. Lay down a second ellipse, but this time hold down the SHIFT key while you drag to preserve the aspect ratio of the original shape (to make a perfect circle).

You've just laid down two black-stroked ellipses with no fill. This is the style of the original shape that you chose to retain by checking Retain style in step 4. You'll find all the first group of basic or primitive shapes have this style.

Now look in the Layer palette. You originally created this file with a transparent raster background.

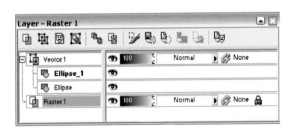

You can see that you now have two layers: the original raster layer and a new vector layer (note the distinctive icons for the different layer types). Vector and raster graphics can't exist on the same layer in Paint Shop Pro so, if a raster layer is active at the time, laying down any vector object will result in the creation of a new vector layer directly above the active raster layer. Alternatively, if a vector layer had been present and active, the shape would have been placed on that layer.

If you expand the vector layer by clicking the plus sign (+) to the left of the layer icon, you'll see that each of the preset shapes is listed. Any individual object will appear as a vector sublayer in the palette. Vector layers can be renamed and dragged just like raster layers, as can individual vector objects.

If you lay down a vector shape without checking Retain style, you can select the colors and other properties to be applied to the shape. Let's do this now.

> *Although you can't vary the opacity of an individual vector object independent of the entire layer, you can click the eye icon to make it invisible. Creating a new vector layer will, however, allow you to lay down an object whose opacity can be independently adjusted.*

6. Open a new image. Select the color, gradient, or pattern you want to use in both Materials swatches.

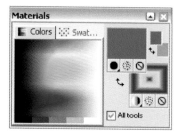

7. Click the Preset Shape tool, if it isn't still active, and select a shape from the first group of basic shapes in the Tool Options palette. We've opted for Star 1.

8. Uncheck Retain style and select any style you like from the Line Style drop-down menu.

9. Enter a stroke width in the Width field. This value is the stroke width in pixels.

10. Go ahead and drag out your shape.

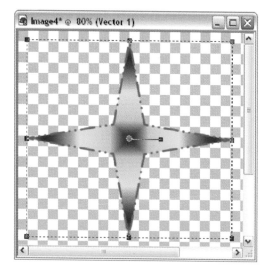

Once you've selected properties for a shape, you can save them as a preset and apply them to any shape you lay down in the future.

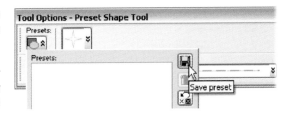

11. Click the Presets button at the upper-left corner of the tool options, and then click the floppy disk icon to the right of it to call up the Save Preset dialog box. You can simply give the preset a name and click OK or, by clicking the Options button, include creator information and a description. Once you've saved the preset, you can recall it by selecting it from the Presets drop-down menu.

So, what if you decide you don't like the look of your new shape? Well, one of the great things about vector objects is that you can edit them without compromising the quality. How, you ask? First, you have to learn about the Object Selection tool.

Object Selection tool

As the name implies, you use this tool to select a vector object.

1. Before you can do anything to an object, you must first select it with the Object Selection tool (O) by clicking the object or clicking directly on the stroke if the object has no fill.

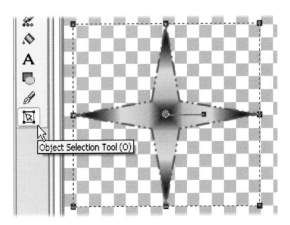

Alternatively, you can drag a selection box around multiple objects to select all of them at once. In this case, the selection box must encompass the objects completely. If even a small portion of an object is outside the box, it will not be selected. Another way of selecting multiple objects is to click each one while holding down the SHIFT key.

2. When you've selected an object, you'll see a **bounding box** surrounding it.

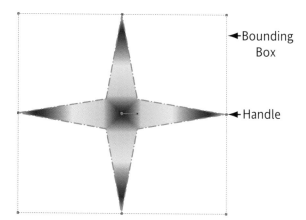

← Bounding Box

← Handle

3. Eight little boxes or **handles** at the four corners and midway between the corners indicate that an object is selected. You can resize a vector object by dragging these handles in or out. Right-clicking and dragging a corner handle will preserve the aspect ratio.

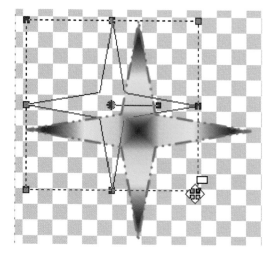

4. Holding down SHIFT or CTRL while dragging a handle applies deformations to the object.

Another reason for selecting a vector object is to change its properties. You can change the fill and stroke attributes of a selected object by modifying the foreground and background swatches as normal in the Materials palette.

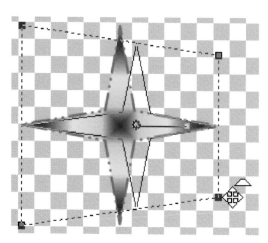

5. You can also edit a selected object's properties
via the Properties button on the Object
Selection Tool Options palette or by clicking the
vector layer in the Layer palette.

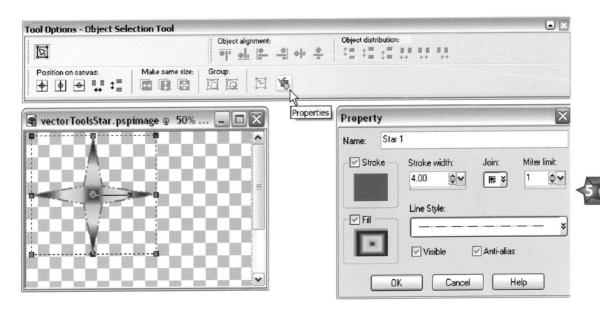

If you change the properties while more than one
object is selected, any attribute you edit will be
applied to all the objects.

Aligning objects

1. Open a new 400x300 image that's 24-bit color
with a white background.

2. Select the Preset Shape tool and draw three different shapes on your canvas.

3. Select the Object Selection tool. Holding down
the SHIFT key, select all of the shapes. The
Object alignment options are now available in
the Tool Options palette.

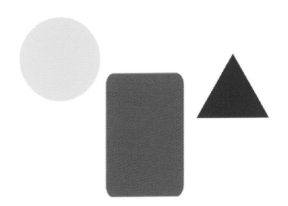

4. Click the Top Alignment button (at the far left of the Object alignment buttons). All of the selected objects align themselves to a common axis defined by the object that's closest to it. In this example, the circle is the highest shape on the canvas, so the rectangle and triangle are aligned to the circle.

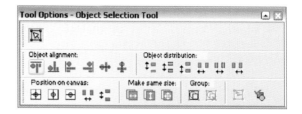

These functions can only be performed when two or more objects or object groups are selected; otherwise, the Object alignment buttons will be grayed out in the tool options. The visually descriptive icons give a good idea of what each function does and how objects can be aligned in different ways: to top, bottom, left, and right axes, and also centered to a vertical or horizontal axis (the two buttons at the right).

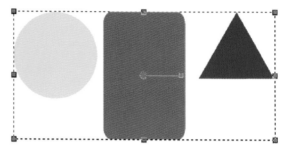

Distributing objects

This function equalizes the space between objects.

1. Start a new image and draw three different shapes on the canvas using the Preset Shape tool, as you did in steps 1 and 2 of the previous alignment example.

2. Select the Object Selection tool and hold down the SHIFT key while clicking to select all objects on the canvas. Like the alignment options, you need to group the shapes first before you can distribute them.

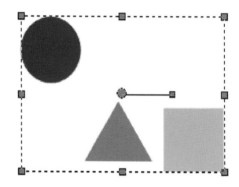

You can vertically distribute objects by their top, center, or bottom edge. The edge or center of the upper- and lowermost objects remain stationary while any objects between them are arranged so that each object is an equal distance from its neighbor, above and below.

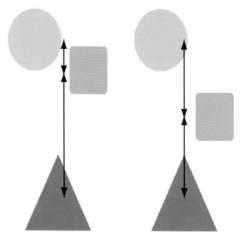

🔲 Before Vertical Center Distribution   🔲 After Vertical Center Distribution

3. Click the appropriate button under Object distribution in the Object Selection Tool Options palette to distribute your objects.

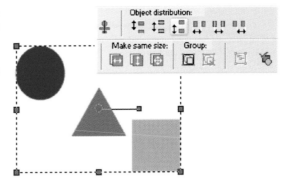

Horizontal distribution follows the same rules on the horizontal axis.

Resizing objects

As well as resizing objects with the bounding box handles, you can use the **Make Same Size** options (these options are also in the Objects > Make Same Size menu). Again, for this to be available, you need to select two or more objects. The three options are Horizontal, Vertical, and Both. When two or more objects are selected and one of these options is applied, all the selected objects will take on the same horizontal, vertical, or both sizes of the uppermost selected object in the Layer palette.

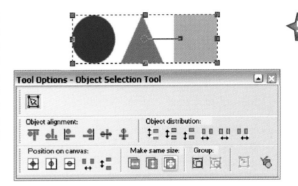

Arranging objects

Objects are arranged from front to back on the canvas, so where they overlap, the object at the front will block out any behind it. You can rearrange this order in a number of ways.

1. Objects at the top of the Layer palette are foremost in the order. You can alter the order simply by dragging the layers into a new order.

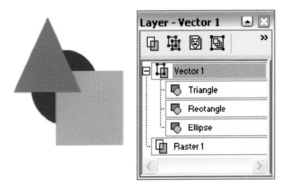

2. Select the object on the canvas that you want to move in the order and then use the commands in the Objects > Arrange menu. For example, Objects > Arrange > Bring to Top will put the selected object on top of the layer.

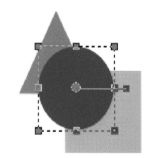

Move Up brings the object past the object directly above it, Move Down moves the object below the object directly beneath, and Send to Bottom places the object at the bottom of the stack. You can move single or multiple selections using these commands.

Vector text with the Text tool

Adding text to images is covered in detail in Chapter One, but text can also be combined with the vector tools. You can apply text to a **path**, which is text that follows a line.

1. To apply text to a path, first lay down a path with either the Preset Shape tool or the Pen tool.

2. Once you've laid down the path, select the Text tool and hover the cursor over the place on the path you want the text to align with (the regular text cursor changes to the text on path cursor).

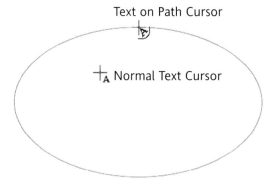

3. Once the path cursor is visible, click to open the Text Entry dialog box and enter your text.

4. You can make the path the text is following invisible by going to the Layer palette, expanding the vector layer (click the plus sign beside the vector layer), and clicking the eye icon.

When you lay down vector text, it remains editable, even after you've deselected the Text tool. You can revisit it by selecting it with the Object Selection tool, right-clicking, and choosing Edit Text from the context menu. The Text Entry dialog box appears and you can make any further changes you like.

Vector text like this isn't the same as most other vector objects; it's more akin to text laid down in a word processor document than a graphic, which is why you can edit it after it's laid down. It's also dependent on the font. That is, if you saved a file with vector text in a certain font in it and tried to open that file on a computer that didn't have the same font installed, you'd be prompted to replace the font with one that is installed.

Also, you can't edit vector text with the Pen tool, but you can get around this by converting the text to **vector objects**.

5. Select the text with the Object Selection tool and choose Objects > Convert Text to Curves. The submenu has two options:

★ As Single Shape

★ As Character Shapes

If you choose As Character Shapes, each letter becomes a separate vector object. As Single Shape converts the entire text entry into a singe vector object. If you have text with different fills and/or strokes, converting it to a single shape will force the text to be all one color, defined by the color of the first character in the text string. Also, you should be aware that you can no longer edit text with the Text tool once you've converted it to curves.

Pen tool

The Pen tool is possibly the most powerful and complex vector tool in Paint Shop Pro. It's both a vector creation tool and a vector editing tool. We'll begin by examining the Pen tool as a vector or node editor.

1. Open a new file with a white background and use the Preset Shape tool to lay down a rectangle shape (check Retain style in the tool options).

2. Select the Pen tool (D). In the Mode area of the Pen Tool Options palette, click the Edit Mode button.

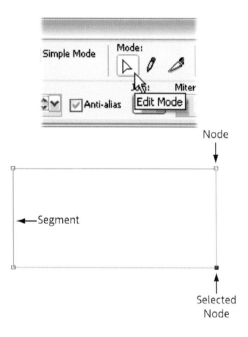

3. The nodes are now visible as little outlined boxes and available for editing. Place the cursor over one of the nodes and click it to select it (the node turns black). As with the Object Selection tool, you can make multiple selections by holding down the SHIFT key while selecting or drag-selecting. Once you select a node, you can move it to any location on the canvas by dragging it. If you have more than one node selected, dragging any of the selected nodes will move them all.

In the case of the rectangle shape, all the **segments** are lines. A segment can be either a line or a curve, and the type of node that controls that segment determines this.

4. Lay down an ellipse shape, select the Pen tool, and click any node. You'll see an example of a node with curved segments.

Notice the little arrow attached to either side of the node? These are the curve control arms, and the ends are the control handles. These define the curve on either side of the node. You can use these to change the curve. If you drag one away from the node, you lengthen the curve and, conversely, if you drag it toward the node, you shorten the curve. Rotating or moving the handle to either side of the node will change the direction of the curve.

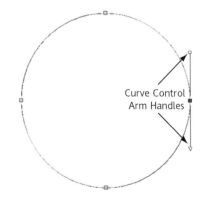

Node types and conversions

The basic types of nodes and line curve combinations are in the Objects > Node Type submenu. Clicking one of these options while one or more nodes are selected will change the selected nodes to that type. The different node types are

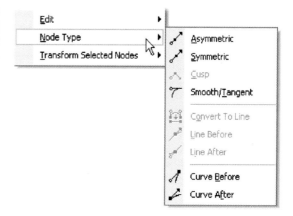

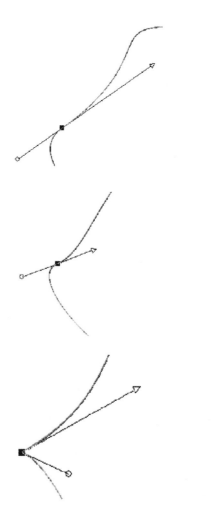

★ **Asymmetric**: Neither curve handle can be rotated without the other rotating in an equal and opposite direction. The curve length of each handle can be adjusted independently.

★ **Symmetric**: Rotating one curve handle has an equal and opposite effect on the other, as with the asymmetric node, but the curve length for both handles is always equal. That is, changing the length of one will change the length of the other.

★ **Cusp**: Each handle can be adjusted for rotation and length independently.

★ **Smooth Tangent**: This is a node with a line on one side and a curve on the other, where the length of the curve is adjustable but the direction of the curve is fixed to that of the line segment.

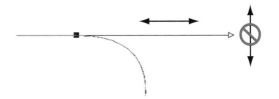

★ **Convert To Line**: This option converts the segments on both sides of the selected node to straight-line segments. If the selected node already has straight lines, this option will be grayed out.

★ **Line Before** and **Line After**: These options convert the curved segment ahead or behind the selected node to a curved segment.

★ **Curve Before** and **Curve After**: These options convert the straight-line segment ahead or behind the selected node to a curved segment.

Drawing and editing shapes

That's all pretty dry stuff so let's have a little fun with this by using Preset Shape and Pen tool node editing to create a simple cartoon character—perhaps a *pen*guin may be appropriate.

1. Open a new image on a white background. Set both the foreground and background swatches to color and black.

2. Activate the Preset Shape tool and set the following tool options:

  ★ Shape: Ellipse
  ★ Retain style: Unchecked
  ★ Create as vector: Checked
  ★ Anti-alias: Checked
  ★ Line Style: Solid
  ★ Line Width: 0.50

3. Lay down a single ellipse about twice as tall as it is wide. Click the Pen tool and put it in Edit mode. Select the two side nodes by drag-selecting around each one, and drag them down about halfway between their original location and the bottom of the ellipse.

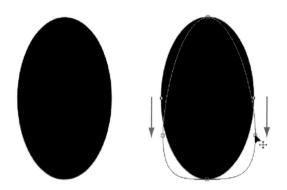

4. Right-click and choose the Edit > Select All to select all the nodes in the path in one fell swoop. (You can also use the selection options in the Edit submenu to cut, copy, paste, and delete selected nodes, as well as to deselect and invert selections.)

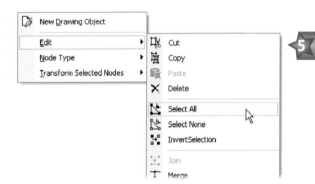

5. With all the nodes selected, select Duplicate Selected from the Transformation Type drop-down menu in the Pen tool options, and enter 0 in both the X and Y fields to make a copy of all the selected nodes. Click the check mark icon to the right of these fields to apply the duplication. The duplicate is now selected, and the nodes' appearance changes to indicate two nodes occupying the same space.

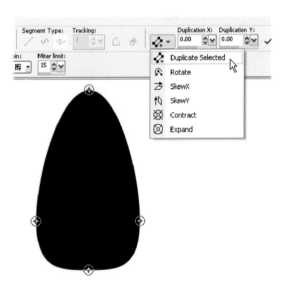

6. Now select Contract from the Transformation Type menu and enter a value in both the X and Y fields (20 pixels is appropriate for our example here, but your entry may vary depending on how big an image you started with). Click the check mark to apply the contraction. If you happen to enter too great or small a value, you can use CTRL+Z to undo it and enter a more appropriate value.

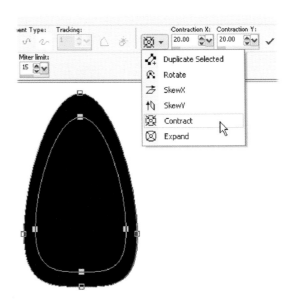

Because the second contour is a duplicate of the original one, both contours are going in the same direction. You can confirm this by clicking a node on each contour and noting the direction of the curve control handle arrows (they indicate the direction of the contour).

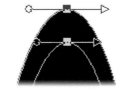

If these contours were going in opposite directions, then any overlapping area, which in this case is the entire second contour, would be canceled out. You would effectively have a path with a hole in it. You can easily change the direction of a given contour by selecting any node on the contour, right-clicking, and choosing Edit > Reverse Contour.

Now that you have something resembling a penguin's body, we'll address the wings.

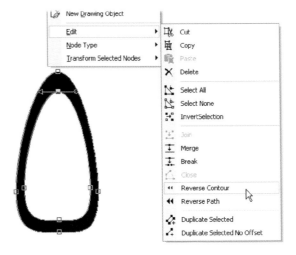

7. With both your stroke and fill still set to a solid black color, use the Preset Shape tool to lay down another ellipse. Drag this one out so it is about four times as high as it is wide.

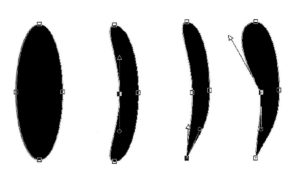

8. Click the Pen tool again and, in Edit mode, select the left side node and drag it inward just past the center of the ellipse. Select the bottom node and rotate both curve handles so they are pointing toward the two side nodes. Finally, return to the left side node and rotate the upper handle outward and lengthen it.

9. Select all the nodes in the wing and select Rotate from the Transformation Type drop-down menu. Enter a value of −15.00 in the Rotation angle field and click the check mark icon. A minus value between 1 and 180 rotates the selected nodes that number of degrees counterclockwise; a positive value rotates them clockwise. The nodes rotate around the mean center position of the selected nodes. Any nodes not selected in the contour will maintain their position.

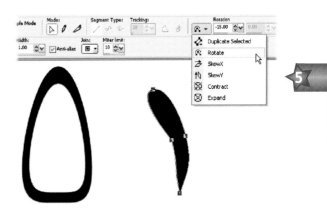

Penguins, like most creatures, are bilaterally symmetrical, so you'll need a right wing.

10. Select all the nodes in the wing, right-click, and choose Edit > Duplicate Selected No Offset. Click-drag one of the nodes while all are still selected to move the entire duplicate contour away from the original. Now right-click and select Transform Selected Nodes > Mirror. Again, with all the nodes selected, drag the new wing over to the body and position it appropriately. Select all the nodes on the other wing contour and do likewise.

Let's take a moment to look at the Layer palette. Notice that there is one background raster layer and one vector layer. If you click the plus sign (+) beside the vector layer, there are two ellipses. These are the body and wing paths you just created.

11. This might be a good time to do some organizing. You can name a path anything you like by right-clicking it and selecting Rename from the context menu. This comes in handy when you're dealing with complex files with many paths. Change the name of the body path to Body and the wings path to Wings.

Your canvas may be getting a little crowded so, if you need more room, open a new image as a working canvas to create additional paths. You can paste them into the original as you go. If you have room on your canvas, lay down the next object somewhere away from the other objects.

12. You'll make some penguin feet now. Change your fill color to an avian foot shade of orange or yellow. Activate the Preset Shape tool and choose the triangle shape. Again, making sure Retain style is unchecked, drag out a triangle about three times wider than it is tall. Drag from upper left to lower right to ensure the correct orientation. Make it large enough to work on easily (with vectors, size really doesn't matter, as you can always resize it later).

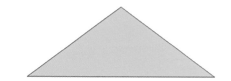

This gives you a rather angular, inorganic shape that's unfit for a penguin's foot, don't you think? The sharp angles are the result of the straight-line segments between the nodes. The solution is to change these to curve segments.

13. Activate the Pen tool, choose Edit mode, and select all the nodes. Right-click and choose Node Type > Symmetric.

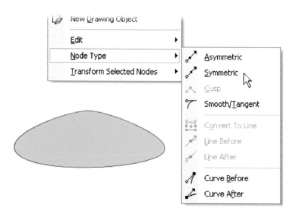

That's a little better, but it still needs some work. With only three nodes, your editing possibilities are somewhat limited. The solution? Add more nodes, of course.

14. When you use the Pen tool in Edit mode, you can add nodes by holding down the CTRL key and placing the cursor over the path at the location where you want the new node. When the cursor is over the path, it changes to the + ADD cursor. When you're at the place where you want to add the node and the cursor changes, simply click and a new node appears. Do this in the middle of the base of the triangle.

15. Add two more nodes as shown here. Select each of these two nodes in turn and drag it inward and toward the center of the foot object.

16. Now that you have your penguin foot, resize the object by selecting it with the Object Selection tool and right-click–dragging a corner handle. Make it an appropriate size to match your penguin body. If you created the foot on a separate image, copy it, Edit > Paste As New Vector Selection into the body image, and then drop it on the penguin.

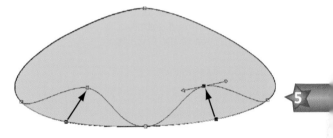

17. After you drop the foot once, paste it again and drop it as the other foot. If you created it on the same image, select it, move it to the body, and then copy and paste as a new vector selection for the other foot. To keep organized, you may want to go into the Layer palette and rename the two triangle shapes left foot and right foot. As you progress, keep giving the various body parts names.

18. For the head, simply lay down another ellipse with a black stroke and fill, and place it on the body.

19. For the beak, you'll want to use the same color as the feet, so activate the Dropper tool (E) and right-click the foot to change the fill color (the stroke should still be black).

20. Lay down a triangle shape, this time dragging from lower right to upper left while holding down the SHIFT key to constrain the aspect ratio to an equilateral triangle. This one should be upside down (compared to the foot).

21. Activate the Pen tool, select all the nodes, and convert them to symmetric nodes. Drag out another triangle constraining the aspect ratio, but this time drag from upper left to lower right so the triangle is upside down compared to the first one. Convert all its nodes to symmetric and move it so that it's above and slightly overlapping the top of the first triangle.

22. Now you'll create the eyes. To make these, lay down three ellipses of varying sizes: first a white one for the eye, then a smaller black one for the pupil, and finally an even smaller white one to simulate a highlight. Make sure you disable Retain style in the Preset Shape tool options for the white ellipses. The preview may look like a white ellipse, but it is in fact a transparent-filled, black-stroked shape. Also, deselect the last ellipse before changing the colors in the Materials palette when you move on to the next one, or these changes will apply to it too. It's impossible to drag out a new shape inside an existing selected shape.

Drag+Shift Drag+Ctrl

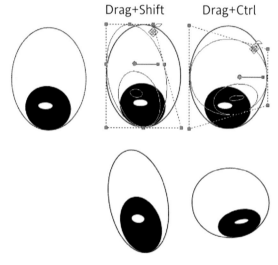

If you like, you can deform the eye by selecting all the objects with the Object Selection tool and using a combination of drag+CTRL and/or drag+SHIFT in the same way you work with the raster Deform tool.

23. If you haven't deformed your eye, simply copy and paste it as a new vector selection to make two eyes. Then resize the eyes if necessary and drag them onto the penguin.

24. If you did deform the eye, you need to make a mirror-image copy for the other eye. As in the last step, copy and paste as a new vector selection. With the second eye selected (ensuring that all three ellipses are selected), drag one of the side bounding-box handles toward the center of the eye and completely through it until you have a mirror copy of the original.

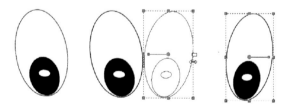

25. Arrange, resize, and select both eyes, and drag them over to the rest of the penguin.

You may recall when you made the body that we went through the reverse contour routine to make a hole to represent a penguin's white breast. This was done more for instructional purposes than practical ones and, if you happen to create this guy on anything other than a white background, he won't look quite right.

26. You can address this by selecting just the body with the Object Selection tool and then activating the Pen tool in Edit mode. Select each of the four nodes that make up the breast contour while holding down the SHIFT key. Right-click and select Edit > Cut. Oops, no more breast.

Not to worry, by cutting the breast you copied the contour to the clipboard. If the body is still selected by the Pen tool, and you try to paste the nodes, you'll just put them back where they were as a contour in the body path.

27. To avoid this, click the Object Selection tool and deselect the body by clicking a blank part of the canvas. Set a white fill and null stroke in the Materials palette.

28. Now return to the Pen tool, click the New Path and Edit mode icons, and then right-click the canvas and choose Edit > Paste. Your penguin should look like it did before you cut the breast, but it now has a separate breast object that can be selected and is white.

29. Save your penguin as a .PspImage file to preserve the vector information, as you'll return to it later.

Drawing mode

The Pen tool is also a vector-drawing tool that you can use to create new paths and contours. For this, you use the Pen tool in **Drawing mode**.

When you use the Pen tool in this mode, the attributes of the path you create are determined by the current settings in the Materials palette and the Line Style and Width options in the Pen Tool Options palette (in the same way as the Preset Shape tool). When the Pen tool is in Drawing mode, you drag out paths, creating segments and nodes as you go. Three different drawing options are available in the Segment Type area of the Pen Tool Options palette:

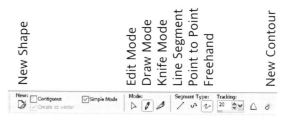

* **Line Segment** allows you to define a single straight line on the canvas by dragging it out. Where you begin dragging is the start of the line and where you release the mouse button is the end of it. Each drag creates a new contour.

* **Point to Point** allows you to click the canvas to create nodes. As you create a new node, a straight-line segment joins it to the previous one you created. If you click and drag, you create a curved segment between the nodes whose direction and length are determined by the direction and length of the drag.

* **Freehand** allows you to simply draw freehand with the cursor and have the path follow it. The other aspect of Freehand mode is **Tracking**. In essence, this smoothes out the lines you draw. A setting of 1 has no effect on the line, whereas a setting of 100 is very invasive. Generally, a setting somewhere between 10 and 20 works well for smoothing out a jittery line.

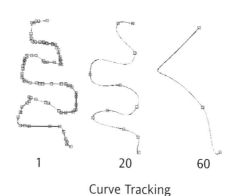

| 1 | 20 | 60 |

Curve Tracking

When in any drawing mode, you have a number of choices regarding creating new paths or contours:

★ **Contiguous**: When in Freehand mode with Contiguous checked in the tool options, you lay down a single contour regardless of the number of drags you make. That is, if you drag out a line and then start a new drag somewhere else on the canvas, the two drags will connect as a single contour. Unchecking Contiguous allows a new unconnected contour with each drag. If Contiguous is checked, and you want to start a new contour, you can click the New Contour icon.

★ **New Shape**: You can start a new path at any time in Drawing mode by clicking the New Shape icon. Remember, all the contours on a single path will have the same colors and other attributes, so if you need a different stroke, fill, or line style for an element of the drawing, you have to start a new path.

★ **Knife mode**: This option is for cutting contours. Drag the Knife mode cursor across a contour, and the contour will break at the point of intersection, creating a start and end node. Knife mode is a click-drag straight-line tool.

Object groups

An **object group** is any number of objects that are grouped together inside a vector layer in the Layer palette. If you expand a group in the Layer palette, the individual objects become visible.

You can click any single object in an object group with the Object Selection tool, and it will select the entire group rather than just the object.

This is handy for editing elements of a complex vector graphic. Once objects are grouped, you can no longer select individual objects with the Object Selection tool. You can, however, select a single object in a group by clicking it in the Layer palette.

Another reason for grouping objects is that it allows you to use the alignment, distribution, and positioning options with complex groups of objects.

1. Take your penguin, for instance. Open him up, select all of him with a drag-select, and copy him.

2. Create a new file and go to Edit > Paste As New Vector Selection. Paste again as a new vector selection and drop this penguin beside his brother.

3. With the second copy still selected, click the Group icon in the Object Selection tool options. He's now an object group, whereas the other guy is just a collection of objects.

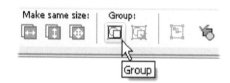

4. Select both penguins by drag-selecting and click the Align Bottom icon in the tool options. The penguin that was grouped remains intact, whereas the ungrouped penguin has fallen apart. All the individual objects align to the bottom of the bounding box.

Making an object group is a very simple matter indeed: simply select the individual objects you want to group by either of the multiple selection methods (drag-select or SHIFT+select), and then click the Group icon in the Object Selection tool options or use Objects > Group. If the objects selected are on separate layers, the group will appear on the lowest layer and any objects included will migrate to that layer.

Exporting shapes

A preset shape file (`.PspShape`) is a normal Paint Shop Pro image file that contains a single vector layer and one or more objects and/or object groups. It contains no raster data at all. As you know, Paint Shop Pro comes prepackaged with a number of shape files. If you point the File Browser (CTRL+B) to the Preset Shapes folder off the main Program Files folder, you can preview and open any of them, just like any other image file:

1. Exporting your own custom preset shapes is a snap. To export your penguin as a preset shape, first open the file. If there's a lot of empty space around the penguin, crop it out.

The first thing to do is group the penguin. If you exported without grouping first, each object in the file would become an individual preset shape.

2. Drag-select the entire penguin with the Object Selection tool and click the Group icon in the tool options. Go to the Layer palette and expand the vector layer. You should see the group with the default name Group 1. Once you export the shape, this is the name that will appear in the Preset Shape tool preview catalog. You can change this to something more appropriate, such as Penguin, if you prefer.

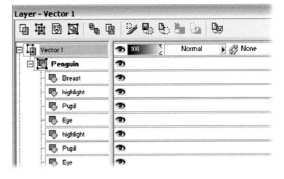

3. Now that you have your penguin grouped and you've given it a descriptive group name, it's time to export. Go to File > Export > Shape. The Export Shape Library dialog box opens, prompting you for a file name, including the .PspShape file extension.

4. Shapes in the Preset Shape tool preview are organized alphabetically according to the name of the file. Give the file any name you like and click OK.

5. Activate the Preset Shape tool and you should find your penguin waiting for you in the drop-down preview. Now that you've safely exported your cartoon penguin as a shape, you have an infinite supply of these aquatic birds at your disposal whenever there's a pressing need for a strange-looking critter.

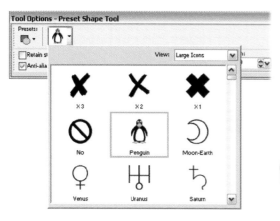

Special Image Effects

In this chapter

We're going to look at the extra touches you can give your images to add certain special effects or looks, particularly those effects that you can imagine but are unable to achieve with a conventional camera. In this chapter, we cover the following topics:

★ Prebuilt and custom Picture Tubes

★ Picture frames

★ The Warp Brush tool

★ The Mesh Warp tool

★ The Deform tool

★ Perspective correction

Picture Tubes

The **Picture Tube tool** is a variation of the Brush tool that allows you to paint using an entirely prebuilt image. Paint Shop Pro comes with a number of Picture Tube files included, and you can collect thousands more online. You can also create your own Picture Tubes.

Some Picture Tubes consist of a variety of different, yet related objects. They can also consist of variations of the same object (color, size, position) or even single objects. The tube is contained in a special file format called `.PspTube`, which is recognized by Paint Shop Pro as a `.PspImage` file, as well as its special Picture Tube file.

1. Open a new 500x500 image that's 24-bit color with a white background. Select the Picture Tube tool from the Tools palette.

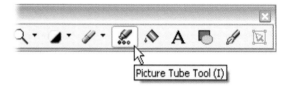

2. Click the drop-down menu in the tool options to preview the currently installed tubes. Paint Shop Pro comes with nearly 100 tubes for you to use.

3. Choose the 3D gold tube.

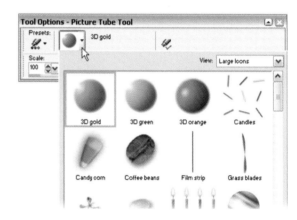

You have fields for Scale and Step, as well as Placement mode and Selection mode. You also have buttons to recall presets (more about these later) and the tube's settings.

The scale of a tube is set to 100 by default. This means that the tube will paint at the same size as when it was originally created in the tube file. You can scale the object between 10 and 250. At a scale of 250, the object will be resized 2.5 times larger than it was originally designed.

Resizing can sometimes be a problem with tube objects; they are raster objects and will appear pixellated at larger sizes.

4. Set the Step setting to 1 in the tool options and click your image. Each click will lay down a single copy of the selected tube.

5. Now drag the Picture Tube tool across the canvas to keep a continuous flow of the 3D gold. The Step setting determines the amount of space between one instance of the object and the next when the tool is click-dragged.

6. Increase the Step to 50 and you'll spread out the instances of the tubes laid down as you drag. This higher Step setting adds more space between instances of the object.

Single Click

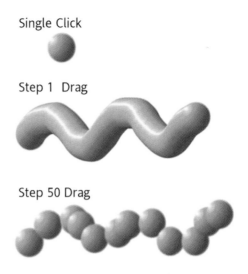

Step 1 Drag

Step 50 Drag

You have two choices for the Placement mode setting:

★ Continuous lays down the individual image at equally spaced intervals determined by the Step value you've set.

★ Random also takes into account the speed at which you drag the mouse. Faster movement lays down images closer together.

Picture Tube files can contain a single image (as you've seen in the case of 3D gold) or any number of different images, such as Marbles. If you browse to your Picture Tubes folder (either My Documents > My PSP8 Files > Picture Tubes or your Paint Shop Pro program files), you can open up a .PspTube file and take a look. If the tube contains a number of images, the Selection mode setting comes into play in the tool options, determining which image is laid down:

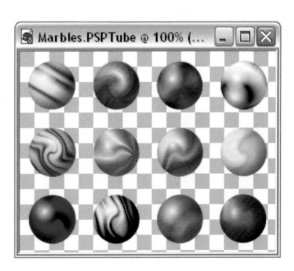

* Random selects the images from the tube file randomly.

* Incremental lays down the images in the order that they appear in the tube file.

* Angular changes individual images according to the direction you drag the mouse. To use this mode, you must drag the mouse—a single click won't lay down a tube image.

* Pressure works with a pressure-sensitive stylus and tablet. The amount of pressure you exert on the pad determines the image selected.

* Velocity varies the selection according to the speed at which you drag the mouse. Again, a single click won't lay down an image.

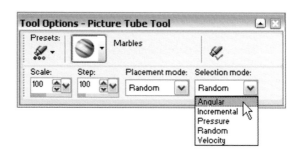

Collecting and organizing Picture Tubes

In addition to the prebuilt tubes, many free tubes are available online. Here are some of our favorites:

* The Original Free Tubes Site:
  www.freetubes.com

* The Graphics Galaxy Search Engine:
  www.thepluginsite.com/search/graphicsgalaxy.htm

* Ron's Toons:
  www.ronstoons.com/tubes/tubes.htm

To organize your tubes, shapes, and other accessories in Paint Shop Pro, open the File Locations dialog box using File > Preferences > File Locations. You can designate more folders to store the various Paint Shop Pro goodies.

The radio button at the far left of the Folders pane defines where any tubes, shapes, and so on that you create yourself are saved to.

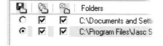

To reduce confusion, you can organize your tubes in categories by folder and turn off the folders you aren't using at the moment. This makes for a less cluttered tube catalog in the Tool Options palette. (See **Chapter** Eight for more information on customizing your preferences.)

Exporting Picture Tubes

You can use Picture Tubes that were made in Paint Shop Pro 6 and 7 by loading them into your Picture Tubes folder.

1. Open `birds.PspImage` from the download files.

2. Go to File > Export > Picture Tube to open the Export Picture Tube dialog box. Notice that the tube file has four images: two across and two down. Set the number in the Cells across and Cells down fields to match these numbers.

The Total cells field should match the total number of objects in the tube file. You can also modify Placement options to your taste.

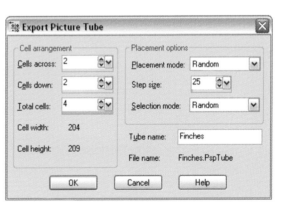

3. Give the tube file an appropriate name and click OK.

4. Now select the Picture Tube tool, look in the tube catalog preview in the tool options, and scroll down until you see your new tube. (If you can't see your tube in the preview, check the location to which you saved the tube in the previous steps and then use File > Preferences > File Locations to ensure that this directory is enabled.)

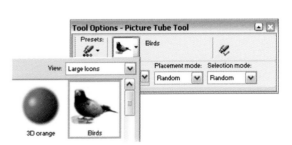

5. You can now use this tube to add a bird or three to any image you like.

> *If you create a new layer to place the tubes on, you have the added flexibility of being able to move the tubes to a precise position with the Move tool.*

Creating your own Picture Tubes

Collecting tubes might be fun, but making your own is even better. You already understand half the battle—how to use the Export to Picture Tube option—but how do you prepare an image so that it's ready to be a tube?

Sometimes you might want to make a tube out of an entire rectangular image but, in most cases, tube objects look best on a transparent background so that they can then be applied over any background color or pattern. Lots of the tubes you can find on the Web are simply objects or pictures but, in Paint Shop Pro 8, you can use tubes to add some functionality that you might not normally be able to use, such as painting with a gradient that's contained on the brush stroke itself. Let's make a gradient brush tube now.

1. Open a new 400x400 image that's 24-bit color with a transparent background.

2. Use the Flood Fill tool to fill this image with any two-color 90° linear gradient fill.

3. Choose the Selection tool. In the Tool Options palette, select Circle from the Selection type drop-down menu and set Feather to 50.

4. Turn on the rulers (CTRL+ALT+R) and use them to place your cursor in the center of the image. Then drag out a selection with a 100-pixel diameter, again using the rulers to guide you (drag down from the 200-pixel mark on the ruler to the 250-pixel mark). This will give you a selection of approximately 200 pixels in diameter when feathering is taken into account.

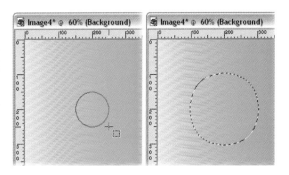

5. Press CTRL+C to copy this object to the clipboard.

6. Open another 24-bit color image with a transparent background, but this time make it 800x800.

7. Go to View > Change Grid, Guide & Snap Properties. In the Current image settings on the Grid tab, set both Horizontal grids and Vertical grids to 400 pixels. Click OK to make these settings.

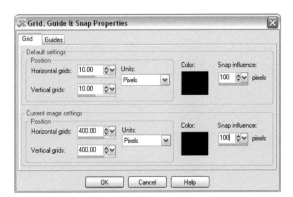

8. Turn the grid on (CTRL+ALT+G) to help you position your tube elements.

9. Press CTRL+E to paste the image you previously copied to the clipboard (in step 5) into your new image. Position this object at the center of the top-left cell of your new image by aligning the cursor with the 200-pixel marks on the vertical and horizontal rulers.

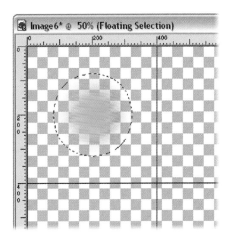

10. Return to your original 400x400 image. Contract the existing selection by 20 pixels (using Selections > Modify > Contract) and copy it to the clipboard.

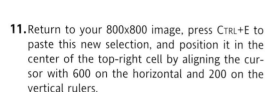

11. Return to your 800x800 image, press CTRL+E to paste this new selection, and position it in the center of the top-right cell by aligning the cursor with 600 on the horizontal and 200 on the vertical rulers.

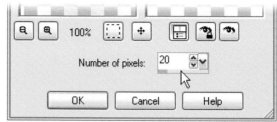

12. Once again on your 400x400 image, contract the existing selection by another 20 pixels. Copy this selection and return to the 800x800 image, pasting it with CTRL+E to the center (align 600 vertically and 200 horizontally) of the lower-left cell.

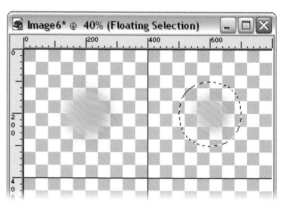

13. Finally, return to the smaller image and contract the selection by *another* 20 pixels. Copy the selection, return to the larger image, and paste the selection in the bottom-right cell (600 vertically and horizontally).

You should now have an 800x800 image with the grid turned on and gradient-filled circles of varying diameters in the four cells. You're now going to export this image as a Picture Tube.

14. Use CTRL+D to deselect everything.

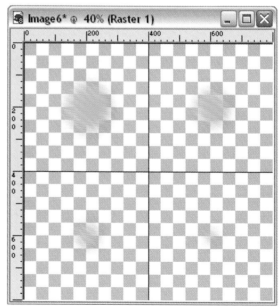

15. Go to File > Export > Picture Tube. Use the settings shown here in the Export Picture Tube dialog box and name your tube something memorable.

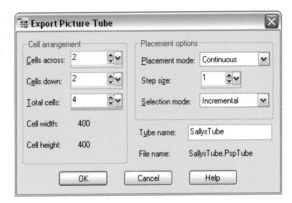

16. Does that tube look kind of boring to you? Wait—select your Picture Tube tool and locate your new tube in the Tool Options palette.

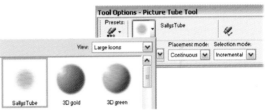

17. Open a new image, and try painting with your tube. Looks like a soft fuzzy worm, right? Try reducing the Scale of the tube and drawing your name or some other text.

This kind of tube works great with a graphics tablet and stylus, if you have them. You can also use it at a large size for quickly filling backgrounds. Try varying the Step size in the tool options to form different effects.

If you'd like your new gradient brush Picture Tube in different colors, you could use the Colors > Colorize feature to quickly colorize the saved image. You would then export the new version as a Picture Tube using the same settings you used previously, only with a new (and even more memorable) name.

Picture Tubes and the
Preset Shape tool

Here we'll show you how to use a preset shape with a custom Picture Tube.

1. Open a new 1352x150 image that's 24-bit color with a transparent background.

2. Select View > Change Grid, Guide & Snap Properties and enter 150 pixels in both the Horizontal grids and Vertical grids fields. Click OK and then turn on the grid (CTRL+ALT+G).

3. Select the Preset Shape tool and choose the Star 1 shape from the Tool Options palette. Uncheck Retain style and make sure Create as vector and Anti-alias are checked.

4. Set your background fill style to a linear gradient, such as the Red-orange-yellow gradient, and set your foreground style to null.

5. Hold down the SHIFT key to maintain the aspect ratio of the shape and start by right-click–dragging from the upper-left corner to the lower-right corner, laying down a star that nearly fills your image space (it doesn't need to be too exact, just large enough to fill the space).

6. Copy this shape to the clipboard (CTRL+C).

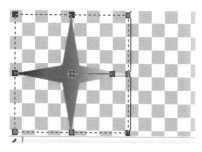

7. Select Edit > Paste > Paste As New Vector Selection (CTRL+G) and drop the star in the second cell (don't worry about placing it accurately in the cell—anywhere inside will do here).

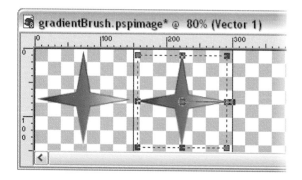

8. Make sure the pasted selection in the second cell is still active (it has a bounding box around it) and select the Pen tool. Select Edit mode in the Tool Options palette, right-click the canvas, and choose Edit > Select All from the context menu.

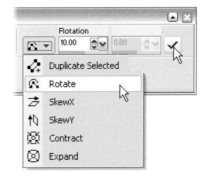

9. In the Pen Tool Options palette, select Rotate from the Transformation Type drop-down menu, and set the Rotation angle to 10 degrees. Click the Apply check mark icon.

10. Copy this rotated selection (CTRL+C), place the mouse cursor in the middle of the third cell, and paste the selection again as a new vector selection (CTRL+G). Click to drop it in the third cell.

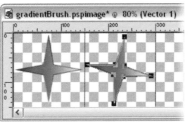

11. All the nodes should still be selected, so just click the Apply icon in the Pen tool options to rotate the new selection by another 10°. (If the Apply icon is grayed out, right-click the canvas and choose Edit > Select All again.)

12. Continue pasting and rotating the gradient star by 10° in each cell. The last star in the final cell should be rotated by 80° from the original star in the first (leftmost) cell.

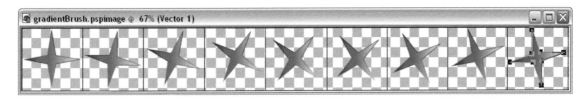

13. When the final cell is filled and the image is rotated, deselect all objects (CTRL+D).

14. Choose the Object Selection tool and click each star object individually while holding down the SHIFT key to select them all.

15. Choose Objects > Align > Vertical Center to align the objects. Now choose Objects > Align > Vert. Center in Canvas to align all the objects across the center of the image. Finally, use Objects > Distribute > Horizontal Center to space all the objects evenly across the canvas.

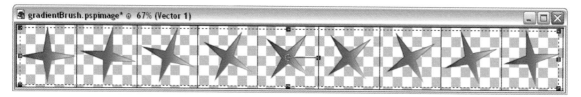

16. Because a tube file must consist of a single raster layer with a transparent background, you must convert your vector layers. You can do this in one operation using Layers > Merge > Merge Visible.

17. Choose File > Export > Picture Tube and export the image with the settings shown here in the Export Picture Tube dialog box.

Try painting with this new tube. We call this an **animated tube**. It's not really animated, but the combination of the incremental setting, a small step size, and the rotated image makes it appear to move as you paint with it. You can apply a single star by clicking once or a whole line of twirling stars by click-dragging.

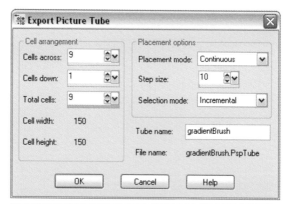

Have fun with the Picture Tube tool and the super-easy image enhancements you can create with it!

Picture frames

The Effects menu has lots of filters (many of which are detailed in Chapter Four) that can enhance your image or give you some ideas and inspiration. Here we'll look at creating special image effects with the built-in Frames tool.

1. Open an image to which you'd like to add a picture frame effect and select Image > Picture Frame.

2. Choose from one of the many prebuilt frames and edge effects in the Picture frame drop-down catalog. Click your choice to see it in the preview pane.

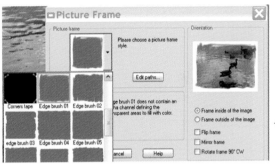

3. You can choose to have the frame inside the image by checking the respectively named box. This won't change the original image dimensions, but you will "lose" image information from the edges of the original image. You can otherwise opt for Frame outside of the image, which adds the frame outside the entire original image, thereby increasing the image dimensions.

Certain frames are not built in the same horizontal/vertical aspect ratio as the image you want to apply them to, so the Flip frame, Mirror frame, and Rotate frame options can be useful in these situations. Some frames contain transparent areas, which you can leave transparent by checking Keep transparent, or you can choose a color to replace the transparency by clicking in the color swatch and choosing a color.

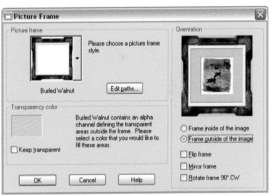

4. You can also apply more than one Picture Frame effect in sequence. Apply the first frame inside the image as usual, and then apply a second frame outside the image, as we've done here, for example.

Deforming images

There are four deformation tools on the Tools palette that you can use to deform an image in different ways.

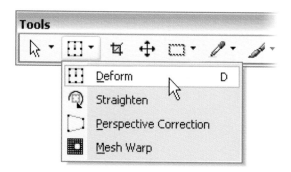

1. Open an image and make a duplicate of the background layer to work on. To use the Deform tool you must be on a regular layer, not a background image.

2. Select the Deform tool (D) from the Tools palette. A rectangular bounding box with a center pivot point and rotation handle superimposes itself on the image.

3. You can resize the content of the image simply by dragging one of the corner or side handles in or out. It resizes along one or both of the vertical and horizontal axes. Right-click–dragging a corner handle maintains the aspect ratio.

4. Try dragging a bounding box corner handle while holding down the CTRL key. It introduces a perspective distortion. Also, SHIFT+drag gives you a shear distortion, and SHIFT+CTRL+drag allows you to freely distort your image.

5. As well as change the size, you can move the content around on the canvas by dragging anywhere inside the bounding box. The image dimensions don't bind you, and you can drag handles and content off the canvas.

6. Rotate your image by clicking the rotation handle in the center of the image and dragging to the desired position (you can also move the pivot point for the center of rotation).

For precise resizing, distortions, and rotations, try entering numerical values into the appropriate fields of the Deform Tool Options palette.

Correcting perspective distortion

Although you can use the Deform tool to perform a perspective deformation, the **Perspective Correction tool** is designed to *correct* perspective distortion that can occur when you take photographs too close to a large subject. This is where parallel lines appear to converge or diverge.

If you're at ground level and take a photo of a tall building, you have to point the camera upward to frame the subject. If the camera's focal plane isn't parallel to the subject, you'll get some degree of perspective distortion. With film cameras, you can fix this by using an expensive specialized tilt and shift lens, or in the darkroom you can tilt the easel under the enlarger. Here, though, you'll use Paint Shop Pro's digital magic.

1. Open a photo that might be in need of some perspective correction and select the Perspective Correction tool. You'll see a bounding box centered in your image.

2. Drag inside this bounding box to move it around on top of the image, and drag on the individual lines to resize it. Dragging a corner handle will relocate the corner without moving any of the other corners. Unlike with the Deform tool, adjusting the bounding box doesn't move the image content.

3. To use the perspective correction, drag the bounding box sides parallel to the lines in the that image you want to make vertical or horizontal. The Perspective Correction tool will adjust the image to make the area of the image at the bounding box lines and beyond vertical and horizontal, while smoothly blending the area within the bounding box.

4. Once you're happy with the bounding box, double-click anywhere on your image to apply the correction. Because the Perspective Correction tool necessarily "unsquares" the image, you'll need to crop it back to a rectangular shape.

As with the Deform tool, you can enter values directly in the Tool Options palette to place the bounding box corners. You can also have the image automatically cropped when the effect is applied by checking Crop image. You may find this tool useful for correcting interior shots.

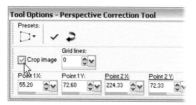

Mesh Warp tool

The Mesh Warp tool is very entertaining and great for creating caricatures from photos and other fun effects. It works by laying a grid down on the image, as defined in the Tool Options palette. At each intersection point of the horizontal and vertical grid lines, there's a control point that you can drag around to warp the image. Because the warp effect is restricted to the four grid quadrants surrounding the control point, the smaller the space between grid lines, the more localized the effect will be.

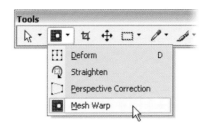

1. Let's have some fun with this tool. Open a portrait photograph to perform some digital plastic surgery. (Because using this filter may be hazardous to your health or marriage, be careful whose photo you choose.)

2. Select the Mesh Warp tool. In the Tool Options palette, set your horizontal and vertical mesh to something appropriate to the size of your image, keeping in mind that too tight a grid restricts the warping effect area, and too wide a grid may not be selective enough. If you check Symmetric, your grid spacing will be equal both horizontally and vertically.

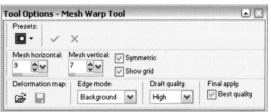

3. Check Show grid and you'll see the grid overlaying your image.

4. To begin the effect, click a handle where the grid intersects and drag your mouse. When you release the mouse, your image will update itself to show the warp effect.

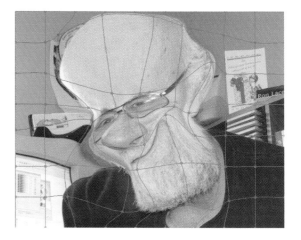

5. The Draft quality menu in the tool options specifies the quality of the image update as you edit. If you're having performance issues, try setting this to one of the lower quality settings. This won't affect the finished product quality, as you long as you ensure that Best quality under Final apply is checked.

6. If you want to undo a single step, select Edit > Undo, but if you want to undo *all* steps, you need to click the red X in the Tool Options palette to reset the image.

7. Once you're happy with your work, click the Apply check mark on the palette. The original grid will appear, but changing tools will get rid of it.

It's fun to use the Mesh Warp tool to resize facial features such as the chin, nose, eyes, and so on. Moving the control points surrounding a feature outward makes the feature larger. Play around with the control points to get a feel for the tool. You can toggle the grid on and off in the Tool Options palette while you work to proof your results in progress, and you can also reset the grid by changing the Mesh field values (be warned, though, that your changes to that point will be applied to the image and the new grid will be set to all straight lines again).

Warp Brush tool

The Warp Brush tool is another warping tool, but instead of manipulating a grid like the Mesh Warp tool, you can paint on different types of warps. This tool is bundled in the Paint Brush tools flyout in the Tools palette. In the Warp Brush Tool Options palette, along with the size hardness and strength options, you have various Warp Modes:

- ★ **Push** stretches out the area encompassed by the brush in the direction you drag the mouse.

- ★ **Contract** shrinks the area in toward the center of the brush area while you hold down the mouse. It's not necessary to move the mouse to use this mode and, in fact, it's usually most effective if you don't move it.

- ★ **Expand** works like contract, but it blows the center of the area out toward the edge.

- ★ **Twirl left** and **Twirl right** give the brush area a spiral warp.

- ★ **Noise** applies random warping as the brush is dragged.

- ★ **Iron out** will progressively unwarp previously warped areas.

- ★ **Unwarp** will completely unwarp previously warped areas.

The Hardness setting defines the amount of feathering at the edge of the brush, much like any of the other brush tools, and Strength determines how aggressively the effect is applied. The Noise setting applies only to the Noise brush. A high setting will make the warp effect more jagged. The Deformation map, Edge mode, and Draft quality settings are identical to those in the Mesh Warp tool.

⭐ Six

A good place to use the warp expand or contract brushes is on the eyes. Take my furry friend here, for instance.

If I make the brush a little larger than his eye, I can contract it so it's a tiny, squinty eye. Or, by using the Expand brush and making the size a couple of times larger than the diameter of his eye, he becomes a cute, dewy-eyed critter.

With a little experimentation with the other warp brushes, you'll be able to create a brand-new species.

Seven

Web Graphics

In this chapter

Now that you've learned how to use all the marvelous tools, created your own graphic masterpieces, and edited your digital photographs, you're going to want to show off your work to your friends and family. It wasn't all that long ago when the average person could present her work to only a handful of people. Today, thanks to the Web, virtually anyone with a computer and Internet connection can publish her work for the world to see. In this chapter, we'll look at a number of Paint Shop Pro utilities that prepare and optimize graphics for the Web:

★ Image slicing

★ Image mapping

★ File formats and image optimization tools

Web graphic file formats

Images and digital photographs of sufficient quality for printing have file sizes that are much too large to be displayed successfully online. A web user would have to wait forever for such images to download. So, before you can publish your work to the web, you need to do two important things:

* **Optimize** your image: Reduce the file size yet maintain as much image quality as possible.

* **Export** your image: Save your image in a web-friendly file format.

Currently, there are three mainstream web formats: **GIF**, **JPEG**, and **PNG**. The format you use depends on the type of image you want to export.

JPEG

The **Joint Photographic Expert Group** (**JPEG**) format is designed to record and compress photographic and other continuous-tone images. JPEG is a 24-bit, 16-million color format, usually with the file extension .jpg. It uses lossy file compression, which reduces file size by discarding some data in the original image. When these files are rendered, the discarded data can result in randomly colored pixels or groups of pixels that are noticeable on the image called **artifacts**. When exporting an image as a JPEG, you make a tradeoff between file size and quality: the more you compress the image, the poorer the quality will be.

GIF

CompuServe's **Graphics Interchange Format** (**GIF**) is an 8-bit, 256-color format and best suited for graphics with limited color palettes and areas of solid color (it doesn't perform well on photographs). Because the limited color palette, **banding** (or dithering) can occur, which is when a large number of colors blended across an area must be reduced to a smaller number in order to break up the smooth flow of color into distinctive bands. GIFs are the best choice for most nonphotographic graphics.

PNG

Portable Network Graphics (**PNG**) format employs nonlossy compression; can be used in 24-bit color, 8-bit grayscale, or 8-bit paletted mode; and supports palette and alpha channel transparency. Unfortunately, it doesn't have extensive browser support; older browsers don't support it at all (pre–Internet Explorer and Navigator 4), and newer browsers don't support PNG transparency. Though its compression of 24-bit images is nonlossy, it doesn't do very high compression. A photographic image will only be reduced to approximately 50% of its uncompressed file size, which is usually unacceptable for web page use (an 800x600 24-bit PNG photograph can weigh in at over half a megabyte). For the latest information on the PNG format, visit www.libpng.org/pub/png/.

Exporting web graphics

File-optimizing tools allow you to edit the various options in each of these formats. You can run these in a wizard format that walks you through the procedure, or you can use the tabbed dialog boxes that provide input and updated previews, illustrating the impact of your settings as you apply them. The file-optimizing tools are in the File > Export submenu.

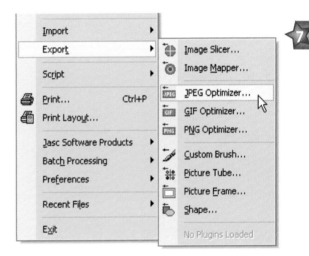

JPEG Optimizer

As mentioned earlier, this tool is primarily for compressing and exporting photographic images. Before you begin the export process, you need to finish editing your photo and resize it to an appropriate size for viewing on a computer monitor. Although a digital camera may be capable of producing 4 or 5 megapixel images, these are much too large to be viewed on computer monitors. The most popular monitor resolutions used today will display less than 1 megapixel, so anything larger won't fit on the monitor without the user zooming out. As a rule, you shouldn't exceed 800x600 pixels when displaying photographs online. Once you've performed your digital darkroom magic and resized your image, you're ready.

1. Open a photographic image and make a duplicate file to work on (SHIFT+D).

> *Overwriting the original image using the optimizing tools will result in an irretrievable loss of quality, so always make sure to work on a copy of your completed high-quality image.*

2. Go to File > Export > JPEG Optimizer. The default compression value is 1 (in the Set compression value to field on the Quality tab). This is the lowest possible level of compression and therefore results in the largest file size.

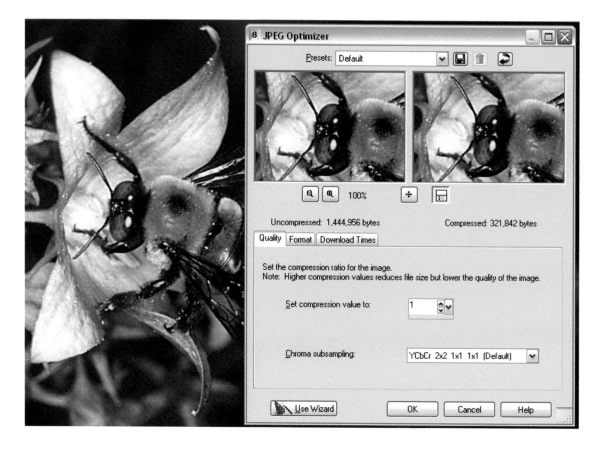

As well as the standard dialog box buttons, you can see the Uncompressed and Compressed file sizes. The compressed size denotes what the file size would be if you saved the image with the current settings. It updates as you make adjustments. The uncompressed value on the left isn't necessarily the original size of your file; rather, it's what it would be if you saved it now to an *uncompressed* format. In most cases, a compression setting of 1 will compress the image to approximately 20% to 25% of its uncompressed file size, but this depends on the complexity of the image. A plain white image compresses considerably more at a given setting than a vibrant multicolored photograph.

3. Adjust the compression value to its maximum of 99 and then take a peek at the preview pane.

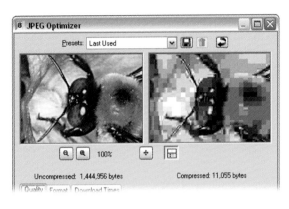

You'll see that the file size has been reduced significantly but so has the image quality. In fact, it's pretty horrible. This is, of course, an extreme example and you'll never need to set the compression this high. However, even at more reasonable settings, you'll see some image degradation in the form of JPEG blocking or artifacts. Blocking is due to the nature of the 8x8 block size used by the JPEG compression standard. High compression ratios result in images with "blockiness" in the blue and red channels. These blocks are especially obvious in the flat areas of an image. In areas with lots of detail, artifacts become noticeable. These are little squiggly areas that slightly resemble ripples on the image.

As with many things, it's necessary to find an acceptable compromise. The uncompressed bumblebee photo in our example is almost 1.5MB—impossible for displaying online. As a rule, individual photos of this size (800x600 pixels) can be compressed to well under 100KB without too much loss in quality by using a compression value between 20 and 30.

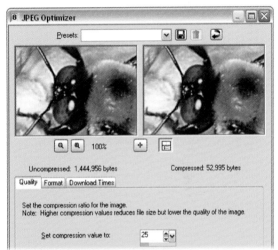

4. Click the Format tab. You have two choices here that impact how the image loads on a web page.

A **standard** JPEG loads onto the page normally, starting at the top and working to the bottom, whereas a **progressive** JPEG will fade in while it's loading. The animation on the palette depicts the effect and will only be apparent on a web page to those with slow Internet connection speeds.

5. Next up is the Download Times tab, which displays the estimated time it will take for your optimized image to download at various connections speeds from 14.4 to 128Kbps. These times are approximate, as there are many variables other than connection speed that can affect download times.

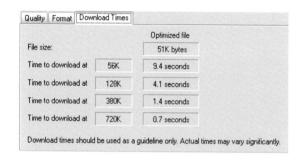

6. Once you've made all your decisions, click OK and you'll see the standard Save As dialog box set to the JPEG format. Navigate to an appropriate folder, give it a name, and you're done.

GIF Optimizer

When you're dealing with nonphotographic images such as vector art or large areas of solid color, GIFs are ideal. One advantage over JPEGs is that GIF is a **lossless** format, if you discount the fact that it's restricted to a maximum of 256 colors. So, because most nonphotographic images contain fewer than or render well with 256 colors, it's a good choice. To find out the number of colors in your image, go to Image > Count Image Colors.

Another advantage is that GIF supports **palette transparency**. This means you can assign one color in the image to be invisible when displayed on a web page, letting the page background show through. This is a particularly handy feature if you're using nonrectangular-shaped graphics on your page, like these guys at www.ronanddave.com.

1. Open a suitable image that you want to optimize as a GIF and duplicate it (SHIFT+D).

2. Go to File > Export > GIF Optimizer.

When you first open the GIF Optimizer, you'll see the Transparency tab. This is where you decide whether to make the GIF transparent and how to define it.

3. If your image already has transparency, check Existing Image or layer transparency to preserve it in the exported GIF. The preview window reflects this by showing the transparency checkerboard.

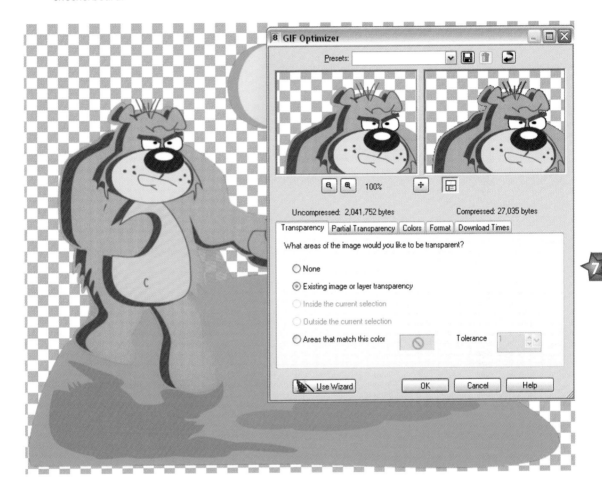

As noted previously, transparent GIFs aren't really transparent; the browser just renders one particular color transparent. If your image already has a transparent area that you want to preserve, you can check Existing image or layer transparency and that color will be assigned to this area and will be the transparent color.

Choosing the correct transparency color is important because that color can appear in the image as fringing around the edges of the transparent areas, particularly when anti-aliasing is used to smooth out edge transitions. Anti-aliasing works by making the pixels of different colors blend together to soften the effect of the transition. So, at the boundary between the black (transparent) area and the image, there will be a few pixels that aren't quite black and won't be rendered transparent. As a result, you get the annoying "fringing" effect. This is hard to avoid, but you can make it less apparent by choosing a transparency color that closely matches the background color of the web page you plan to use the graphic on. To choose the color, go to the Partial Transparency tab, check Yes, blend with the background color, and then click the Blend color swatch.

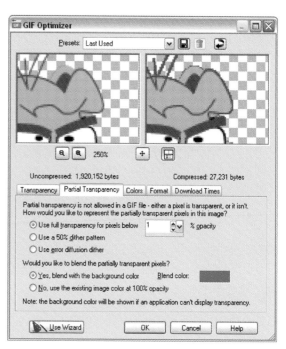

If your image doesn't contain a transparent area, you can assign an existing color, such as the background color, as the transparency area. Check Areas that match this color on the Transparency tab and pick the background color right off your image with the eyedropper. The Tolerance field lets you adjust the aggressiveness of the transparency on the edges and, though increasing this will reduce fringing, it will also decrease the smoothing affect of anti-aliasing.

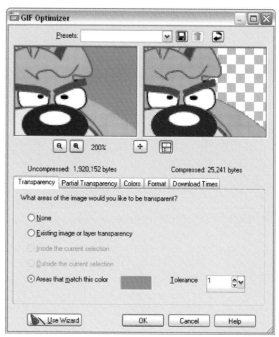

The Partial Transparency tab allows you to fake semitransparency. It's "fake" because the GIF format doesn't actually support partial transparency. The partial transparency options allow you to alter the color of the pixels in the partially transparent area. The Use full transparency for pixels below field renders the partially transparent pixels with an opacity value below the value entered in the field. A value of 100% will therefore render the entire image transparent. **Dithering** is the process whereby the color of a single pixel is determined from the color of surrounding pixels:

★ **Pattern** dithering uses dots to create a pattern to smooth the area between two colors.

★ **Diffusion** creates a series of bands between the two colors.

4. Use the preview pane to decide which is best for your particular graphic.

5. Your blend methods are the following:

   ★ With the background color if you select Yes, blend with the background color

   ★ With the existing background transparency color if you select No, use the existing image color at 100% opacity

6. Next up is the Colors tab, which allows you to choose the method of reducing the colors in your image and even set the number of colors it includes.

7. If the image contains any continuous tone areas (such as gradients), set How many colors do you want? to 256 to ensure the smoothest possible blends. However, if fewer than 256 colors are already present (remember, you can count them with Image > Count Image Colors), reducing this number gives you a smaller file size.

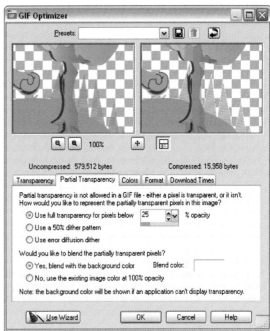

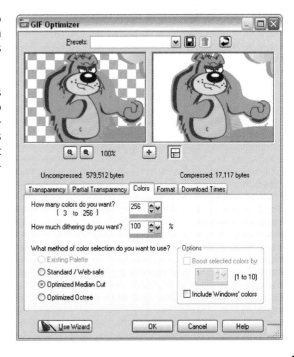

8. Whether you use dithering (and how much you need) depends on the image and, again, if any continuous tones or gradients are present. If there aren't any, enter 0 in the How much dithering do you want? field. If there are, set an appropriate value to eliminate any apparent banding. You can determine this by focusing the preview pane on any gradient areas in the image.

Always go with the smallest value that achieves the optimum results. Too much dithering can cause random pixels to change colors in areas of solid colors. This can manifest itself as speckling, as you can see here on the bear's chest.

In the What method of color selection do you want to use? area, you have as many as four options:

9. If the image is already an 8-bit or less grayscale or paletted image, you can select Existing Palette and no changes will be made to the colors. If it's a 24-bit, 16-million color image, then you have to choose a color reduction method.

10. The Standard/Web-safe colors are a throwback to the days when many computer monitors supported only 8-bit color. Early browsers displayed a limited number of colors and altered any image they loaded to use these colors. The web palette reflects these colors, restricting you to the 216 specific colors, including only 6 shades of gray, which can be displayed by those browsers.

11. Use Optimized Median Cut if your image contains many colors and gradients, or other continuous tone areas, and needs the colors to be reduced. If you've used dithering, this method will reduce the likelihood of speckling.

12. If your image contains around 256 colors or fewer, use the Optimized Octree method.

Today, very few people use those browsers or 8-bit monitors, so the constraints applied by this option are unnecessary unless you know your images will be deliberately viewed in this manner. Using web-safe colors will almost certainly make your graphics look different than you intended because of the limited number of colors available.

13. Boosting selected colors gives them more weight by the factor you enter in the Boost selected colors by field, between 1 and 10. To use this, you must have an active raster marquee selection on the image to define the selected colors. Check Include Windows' colors and use Optimized Median Cut as the color selection method.

The Format and Download tabs perform the same functions you saw in the JPEG Optimizer. Clicking OK at the bottom of the GIF Optimizer will bring up the usual Save As dialog box.

PNG Optimizer

Because PNG supports both 24-bit and 8-bit palette-based formats, your first decision is to choose one.

Open the PNG Optimizer with File > Export > PNG Optimizer. On the Colors tab, you have your choice of image type.

* Palette-Based is the same as the GIF format and is limited to a 256-color palette in which, like the GIF Optimizer, you can restrict the number of colors and apply dithering. When creating a palette-based PNG file, you have the same color selection choices and options as you do with the GIF Optimizer.

* Greyscale (8 Bit) converts the image to 256 shades of gray.

* 16.7 Million Colors (24 Bit) is the full color range format. As mentioned earlier, PNG compression for 24-bit files isn't for general web use.

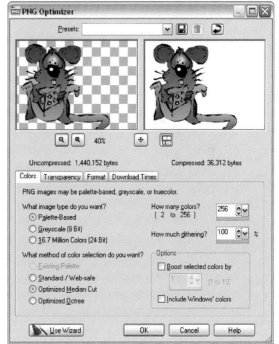

On the Transparency tab you can choose No transparency, Single color transparency, or Alpha channel transparency. In either of the latter two, you have the option of using existing image transparency or picking a transparent color as you do with the GIF Optimizer. In addition to these, if you have an active marquee selection on the image, you can choose to make the area outside the selection transparent.

Alpha channel transparency allows you to define true partial transparency. This lets you use feathered selections to define transparent areas or have drop shadows over existing transparency displayed correctly without the fringing associated with GIF files. You must, however, use 16.7 million colors for this option which, as mentioned earlier, isn't widely supported by browsers.

The Format and Download Times tabs mirror those of the GIF and JPEG Optimizers.

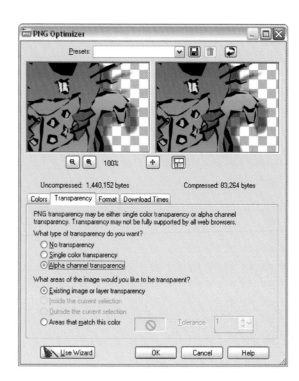

Image Slicer

Another useful web tool is the **Image Slicer**, which you can use to slice a large image into several smaller ones, much the same as you might cut up a picture on a piece of paper. This tool is used exclusively for posting images to web pages. You might want to do this for a number of reasons:

* To break down a large image into smaller parts that will appear piece by piece if the viewer has a slow Internet connection, thereby keeping the user's interest

* To optimize different areas of the same graphic independently

* To include rollover buttons on larger images, such as a web site navigation bar

You may have an image that includes both photographic and limited color elements. By slicing up the image, you can save different portions in the most appropriate format and even adjust the settings of a single format to optimize different areas.

There's much more to image slicing than simply cutting up a picture, though. You also have to put the sliced images back together on the web page. You do this with a Hypertext Markup Language (HTML) file that loads in your browser and tells it how and where to display text and images on a web page. Sliced images are displayed seamlessly on a web page through the use of tables, much the same as you may have used with your word processor. The size and configuration of the table cells need to reflect how the image was sliced. Fortunately, you don't have to learn how to write HTML files to use the Image Slicer, because not only will Paint Shop Pro slice the image for you, it will also write the HTML code.

We'll use this tool to slice and optimize an image for the web that's built of both graphics and a photograph. To follow along with your own work, open or create an image that contains both graphics and a photograph.

Assume that you want to make a web page for a small business. In this example, we have a photographic element (literally) that would be best rendered as a JPEG, along with some text elements that might be better suited to the GIF format. A navigation bar is included that will need to contain hyperlinks to other web sites.

1. Open your image in Paint Shop Pro and go to File > Export > Image Slicer. You might want to maximize the dialog box to give yourself more space to work with in the preview window.

The first thing to notice is that, unlike most dialog boxes in Paint Shop Pro, there's a single image pane. This is because the Image Slicer doesn't introduce any viewable changes to the image. The preview pane is actually your work area. You can zoom in and out and navigate around the image using the familiar buttons. Below the zoom and navigation buttons are the slicer tools.

You can use the Selection tool (the selected arrow here) to select individual cells for editing once you've performed some slicing.

2. Immediately to the right of the Selection tool is the Grid tool. Select it and then click anywhere in the image window to bring up the Grid Size dialog box.

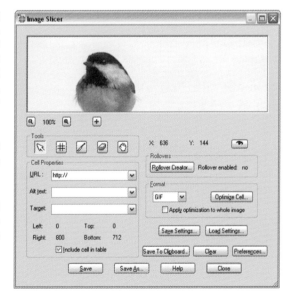

3. Enter the number of rows and columns you want to slice the image into, and it will arrange them equally on the image. Red lines show the slices. A selected cell is indicated by a green outline.

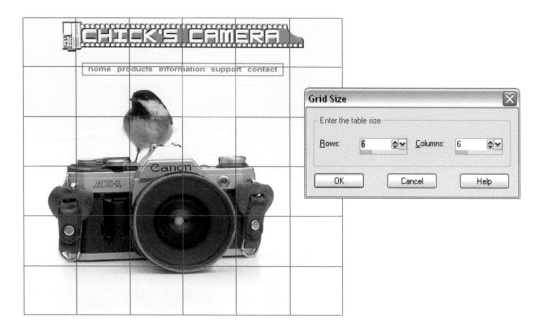

The Edit menu is unavailable when the Slicer is active, but CTRL+Z will still undo the last action and the Clear button will clear out all actions.

The Grid tool is fine for making nice, evenly sliced cells over the entire image, but it doesn't work for splitting individual cells into smaller units. For this, you use the **Slicer**. This makes a single slice starting at the closest existing slice away from the direction of the drag and ending at the closest existing slice ahead of the point the drag ends. If there's no slice in either or both of those areas, the slice will extend to the edge of the image. The slice will be horizontal or diagonal depending on which direction you drag the cursor.

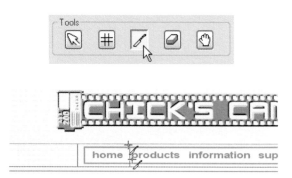

4. The **Eraser** tool is next in the Slicer. If you click this tool directly over a slice, it will remove the slice. You know you're directly over a slice when the cursor changes from the normal arrow to an eraser icon.

Because of the nature of tables, this means that all cells must be rectangular; the Eraser tool won't allow you to remove slices that violate this rule. When you try to do so, it presents an eraser cursor overlaid with the null symbol.

5. The hand icon is the standard pan tool, which you can use to drag a zoomed-in area around. X and Y denote the horizontal and vertical coordinates of the cursor in pixels for any tool, from the top-left corner of the image.

Once cells are created, the cell will bind the Slice and Grid tools. Clicking in a cell will create slices inside only that particular cell. As a result, by creating two horizontal slices above and below the navigation bar, we can go into that cell and create a number of vertical slices to make each word in the text a separate image without slicing anything outside that cell. This allows us one cell for the photo of the bird, a separate one for the banner, and individual cells for each of the links on the navigation bar.

6. Now you can include the links for the navigation bar. To apply a hyperlink to a cell, first select the cell in the image window and then go to the Cell Properties area in the Image Slicer dialog box.

7. Enter the web address in the URL field. You can use either the full address of the page such as http://www.chickscamera.com/products.html or a relative address such as products.html.

The link doesn't necessarily have to be a web page URL. You can also enter an e-mail link by typing in mailto: followed by the e-mail address of the contact, such as mailto:ron@ronstoons.com. When this link is clicked, the user's e-mail client opens up with a new e-mail addressed to ron@ronstoons.com. You can also pre-fill the subject line of the e-mail. For example, enteringmailto: ronstoons.comsubject=Zero to Hero will include the text "Zero to Hero" in the e-mail's subject.

8. You can enter something descriptive about the link or image in the Alt text field. This text will appear on the web page as a little pop-up, similar to a tool tip in the browser when you hover your cursor over an image.

The information you enter in the Target field determines how the link will open. You can select the following options from the drop-down menu:

★ _blank opens the linked page in a new browser window.

★ _parent opens the linked page in the parent window or frameset.

★ _self opens the linked page in the same browser window or frame occupied by the link.

★ _top opens the linked page in the current browser window as a full page and removes any frames.

The Left, Top, Right, and Bottom numbers indicate the location in pixels of the selected cell. The Include cell in table check box actually includes the sliced image piece in the HTML table. If this is unchecked, that cell will be blank on the web page. You might want to do this if you wish to use some regular text in this area of the web page instead of an image. If you do uncheck this box, no link can be assigned to that particular cell.

9. Clicking the eyeball icon allows you to proof your settings by launching your browser and opening the web page.

10. In the Format area of the Image Slicer dialog box, you can decide what file format you want a particular cell to be: GIF, JPEG, or PNG. In our example, we make the photographic cell of the bird a JPEG and the remaining cells GIFs. We select a cell and apply a format.

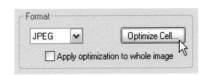

11. Clicking Optimize Cell brings up the familiar Optimizer dialog box for the selected format, where you can address the output settings for the image slice.

12. If you want to output all the slices to the same file format and optimization settings, simply select one cell, check Apply optimization to whole image, and apply your settings. All the slices will be exported to the selected file format and optimized to those settings.

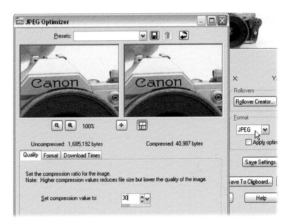

13. Clicking the Save Settings button opens the **Save Slice Settings** dialog box for the **JSD** format (Jasc's slicer format). This will save all slice location, rollover, and file format information, but *not* the images. Once saved, this information can be recalled to the same or a different image, and edited by clicking the Load Settings button. This way, you can modify an existing web page without having to start from scratch.

14. Clicking Preferences will bring up the Slice Preferences dialog box. Here, you can customize your slice colors, the number of entries in the drop-down history list, and whether or not you're prompted for a separate image folder when you save your completed HTML and image slices using Paint Shop Pro, as opposed to using the clipboard.

15. Click Save To Clipboard if you want to paste the HTML into an editor such as Dreamweaver.

You'll be prompted to select a folder to save the images in. The name you choose will be a prefix followed by a numbered description of the row and column in the table the image appears. For instance, if you chose `chickscamera` as the file name, the image on the first column in the first row would be assigned the name `chickscamera_1x1.gif`, the first file on the second row would be `chickscamera_2x1.gif`, and so on. Meanwhile, the HTML table information that instructs the browser how to reassemble the images is copied to the clipboard. Use this option if you want to use another program to create and edit the web page by pasting the clipboard contents into that program. You can use any text editor (for example, Notepad) to assemble an HTML file, or you can use a dedicated editor (for example, FrontPage Express, which comes with Windows).

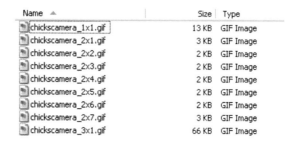

When you save the HTML file from an editor, be sure you use the same root folder you instructed Paint Shop Pro to use.

16. To have Paint Shop Pro create the complete web page, including the HTML file, click the Save As button. If you didn't check Prompt for image folder on Save or Save As in the Slice Preferences dialog box, all the images will be saved in the folder you choose for the HTML file and will use the name of the original image file as a file name prefix for the individual sliced images. Once you've saved the complete page, you can make changes to it in the Slicer and click Save to apply them.

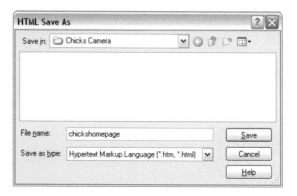

17. If you did check that box, after you decide on a name and folder for the HTML file and click Save, a second dialog box pops up asking for a directory and prefix name for the images.

Unless you have a web site directory structure already set up, it's best to use or create a subfolder away from where you saved the original HTML file.

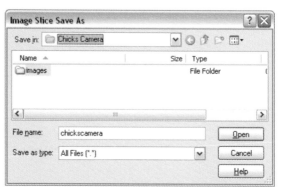

Adding rollovers to your web graphics

Using the **Rollover Creator** in the Image Slicer dialog box, you can assign different images to a selected cell to coincide with a user's particular mouse state. This is a common practice on many web pages and is mostly used for the "mouse over" state, where a button changes appearance as the mouse cursor moves over it.

Before you use the Rollover Creator, you need to prepare the appropriate images for each mouse state. Although you're able to save up to six different mouse states, you don't have to choose them all; just the mouse over state is sometimes enough. The mouse states are

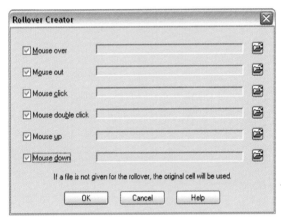

* **Mouse over**: The chosen image is shown when the cursor moves over the cell.

* **Mouse out**: The image displays after the cell has been moused over and the cursor moved off the cell (in most cases, this is the original cell image).

* **Mouse click**: The image displays when you click the mouse.

* **Mouse double click**: The image displays after a double mouse click.

* **Mouse up**: The image displays while the mouse button is depressed.

* **Mouse down**: The image displays while the mouse button is depressed.

You'll have to know the size of the cell you want to make a rollover image for in advance, in order to make it the correct size. Because of this, it's best to do your slicing first and save it in two formats:

* A completely sliced creation with images and an HTML file

* A JSD file (via the Save Settings button) that you can reload after you create the rollover images

You can determine the size of a cell by subtracting the Left value from the Right and the Top value from the Bottom in the Cell Properties area of the Image Slicer dialog box, but perhaps the best way to do this is to use the saved sliced images for the cell in question. This way, you'll have the correctly sized image and you can make subtle changes to it, such as changing the text color to make the rollover more effective.

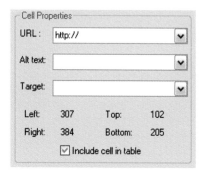

1. Whichever method you use, save the image with a new name to the image directory where you saved the original images from the Slicer. Give it a recognizable name—for example, you can add the word "rollover" to the original file name (to make `chick_2x3rollover.gif`, for example).

2. Once you've edited and saved the rollover image file(s), open the original file you sliced and go to File > Export > Image Slicer. Now select Load Settings in the Image Slicer dialog box and load the JSD file you saved.

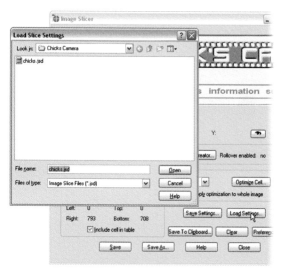

3. Select the cell you made the rollover image for with the Arrow tool in the preview pane and click the Rollover Creator button. The familiar possible mouse states appear.

4. Simply check the box for the state(s) to which you want to apply a rollover and click the folder button to the right of that state to bring up a file selection dialog box, where you can navigate to the folder containing your images.

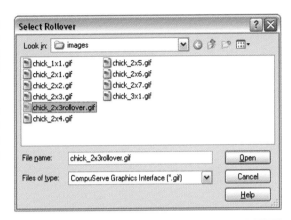

In our example, we created a rollover image from `chick_2x3.gif` (the third cell in the second row) by changing the text color to black and saving it as `chick_2x3rollover.gif`. We then assigned it to the mouse over state for the 2x3 cell.

> After you set any image for the mouse over, you should make sure you also assign an image to the mouse out state, so that the button returns to its original appearance when the user's mouse rolls off the button. Usually this image is the original slice and, in our case, this is *chick_2x3.gif*. If you don't do this, the image won't change back to the original state after the mouse over image occurs.

5. Once you've assigned all your rollovers to all the cells you want, click OK in the Rollover Creator and Save in the Image Slicer dialog box. The web page will be saved complete with rollovers. You can also use the clipboard method if you want to use an HTML editor. You can look at Chick's page by pointing your browser to www.ronsfotos.com/chicks.

Image Mapper

The Image Mapper is another method of assigning hyperlinks to graphics on web pages. Basically, this method defines hotspots on a single image that are defined in the HTML file with coordinates to which hyperlinks are assigned. Once an image-mapped web page is loaded in a browser, clicking a hotspot will send you to the linked page. Image mapping doesn't slice up the image and, when you save the image-mapped page, you'll have only one image file.

1. Open an image that you could use for a web page and go to File > Export > Image Mapper.

Notice that it shares a lot of the same elements with the Image Slicer. You'll also be pleased to know that these elements operate in much the same way. The main difference is the choice of tools. The selection and pan tools work the same as in the Slicer but, unlike the Slicer, you don't define cuts in the Image Mapper—you define **areas**. The Mapper has three tools that can accomplish this.

2. The Polygon tool is a point-to-point line tool. Click and move the mouse in the image pane to draw straight lines. You can close the area either by double-clicking or clicking back at the point where you first started.

3. With the other two selection tools (the rectangle and circle icons) you can select a rectangular or circular area, respectively, by dragging out a shape in the image pane.

4. Once you've defined an area, you can drag it to a new location on the image using the Move tool (the four-headed arrow).

5. After you define an area, use the Cell Properties fields in the Image Mapper dialog box to assign a URL. Here, we've added a mailto: command for the Contact button at the right of the navigation bar.

6. When you've finished defining all the hotspots and assigning them URLs, you can save these settings as a JMD file in the same way you saved Image Slicer settings (by clicking the Save Settings button). Move on to the Format area of the dialog box, choose the best file type for the image, and optimize it. We've gone for JPEG here.

7. Finally, choose the save option you prefer. If you want the image map to be an entire page, use the Save or Save As option. If you want to include an image map in an existing HTML file you're creating, use the Save To Clipboard option.

> *Although the Rollover Creator is available in the Image Mapper after a hotspot is defined, it isn't of any practical use. You can't roll over a hotspot, so if you apply a mouse over state to a hotspot, the entire image— not just the hotspot—would change to the rollover state image.*

Paint Shop Pro 8:
Have It Your Way

In this chapter

Paint Shop Pro 8 includes several new features that can enhance your ability to design quality graphics quickly and use advanced tools even if you aren't yet comfortable with them.

Even if you're quite familiar with the Paint Shop Pro 8 interface at this point, this chapter will take you on an in-depth tour and investigate some features that can help you work more efficiently:

★ Using scripting

★ Configuring and optimizing all the toolbars you can use

★ Setting up your Paint Shop Pro workspace efficiently and comfortably

★ Adjusting your program preferences

Scripts

Scripts allow you to automate repetitive tasks, so that instead of using a number of commands and keystrokes, you can click a button or two and accomplish the same process in seconds. You can use scripts for common tasks in many different processes.

A typical task is resizing an entire directory of digital photos to the same size. You may even want to place them on a suitable background with a caption or title. You could complete the process by saving each photo as a JPEG image with a certain amount of compression. A task like this, involving 100 photos or more, might take days to complete, but in Paint Shop Pro 8 you can do it in seconds using a few preinstalled scripts. You can even write a single script that accomplishes the entire project.

Scripting in Paint Shop Pro is handled by a programming language called Python, but it's not necessary for the average user to understand it or any other programming language, as there are some simple tools that can make anyone a scripting genius. We'll start with the Script toolbar itself (View > Toolbars > Script):

The Select Script drop-down menu displays all the scripts contained in the Scripts folder of Paint Shop Pro. As with many other features, you can use scripts stored in other folders too, as defined in File > Preferences > File Locations.

It's always important to remember that scripts are written in a computer language and therefore can be used by someone with malicious intent to harm your computer. So, first and foremost, never run a script from a source you don't trust. Even a script that's not intended to harm your computer could still alter things enough to confuse and irritate.

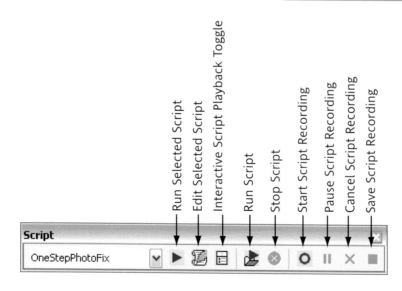

Paint Shop Pro arrives on your doorstep with a default configuration designed to protect your computer from malicious scripts: **Python Restricted Execution mode**. Scripts can be of two varieties: **Restricted** or **Trusted**. Restricted mode prevents a malicious script from doing major damage to your computer, but it still won't prevent pesky furniture rearranging inside Paint Shop Pro itself.

Trusted scripts run with Restricted mode off and for this reason can be considered potentially harmful. Most scripts in Paint Shop Pro run in Restricted Execution mode. However, some trusted scripts need to be run with Restricted mode *off*, although you don't need to worry about toggling anything on or off. Just place scripts that should be in Restricted mode in the Scripts-Restricted folder, and Paint Shop Pro will automatically manage the execution mode. Trusted scripts are stored in the Scripts-Trusted folder, which can be in a number of locations:

★ The Paint Shop Pro 8 program folder

★ My Documents/My PSP8 Files/Scripts-Trusted

★ Another folder that you've created yourself

The best defense against harmful scripts is to not accept any scripts at all, but write your own instead, or use one of the many scripts built into the program. *Do not* accept scripts that must run from the Scripts-Trusted folder unless you're absolutely sure of the script's integrity.

> *If you're feeling clever, you can open any script in a text editor, such as Notepad, and examine it before you run it. Although the code elements might look like mumbo-jumbo, you should be able to pick out something like* `format C:` *(not something we want to do!).*

Editing photographs with scripts

1. Open an image (use a duplicate image here so there's no danger of affecting your original).

2. Activate the Script toolbar using View > Toolbars > Script, and select a handy little script called GreyscaleInPlace from the Select Script drop-down menu.

3. Click the Run Selected Script icon, and the image will be converted to grayscale quickly. This script runs in **Silent mode**, which means that you won't see any functions performed (it will all be done without any further interaction from you), and up pops the finished result.

This script converts any image to grayscale and then converts it to 24-bit color, because a normal grayscale conversion converts the image to 8-bit color.

Adding captions to photos

1. Scroll down the Select Script drop-down menu in the Script toolbar and choose SimpleCaption. Make sure the Interactive Script Playback Toggle button is active and click the Run Selected Script icon. You'll be prompted to enter a caption.

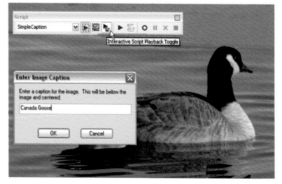

This is an example of a script running in **Interactive mode**.

2. Enter an appropriate caption and click OK. The rest of the script runs.

This script gives you a final image that's mounted against a subtle gray background, with a drop shadow and a caption. The background and shadow are added in Silent mode.

Canada Goose

Recording your own scripts

Using the built-in scripts gives us lots more functionality. Although the folks at Jasc have provided lots of scripts to make our lives easier, we can make our own personal scripts too.

1. Open any picture. Make one or use a favorite—it doesn't matter. Crop or resize it to 600x600 pixels, but don't worry about maintaining the aspect ratio. It's not important that the picture maintains any realism for this example.

2. Click the Start Script Recording button on the Script toolbar.

3. Go to Effects > Texture Effects > Weave and accept the default settings, which should look like those shown here:

If your current settings don't match these, click the Reset icon in the Weave dialog box, and they'll quickly be reset.

4. Click OK to apply the effect.

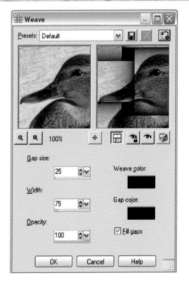

5. Now go to Effects > Reflection Effects > Kaleidoscope, and click the Reset icon to change all the settings to the default state. Set Number of petals to 4, as shown here. Click OK to apply the effect.

6. Go to File > Save As and browse to the Programs/Jasc Software Inc/Paint Shop Pro 8 /Patterns folder. Save this file as a .PspImage file with a descriptive name.

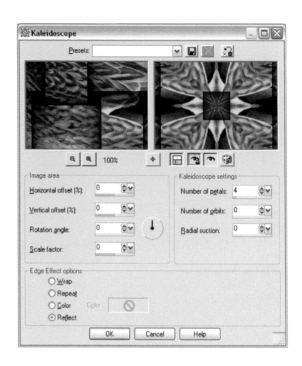

Upon installation, Paint Shop Pro creates some user folders in My Documents/My PSP8 Files on your computer. It also creates similar folders in the Program Files/Jasc Software Inc/Paint Shop Pro 8 folder. Both folder paths are configured upon installation to be "seen" by the program, so any image element stored in either type of folder will be used by Paint Shop Pro.

By default, any image elements included with the program are stored in the Program Files folders. Any user-created image elements are saved automatically in the My Documents folders. You can change these folders to those of your own choosing in File > Preferences > File Locations, or you can click the Edit Path button in any dialog box where you wish to change the save-to path.

7. On the Script toolbar, click the Save Script Recording icon.

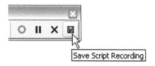

8. Give your script a descriptive name and save it in the default Scripts-Restricted folder (Program Files/Jasc Software Inc/Paint Shop Pro 8/Scripts-Restricted).

Ta-dah! Your first script. This pattern should now be available to you in your Patterns folder and in the Materials palette, or anyplace you can access your Patterns folder from inside Paint Shop Pro, such as the Sculpture effect.

Using your personal scripts

Now let's test out your handmade script.

1. Open another image and choose your script from the Select Script drop-down menu in the Script toolbar.

2. Run the script by clicking the Run Selected Script button in the toolbar.

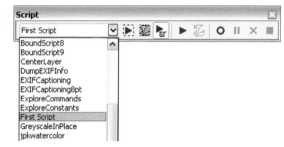

The script will stop at several points to allow you to make adjustments to the effects. Just click OK if you don't want to make any changes and save the pattern as you did at the end of the previous example.

How easy is that? You can pause or cancel script recording using the buttons at the far right of the Script toolbar, and you can choose to use any script in either Interactive or Silent mode by toggling the button on the Script toolbar.

Paint Shop Pro 8 ships with some very useful scripts:

★ The **OneStepPhotoFix** script does amazing things with your photos.

★ **PaletteFromImage** produces a 256-color palette from an image.

★ **EXIFCaptioning** adds **Exchangeable Image File Format** (**EXIF**) information to the image as a caption. EXIF is a commonly used digital-camera file format that records information such as exposure time and aperture settings (see www.exif.org for full details).

★ **BevelSelection** adds a bevel and drop shadow to any selection. And there's many more!

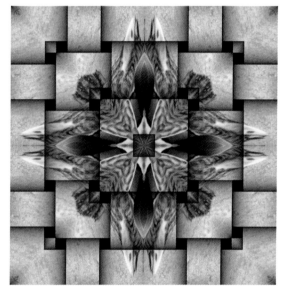

Script Output palette

This palette will show you the progress of any scripts you run. If space is at a premium, you might consider turning it off and only turning it on (F3 to toggle) as needed when you're recording scripts. This palette will automatically open if a script has errors in it, and the errors will be highlighted in red. If you're feeling adventurous, you can use this information to help discover why the script didn't work or perhaps edit the script so that it *will* run!

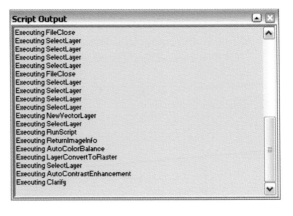

Script Editor

You can open the Script Editor to see the workings of a script (either one of the defaults or one you've recorded) by clicking the Edit Selected Script button.

You can change the mode that each step of the script works in (Silent or Interactive), and enable, disable, and edit each stage of the script.

If you know a little bit of the Python language, you can edit the script directly. Click the Text Editor button and the script will open in Notepad (or another text editor you set up at File > Preferences > File Locations).

If you'd like to learn more about the language used to record scripts, check out www.python.org.

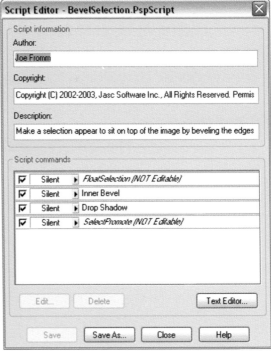

Workspace files

Workspace files let you save your preferred workspace setup and palette organization. Let's begin by saving your current settings so that no matter where you go exploring, you'll be able to restore your workspace to your current configuration.

1. With Paint Shop Pro open, but with no images open, go to File > Workspace > Save (or use the shortcut SHIFT+ALT+S).

2. When the Save Workspace dialog box opens, name your workspace something descriptive and click Save. The workspace files save to the My Documents/My PSP 8 Files/Workspace folder, unless you've configured it differently.

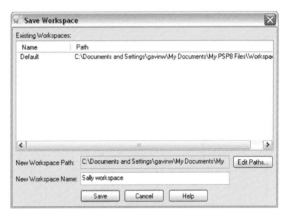

Now, no matter what changes you make to the interface, you'll always be able to restore it to exactly the way you left it.

> *Don't overwrite the file named* Default.PspWorkspace. *Loading this workspace will return Paint Shop Pro to its default settings.*

3. Let's totally mess up the picture and turn *everything* on in the interface. Press SHIFT+CTRL+T, and all the possible toolbars and palettes in the default Paint Shop Pro configuration open in your workspace.

This is a good way to retrieve a toolbar or palette if you just can't seem to find it. This little trick brings them all back front and center. If you've made custom toolbars, this trick won't retrieve those, but if you reload your saved workspace file with the custom toolbars, you'll get them back.

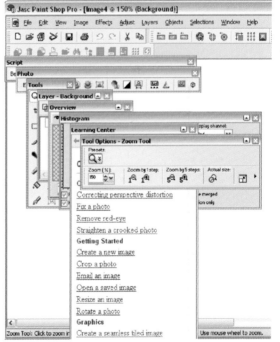

Customizing palettes

Now that you have all the toolbars and palettes open, we'll examine how to customize them to your liking.

Tool Options palette

You should be quite familiar with the operation of this palette as it relates to tools you've used throughout this book, but you may not know that you can configure the palette itself. You can dock it to a side of the workspace, let it float freely on the workspace, or even put it outside the workspace window.

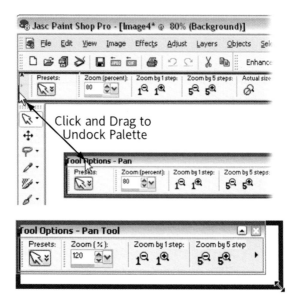

1. If the palette is already docked at the top or bottom of the workspace, you can float it by clicking and dragging the double vertical dotted line at the left side of the palette. (If the palette is docked to the side, then the double line is at the top of the palette.)

2. If the palette is already floating, you can resize it on any side by click-dragging the edge, just like any regular Windows window. As you resize the palette, you drag out the feature groups, replacing the flyout arrows.

You can resize the Tool Options palette to its most effective shape for your own needs. You can also move feature groups within the palette to make the most efficient use of the space available.

3. To drag a feature group, click the dotted vertical divider bar at the left end of the group, and drag the group to the area on the palette where you'd like it to stick. If, after you do this, the palette is taller than the feature groups require, it will resize automatically.

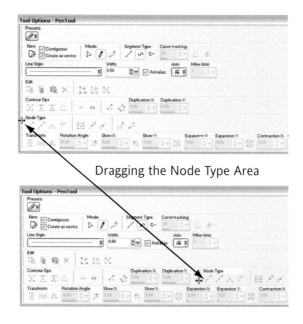

Dragging the Node Type Area

Quick Guides palette

Now let's take a look at the next palette in the group: the **Learning Center palette** (F10). This palette contains a series of **Quick Guides**, which allow you to walk through HTML tutorials, including active links that help you perform a task as you go along. Some basic Quick Guides are included with Paint Shop Pro 8, and you can download more at the Quick Guides Home at www.jasc.com. You can also print the Quick Guides directly from the Learning Center.

Magnifier

The Magnifier is a handy little zoom tool you can toggle on or off by pressing F11 or right-clicking a toolbar and selecting Magnifier. Once the Magnifier is activated, a small window opens, giving you a 5x zoomed view of a 30x30 pixel area centered on the cursor's location.

Customizing toolbars

There are eight standard toolbars, all of which you can toggle on and off from View > Toolbars. You can also use the following shortcut keys:

- ★ B: Browser toolbar
- ★ E: Effects toolbar
- ★ H: Photo toolbar
- ★ S: Script toolbar
- ★ T: Standard toolbar
- ★ A: Status toolbar
- ★ O: Tools toolbar
- ★ W: Web toolbar

If you float any toolbar, you can resize it from the long strips to rectangles by grabbing any side and dragging.

If a toolbar doesn't contain some icons for commands you use frequently or it's cluttered with icons you never use, you can customize it with exactly the icons you want.

1. Right-click the title bar of any toolbar and select Customize. The Customize dialog box opens on the Commands tab.

In the Categories field on the Commands tab, you can narrow your search for appropriate buttons by picking a specific category of commands listed by menu. You can select All Commands too, which is at the bottom of the list. The commands available to the selected menu appear in the right pane, and you can add any of these to your toolbar by simply dragging them over to it.

2. As you drag the icon to the toolbar, you'll see a small black vertical divider. When you release the mouse, the icon will be added wherever the divider is when you drop it. In the case of a rectangular toolbar with several rows of icons, the icon will be added to the next row if it's at the edge of the toolbar.

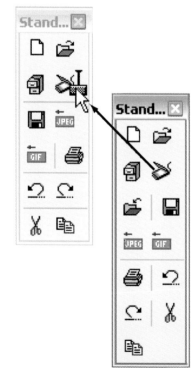

3. To add a separator to a toolbar, drag an icon slightly down and to the right (*slightly!*) on the toolbar as you're customizing it, and a separator will be created to the left of that button. You can also add a separator by right-clicking the icon in question and choosing Start Group.

4. If you want to remove an icon from a toolbar, just click it, drag it off the toolbar, and drop it anywhere. Voila!

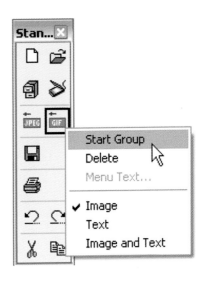

Creating new toolbars

Okay, you've customized all your current toolbars, but what if you want to create some special ones of your very own? Not a problem!

1. Right-click the title bar of any toolbar and select Customize. Select the Toolbars tab and then click the New button.

2. You can now give your toolbar a name. You may want a specialized toolbar for vector tools or selections, for instance. Name your toolbar and then click OK.

You'll see a small toolbar without icons appear on the workspace.

3. Now go to the Commands tab again, where you can drag icons over to the new toolbar in the same way you customize an existing one.

4. Once you have all your toolbars and palettes configured, docked, or floated as you wish, go to File > Workspace > Save and save this workspace configuration. Name this workspace something descriptive to distinguish it from the original workspace you saved before you started rearranging all the furniture. Don't forget to do this! If Paint Shop Pro 8 crashes, or if you drag a toolbar so far off-screen you can't retrieve it, you'll need that workspace file again.

You can set up different workspace files for different tasks. For example, when photo editing, you may want to customize your Photo toolbar and not require the Web tools in the workspace at all.

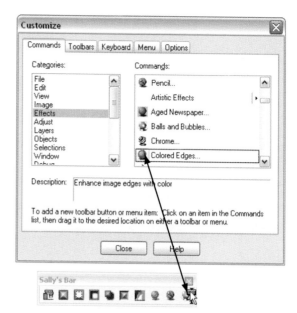

> *You can launch Paint Shop Pro directly from a workspace file if you like, and you can save workspace files to your Desktop or Quick Launch toolbar, so that just clicking the desktop icon for a particular workspace file will launch Paint Shop Pro in that configuration.*

Program preferences

Another feature that adds flexibility to the program is the ability to customize the way in which the program handles certain actions and processes.

Go to File > Preferences to see the many types of feature preferences. Select File > Preferences > General Program Preferences and you'll see a tabbed dialog box with ten different preference subcategories.

Undo

The preferences on the Undo tab allow you to enable or disable the Undo and Redo features under the Edit menu. Here, you can set the size of the disk space allocated to the Undo feature and the number of Undo steps the program will save for a particular image. This may be important if you're using a computer with limited memory or space resources. The more resources you devote to Undos, the less is available for other uses. Compressing will reduce the disk space needed, but it may also impact your computer's performance.

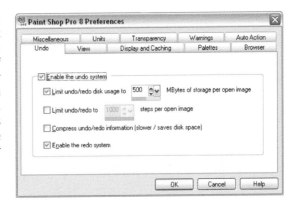

Display and caching

The Display and Caching preferences control the following:

★ Display of the color tool tips whenever you use the Eyedropper tool

★ Use of precise cursors

★ Whether tool outlines are displayed when you use one of the Brush tools

★ Whether you see the Pen tool's control handles when you use it on a raster layer

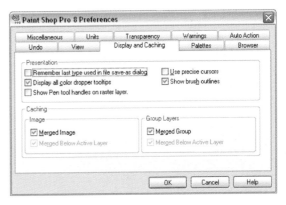

Perhaps the most useful option here is Remember last type used in save-as file dialog. Because many users consistently save images as one particular file type, such as JPEG or PNG, enabling this option will save a little time when saving image files. You won't have to scroll through that 9-mile-long list of possible file types that Paint Shop Pro can save!

Palettes

You've already used the Palettes tab to enable or disable docking of some palettes. You can also use this tab to control how Paint Shop Pro displays color information in both the Materials palette and tool tips. RGB will update the Eyedropper tool with red/green/blue values, and HSL will use hue/saturation/lightness values. Decimal or Hexadecimal display will display the HSL and RGB color values in decimal or hexadecimal format. Because web browsers use hexadecimal format, you may prefer to display colors in this form when you're

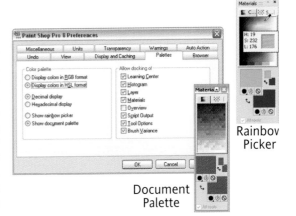

Rainbow Picker

Document Palette

creating art destined for the Web. Checking Show rainbow picker will show all the colors available in the Color palette, whereas checking Show document palette will show only the image colors included in a paletted image, such as a 256-color GIF. If you have a 24-bit 16-million color image, you'll see the Rainbow Picker regardless of which option is selected.

Browser

The Browser preferences affect how thumbnails of your images are displayed in the Image Browser. You can set the size of the thumbnails to as large as 150 pixels on a side and display tool tips for the thumbnails. You can also modify the Browser appearance itself and choose to have the thumbnails automatically updated whenever you make a change to an image.

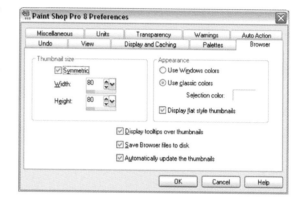

Auto Action

The Auto Action tab will allow you to tell Paint Shop Pro what to do when you ask it for the impossible. For example, if you're working on an 8-bit 256-color image, you can't create a new layer unless you increase the colors to 16 million. If you try and do this, you might see a warning message.

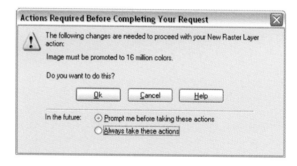

This would happen if you had Convert to 16-million colors set to Prompt (the default). If you set it to Always, Paint Shop Pro automatically increases the colors whenever you initiate an operation that requires this action. If you set it to Never, any operations that require this action are grayed out or unavailable. The three buttons at the bottom left of the palette apply the settings to *all* the auto actions.

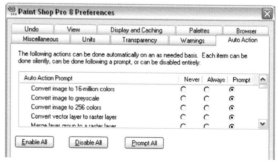

Warnings

The Warnings tab is pretty self-explanatory. It allows you to customize what warning messages are displayed for particular events.

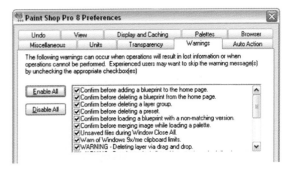

Transparency

In the Transparency tab, you can pick the grid size and colors of the transparency checkerboard. If you find the grid distracting, you can replace it with a solid color by selecting identical colors in both the Color 1 and Color 2 swatches. There are also settings in the Grid Colors Scheme drop-down menu that will give you a solid color image canvas instead of a grid.

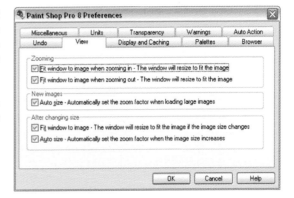

View

Under the View tab, you'll find several settings that control how your window resizes itself when you change the Zoom view or size of an image. Check the options and the window will resize itself around the zoomed image.

Checking the Auto size option will automatically open a large image to a zoom factor that will allow the entire image to be seen.

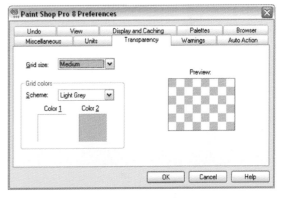

Units

Under Units tab, you can define how the various palettes and rulers that display units of measurement will do so:

* ★ Pixels

* ★ Inches

* ★ Centimeters

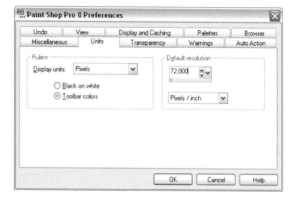

Miscellaneous

Finally, the Miscellaneous options let you decide the number of recent files to be displayed at the bottom of the File menu, as well as what to do with clipboard data when you close the program. For most modern tablets, including the Wacom models, you'll want to check Disable pressure support for puck-type pointing devices.

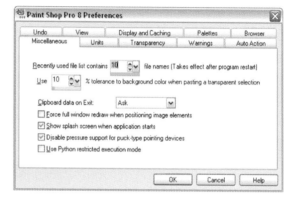

Hero One
Digital Divorce

In this chapter

This section of our book is devoted to real-world projects—the types of tasks people typically want to accomplish, whether for work or pleasure. In this chapter, we'll show you how to manipulate a photo that could be "just right," if only it didn't have that pesky ex-husband or bratty neighbor kid in it, and turn it into a photograph worthy of your treasured photo album. We'll cover the following topics:

- ★ The Freehand Selection tool

- ★ The Manual Color Correction tool

- ★ The Deform tool

- ★ The Background Eraser tool

- ★ Alpha channel selections

Let's start with this shot of some friends at the movies (`moviefriends.tif` in the download files). It might be a nice photo, but wouldn't it be good if we could remove the guy in the back row from the picture?

1. Begin by opening the image in Paint Shop Pro. Take a look at the various elements in the photo.

This is the new image you're going to try and create, with the boy banished from the background.

2. You'll make good use of the Layer palette in this project. Make sure it's visible (F8) and promote the Background layer to a full layer (Layers > Promote Background Layer).

3. Add a duplicate layer to the image (Layers > Duplicate).

4. Activate the Freehand Selection tool and set the following options:

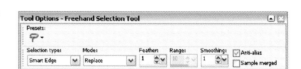

   ★ Selection type: Smart Edge
   ★ Mode: Replace
   ★ Feather: 1
   ★ Smoothing: 1
   ★ Anti-alias: Checked

5. You'll use the seat back directly in front of the pesky boy to replace the seat he's occupying. Refer to the image here, and begin by clicking at the top-left corner of the seat back, behind the boy in the red shirt. Click again at the points indicated in the image. Drag down in a straight line until you're nearly at the top of the next seat row.

6. Click to set the Smart Edge "point" at the bottom-left corner of the visible seat back, and then drag right to the edge of the empty seat back behind the guy in the red shirt. Click again and drag up to the top of the seat back. At this point, double-click and the selection should complete itself by forming the last side of the selection and snapping to the top seat-back edge. The completed selection should be fairly rectangular in shape.

7. Save this selection to an alpha channel (Selections > Load/Save Selection > Save Selection to Alpha Channel).

8. Now copy the seat back with CTRL+C, use CTRL+L to paste it as a new layer, and rename it Seat Back 1.

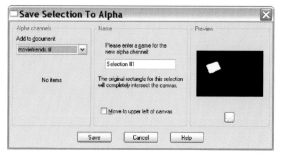

9. Deactivate the selection (CTRL+D) and, using the Move tool, click the new seat back area on the Seat Back 1 layer and try and move it into position over the boy's seat. Don't worry if it's not too exact.

You should now have three layers in your palette: the original image on the bottom layer, a duplicated layer over that, and a third layer containing just the selected seat back.

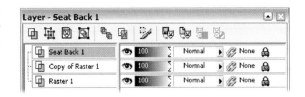

10. The new seat back is a bit too large to match the scale of the other seats in the boy's row. Make the Seat Back 1 layer active and then choose the Deform tool (D). A bounding box appears around the seat back.

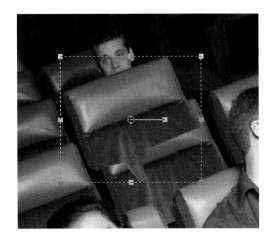

11. Lower the opacity on the Seat Back 1 layer to 70 so that you can see through to the underlying seat back and scale your selected seat to match it.

12. Now that you can see through the seat back, right-click the bottom-right node of the deformation bounding box and drag inward to match the size of the selected seat back to the boy's. You also need to align the seat back with the boy's, which you can do simply by dragging the bounding box.

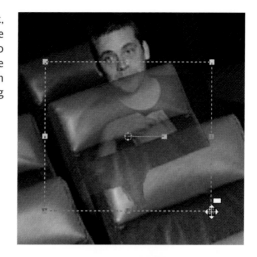

If you need to rotate the seat back to align it correctly, hover your mouse cursor over the center pivot handle until you see the rotate icon, and then click and drag the box in a circular motion.

Tidying up the selection

The new seat back might be a little rough around the edges, and there may be other elements in the photo that currently give away your trickery, so you'll need to spend a little time cleaning up these clues.

1. Increase the layer opacity of the Seat Back 1 layer back up to 100%. You may also need to clean up the edge of the new seat back. If you do, grab the Eraser tool, set the size to 4, and set Shape to Round. Carefully erase any stray yellow or light-colored pixels from the top edge of the seat by clicking them one by one with the Eraser tool. If necessary, zoom in to 600% or more to view the pixels you're trying to erase.

2. Go to Selections > Load/Save Selections > Load From Alpha Channel and load the saved selection, making sure you're still on the Seat Back 1 layer.

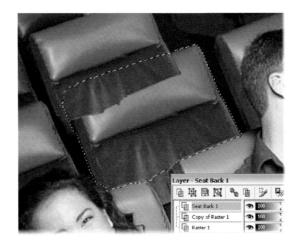

3. Press DELETE to erase any portion of the seat back that falls within the selected area. This should now give you a well-defined edge between the first and second rows.

Matching colors

Now, despite your efforts, the boy is doing everything he can to stay in the photo. A bit of the boy's arm is still visible between the seats, not quite covered by the seat texture, a telltale clue that you've been pasting him out. You can cover this up using the Clone Brush tool.

1. Select the Clone Brush, and set the following tool options:

- ★ Size: 30
- ★ Shape: Square
- ★ Hardness: 40
- ★ Rotation: 70
- ★ Opacity: 50
- ★ Sample merged: Checked

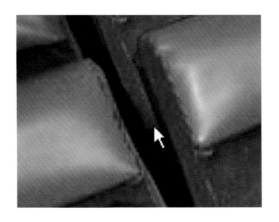

This allows you to sample a clone area from a layer below a transparent layer—very handy.

2. Right-click the left edge of the seat above the boy's arm to sample the color, and then left-click in the area you want to correct. Brush and click to add some of the seat back texture and color over the remaining arm. Keep resampling darker colors and painting them on the arm, gradually fading it into the black area.

3. Now let's match the color of the new seat back you created to the seat back next to it in the same row as that pesky boy you're eliminating. Ensure the Seat Back 1 layer is active and go to Adjust > Color Balance > Manual Color Correction.

4. Sample an area of the new seat back to use as the source color. Click the Source swatch, hold down the CTRL key until you see the eyedropper icon, and then drag over the seat back you want to sample. Click to set this color as the source color.

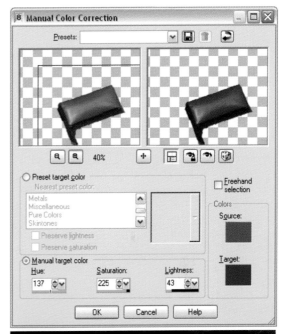

5. Select Manual target color, hover your mouse cursor over the Target color swatch until the eyedropper icon appears, and then hold down the CTRL key. Now move the eyedropper cursor to the seat back to the left of the seat back you've created, and click to sample a color from the top area of the leather back for the target color. Proof this color on the new seat back by clicking the Auto Proof or Proof icon, if you don't have one of them already activated. Once you're satisfied with the color, click OK.

6. Duplicate the Seat Back 1 layer to use for the final seat in the row furthest back, to remove the rest of that pesky boy's head. Name this duplicated layer Seat Back 2.

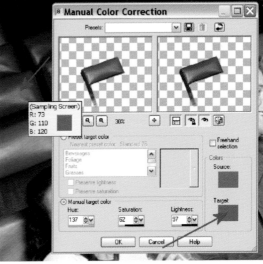

7. Activate the Seat Back 2 layer, deselect any existing selection, and use the Move tool to move the new seat back into position over the boy's head.

8. Lower the Seat Back 2 layer opacity to 70% and activate the Deform tool. Resize and rotate the new seat back into position as you did for the first seat. In the Layer palette, drag Seat Back 2 *beneath* Seat Back 1.

9. Using the Manual Color Correction tool again (Adjust > Color Balance > Manual Color Correction), modify the color of this new seat back using the same process you did for the first seat back. In this case, use the seat to the left of the new seat back as the source color.

If you have any remaining lighter colored pixels around the seat back edges (will that boy *never* leave?), use the Clone Brush to clean up the edges with the same settings you previously used to clone the boy's arm out of the picture.

Adding realism

Well, now the boy's finally gone, but the new seat backs could use a little touch of realism (they are, after all, duplicates of the first empty row). Let's merge the two new seat back layers into one.

1. In the Layer palette, turn off Raster 1's visibility and Copy of Raster 1. Make the Seat Back 1 layer active, right-click it, and choose Merge > Merge Visible.

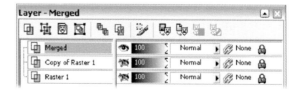

2. Activate the Warp Brush tool. Set Size to 30, make sure the new Merged layer is active, and alternate between the Expand, Contract, and Push modes to add a few bumps and dents to the two new seat backs, so that they don't seem exact copies of the original.

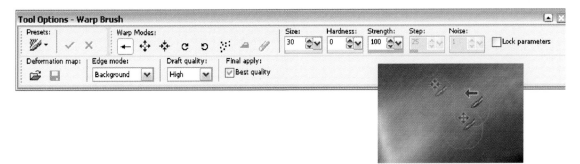

3. Now turn the visibility for Layer 1 back on and you've finally "divorced" that guy right out of the photo. But what if you'd like to add someone? Go to Layers > Merge > Merge Visible and let's move on.

Adding elements to the photo

Sometimes somebody doesn't make it into a favorite photo but, through the magic of Paint Shop Pro, you can make it look like that person attended the event. Our movie-loving kids here hate to go anywhere without the family pet (plus he's a good deterrent should that guy show up again!).

We'd like to let Sparky here go along for the show, but first a little preparation work is required for which the Background Eraser tool is perfect.

1. Open Sparky's image (dobie.tif in the download files). In the Layer palette, promote the background layer to a full layer (Layers > Promote Background Layer).

2. Activate the Background Eraser tool and set the tool options as shown here:

3. Begin erasing around Sparky. Keep the center point of the brush outline away from the edge of the dog, and drag around the perimeter. You may get a better result if you complete a brush stroke, release the mouse, and then begin another brush stroke.

Once you've removed the majority of the background, you can use Remove Specks and Holes to get those remaining background specks.

4. Activate the Magic Wand tool and select the transparent background portion of Sparky's image. Go to Selections > Modify > Remove Specks and Holes. Check Remove Specks and Holes and set the Square area dimensions to 50x100, as shown here.

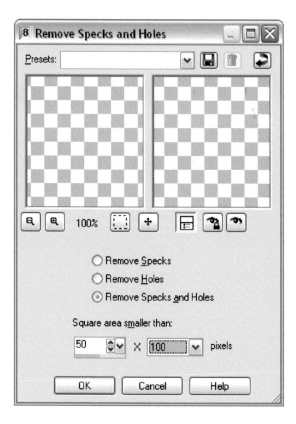

5. Once you've modified the selection and removed the holes, invert the selection (SHIFT+CTRL+I) to select just Sparky. If you find that you still have some background areas selected besides Sparky, grab the regular Eraser tool and erase them. If it's difficult to see these specks on the standard checkerboard background, go to File > Preferences > General Program Preferences and, on the Transparency tab, change the background scheme to a starkly contrasting color.

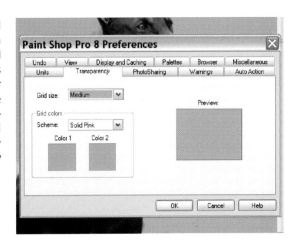

6. Let's move Sparky into the photo. Copy and paste him as a new layer (CTRL+L) into the movie kids image.

Now Sparky is way out of proportion for this photo and his color's all wrong. Decide where you want Sparky to sit at the movies (although he does like to be up front, especially if the movie trailer is *Lassie* or *Rin Tin Tin*). This time you need to maximize the image and zoom out to use the Deform tool (otherwise, you can't see the corner handles to grab them).

7. Zoom down to 50% and maximize the image. Select the Deform tool. Right-click a corner handle of the bounding box and drag inward to resize Sparky. Rotate him slightly so that he's "sitting" in the seat in front of his friends.

Now it's time to adjust Sparky's coloring, as he doesn't quite match the lighting of his new surroundings. Let's warm him up a bit.

8. Go to Adjust > Color > Automatic Color Balance. As Sparky is now indoors in a movie theater with overhead fluorescent lighting, you want to warm him up a bit. Set Illuminant temperature to 5100, set Strength to 30, check Remove color cast, and proof the color change on the photo.

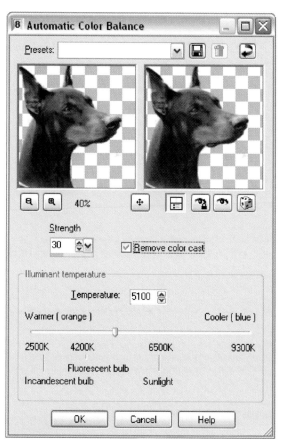

9. Sparky just needs a bit of a shadow now, so go to Effects > 3D Effects > Drop Shadow. Use the shadow behind the girl looking at the camera as a guide to the light source direction. Apply a black shadow with high Blur and Opacity values. Make sure Shadow on new layer is checked.

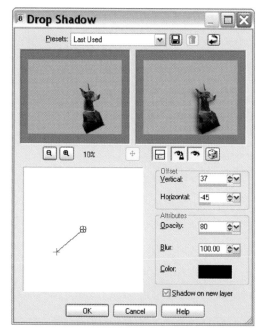

10. On this new layer, you want to remove any shadow that has been created at the top of Sparky's head and his left side. Ensure the newly created Raster 1 Shadow 1 layer is active, grab the Eraser tool, and erase any shadow on those sides of Sparky.

11. Let's tie up all the loose ends. Go to Layers > Merge > Merge All (Flatten).

This merges all the layers and allows you to complete the final step for this image: a shot of the OneStepPhotoFix script.

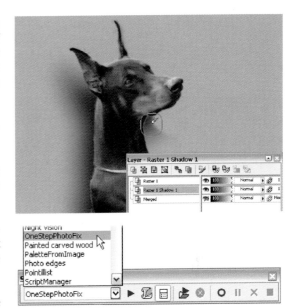

12. Make sure the Script toolbar is visible (View > Toolbars > Script). Click the arrow to the right of the script display box and choose the OneStepPhotoFix script.

13. Click the Run Selected Script icon and let the script balance the color, saturation, and contrast, as well as the sharpness of the photo.

⭐ Hero One

There you have it: one photo inhabitant divorced and another added!

Hero Two

Creating Logos with

Vector Graphics

In this chapter

You've already learned that Paint Shop Pro is a capable vector graphics program, as well as a paint and photo editor. This sets it apart from most consumer computer graphics software on the market today and makes it possible for users to create high-quality, scalable computer illustrations that can be used in a variety of ways. In this chapter we'll cover the following topics:

* ★ Combining vector shapes with text by creating a vector logo

* ★ Using vectors to create and print business cards

* ★ Printing multiple images using the Print Layout utility and templates

* ★ Exporting vector graphics as clip art to use with other applications

Vector graphics were the first type of computer graphics to be widely used by graphic artists and are still the tool of choice for most. Most of the nonphotographic images you see in magazines, newspapers, and books began life as vector illustrations. Although Paint Shop Pro isn't quite as powerful as dedicated vector drawing programs such as Adobe Illustrator and CorelDRAW, you can still create professional vector illustrations using it.

Creating a vector logo

1. Begin by opening a new 700x400 image with a white raster background. Set the foreground/stroke to null and make the background/fill a solid color of your choice. This will be the color for the logo but, because of the nature of vector graphics, you get to change your mind about this at any point along the way.

> *Although transparency is a useful tool, the checkerboard can be distracting. It's often a good idea to start with a white background to give a cleaner view of your work. You can turn off or delete the background at any time during the project.*

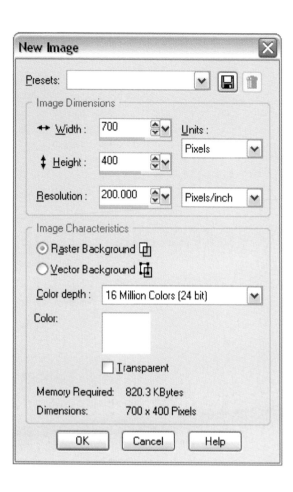

2. Activate the Preset Shape tool, uncheck Retain style so your color of choice will be applied, and check Create as vector and Anti-alias. As you have a null stroke, the Line options don't matter.

3. Select the Ellipse shape from the Shape list and drag out an ellipse approximately 300x150 pixels. An easy way to do this is to keep an eye on the cursor coordinates at the bottom-right of the task bar. Start your drag at about x:200, y:100, and drag downward and to the right to x:500, y:250. Absolute accuracy isn't necessary, so don't be too fiddly about this.

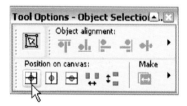

4. After you've laid down the ellipse, switch to the Object Selection tool and click the Center on canvas button in the Position on canvas area of the Tool Options palette.

This may be a good time to make sure you've checked the All tools box in the Materials palette. This ensures that your color choice is maintained, whatever tool you use.

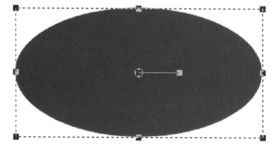

5. Deselect the ellipse by clicking an empty part of the canvas with the Object Selection tool.

6. Activate the Text tool. Because different fonts can require different settings to make this project work, start off using the same font and settings we use and later, once you get the method down, experiment with more personalized choices to exercise your own creativity. In the Create as field, choose Vector; set Size to 32, Stroke width to 0, Font to Arial, and Font Style to bold; and center the alignment. Leave Kerning at 0 and set Leading to –350.

The term "leading" (pronounced ledding) refers to metal lead and comes from the practice of using lead strips of varying widths to separate lines of text in the days of metal type.

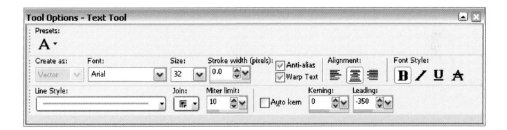

7. Place the cursor over the top center of the ellipse (approximately x:350, y:125). The cursor changes from the regular text cursor to the "rocking A" text on a path cursor. Click the mouse when you're there to bring up the Text Entry dialog box.

8. Type in a few words made up of 10 to 12 characters. The text is centered on the top and follows the path of the ellipse, but it's sunk about halfway down into it because of the leading value you used. If you chose a different font, you may have to adjust the leading value and/or the font size to get the same effect. By highlighting the text in the Text Entry dialog box, you can adjust these settings if needed and the canvas will update to let you know if you have it right. Click Apply in the Text Entry dialog box when you're satisfied.

When you apply the text, it should be selected. If it isn't, activate the Object Selection tool and select it.

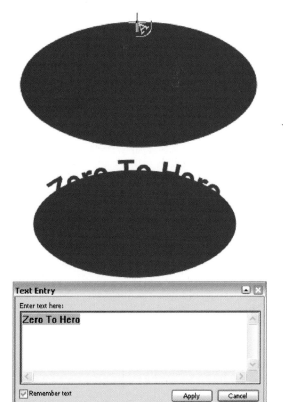

Now you want to make the text a vector path. This will change it to nodes and segments independent of the font file and allow you to combine it with other contours in a single vector object.

9. Go to Objects > Convert Text to Curves > As Single Shape to combine all the characters into one vector object.

10. Now you want to combine your text with the ellipse to create a single object. Ensure the text is still selected and activate the Pen tool in Edit mode. You should now see the text with its nodes.

11. Select all the nodes in the text, either by drag-selecting or choosing Edit > Select All from the right-click context menu. Right-click again and choose Edit > Cut. This copies the nodes to the clipboard and removes them from the canvas.

12. Although there's nothing visible, the object still exists in the Layer palette so, for the sake of neatness, you may want to delete it by expanding the Vector 1 layer, right-clicking the layer containing the text, and selecting Clear.

Now you'll combine the copied text with the ellipse.

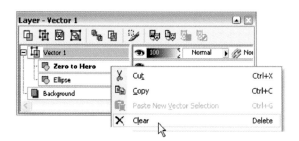

13. Click the ellipse using the Object Selection tool and then activate the Pen tool, again in Edit mode. Right-click the ellipse and choose Edit > Paste. Your text reappears, but this time as part of the same object as the ellipse.

Unfortunately, when you paste nodes into an object in Paint Shop Pro, it offsets them 10 pixels to the right and below the original position, so you have to nudge them back to where they should be. This is easily accomplished by using the arrow keys while holding down the CTRL key. This combination nudges the selected nodes 10 pixels in the direction of the arrow key used.

Nodes Pasted out of Position

14. Press CTRL+up arrow key and CRTL+left arrow key to relocate the text to its original position. (Pressing the arrow keys *without* holding down the CTRL key will nudge the selected node by 1 pixel at a time.)

Though that's all fine and dandy, it doesn't appear to be any different from what you had a couple of steps ago. You may recall from Chapter Five that when contours going in opposite directions overlap, the overlapping fill area is canceled out. As you can see, the overlapping area in your object isn't canceled out, so the ellipse contour must be going in the same direction as all the text contours.

15. To remedy this, simply select any node in the ellipse contour, right-click, and choose Edit > Reverse Contour. Deselect the ellipse and now your overlapping text area is canceled out.

Adding extra detail

Perhaps you now want to add some more text to your logo, such as a company name and address.

1. Go back to the Text tool and change the font size to 12 and Leading back to 0. In the Materials palette, change the fill color to something that will contrast against the ellipse color. While holding down the ALT key to prevent text on a path, click somewhere just above and left of center and enter two or three lines of text. Go to the Object Selection tool and move the text to a better position if necessary.

2. With the text selected, right-click and choose Convert Text to Curves > As Single Shape.

3. With the Pen tool selected, right-click and choose Edit > Select All.

4. Now right-click the text and choose Edit > Cut.

5. Use the Object Selection tool to select the ellipse.

6. With the Pen tool, right-click and choose Edit > Paste.

7. Use CTRL+up arrow key and CTRL+left arrow key to nudge it back into position.

You have some empty space over on the lower-right side that you can add a graphic to.

8. Activate the Preset Shape tool and select a suitable single object shape. These are all black in Paint Shop Pro—the multicolor shapes are made up of object groups and aren't suitable for this procedure.

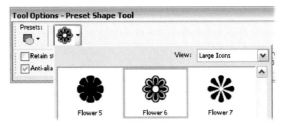

Single Object Shapes

9. Choose a suitable shape and lay it down where you want it. You'll have to start the drag outside the ellipse, as the Preset Shape tool won't start an object inside another. If you can't locate it just where you want it, switch to the Object Selection tool and move it as needed.

Now you need to go through the cut, copy, and paste procedure again. It may or may not be necessary to reverse the contour depending on the shape you used. When you paste the nodes into the ellipse, if it's already cut out, don't reverse the contour. As a reminder, here's the process again:

★ Select the shape with the Object Selection tool.

★ Activate the Pen tool. Right-click the shape and choose Edit > Select All.

★ Right-click again and choose Edit > Cut.

★ Select the ellipse with the Object Selection tool.

★ Activate the Pen tool, right-click, and choose Edit > Paste.

★ Nudge the shape back with the CTRL+up and left arrow keys.

★ Reverse the contour if necessary.

10. Finally, you can add some additional text, such as a name and a web page URL.

With a little imagination, but not necessarily any great drawing ability, you can use these methods combined with the Pen tool to come up with all sorts of imaginative vector graphics:

Printing with templates

So, after you've made all these interesting vector shapes, you're probably wondering what to do with them. Vector graphics are great for print projects. They can be scaled without loss of quality, so a single graphic can be put to a variety of uses in print. If you've ever used clip art in a newsletter or poster, chances are it was vector.

Let's take the vector logo, use it as a business card, and print it right here in Paint Shop Pro.

1. Select the logo and added text with the Object Selection tool, right-click, and select Group.

2. Right-click and drag (to maintain the aspect ratio) one of the corner handles, so the object completely fills up the workspace. Once it's resized, click the Center on canvas button in the Position on canvas area of the Object Selection tool options.

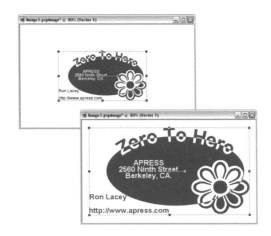

We started with a 700x400 image for a reason: Avery and other companies make perforated business card stock at 2 x 3 1/2 inches, which is the size of our graphic at 200 ppi. This stock includes Avery product numbers 8371, 8372, 8374, 8379, and 8376, among other specialty stock, and Paint Shop Pro has print templates for many Avery products, including the business card stock.

3. Go to File > Print Layout to open the Print Layout utility. There's a blank white representation of your print paper in the work area and any open images on the left sidebar. If you want, you can drag any open image from the sidebar to the blank paper and drop it in position. You can also drag and drop any number of the same image.

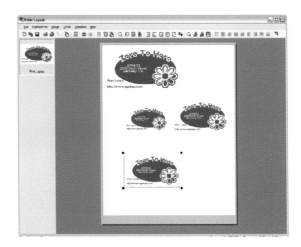

Any image you drag over will be selected, as indicated by the bounding box, and dragging any corner in or out will resize the image while maintaining the aspect ratio. Pressing the DELETE key or right-clicking within a bounding box and choosing Remove from the context menu removes a selected image. The context menu also gives you zoom options and allows you to rotate, remove, and position the selected image on the page.

4. Because your logo is already the correct size, you can call up the print layout template for the Avery business card stock. Go to File > Open Template to see the Templates palette.

5. Highlight Avery in the category field and locate template 8374 in the preview pane. Double-click the preview thumb to load the template onto the workspace.

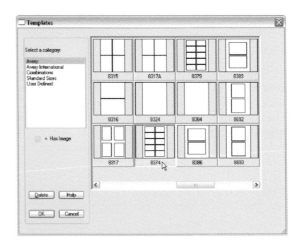

6. You can now drag your image from the sidebar into a cell on the template. In our case, the image will fit the cell exactly but, if the image were larger than the cell, only the portion within the cell would appear or be printed. In cases where the image is larger or smaller than a given cell, you can use the Cell Placement options from the context menu to locate it within the cell. The Cell Placement menu replaces the Image Placement menu when you use a template rather than a blank page.

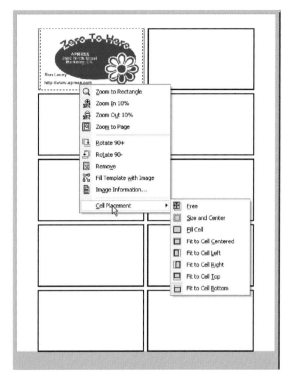

7. You can drag the image from the sidebar to each individual cell, or you can fill all cells in one fell swoop by right-clicking in a cell and choosing Fill Template with Image.

8. Once done, you can check your printer options with File > Print Setup and then use File > Print to commit your creation to paper.

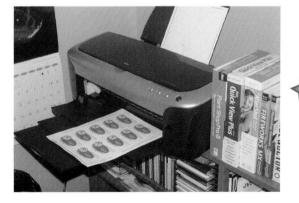

If you don't want to print right away or you think you may need to make more copies at some time in the future, you can save the template compete with images.

9. Choose File > Save Template to bring up the Save dialog box, where you're prompted to give the template a name. To save the images with the template, simply check the Save with images box.

10. When you want to reload the template, you'll find it listed in the Select a category area of the Templates dialog box, filed under User Defined. Templates with cells containing images have those cells highlighted in cyan in the Templates dialog box. You can also remove templates from this dialog box by clicking them and pressing DELETE.

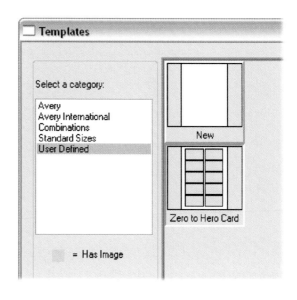

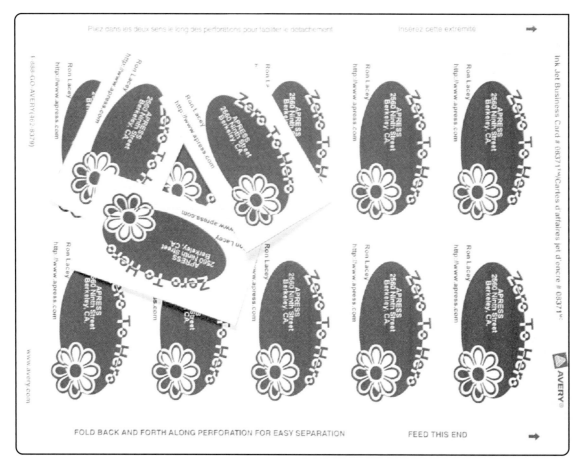

Exporting vectors as clip art

If you've ever produced a newsletter, poster, or birthday card using desktop publishing software such as MS Publisher, or if you've ever composed a letter in your word processor using clip art, it's likely that the graphics you imported were vector clip art. Most clip art collections sold are made of vector graphics, usually in Windows Metafile Format (.wmf) or Extended Metafile Format (.emf). The reason for this is the **scalability** of vector graphics. Because this art is often used for enhancing printed documents, the creators have no idea how big an image the user will need: a tiny postage stamp–sized image to use in a letterhead or a large graphic for a banner or poster?

Because neither the .emf nor the .wmf file format supports gradients, patterns, or textures, it's best to use solid color objects for exporting. Anything else can yield unexpected results.

You can export your vector art to .wmf or .emf format in Paint Shop Pro from the Save or Save As dialog box. If your publishing software supports .emf, this is the preferred format.

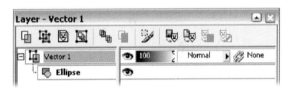

1. Crop your image tight to the drawing and delete any raster layer, including the background layer if you have one.

2. Go to File > Save As and choose the appropriate format (either .emf or .wmf).

3. Click the Options button in the Save As dialog box and select Save bitmap and vector data (after you set this option once, the save options will default to it whenever you save to this format again).

4. Choose a file name and a location to save the file to.

Now you can use your favorite desktop publisher to create personalized newsletters and other print projects.

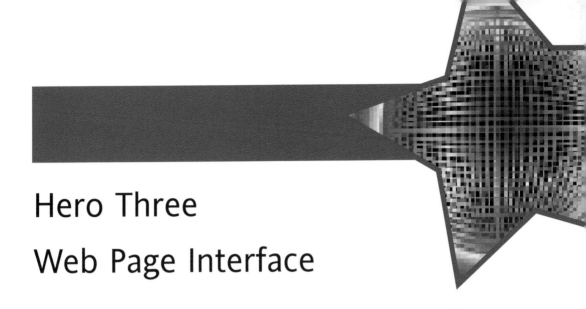

Hero Three

Web Page Interface

In this chapter

We're going to use Paint Shop Pro to create graphics for a typical home web page. Specifically, we'll create web navigation elements using vector tools and the Effects menu to produce a high-tech look, which we'll then optimize and export using the web graphic tools. In this chapter we cover the following topics:

- ★ Designing a banner

- ★ Creating reusable buttons from templates

- ★ Using the Image Slicer

- ★ Creating rollovers

Creating editable buttons

One thing you're going to need on your web page is link buttons and, at some point down the road, you'll want to add pages to your web site, so you'll need to add or change link buttons. Using vector text and presets, you can re-create the same buttons and editable text for future expansion.

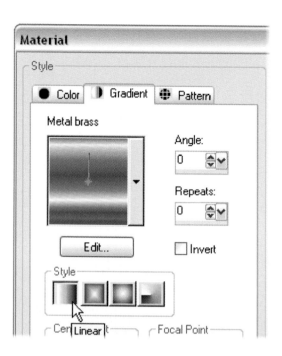

1. Open a new 600x600 image on a black raster background. Check All tools in the Materials palette, set the foreground to null, and set the background to gradient. Choose Metal brass in the Material Picker. Make it a Linear style and make sure Angle and Repeats are both set to 0.

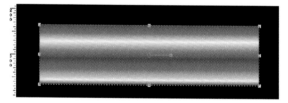

2. Use the Preset Shape tool and, in the tool options, uncheck Retain style and ensure Create as vector and Anti-alias are checked. Lay down a 400x100 rectangle.

3. In keeping with the industrial look you're going for, you'll add some rivets to the button. Return to the Preset Shape tool, select Button 027 from the shape list, and check Retain style. Lay down a 15x15 shape on an empty area of the canvas.

4. Copy the object, paste it as a new vector selection (CTRL+G), and drop the copy just inside one of the corners of the rectangle. Paste two more times so you have four shapes, and place one inside each corner.

5. Select the two upper rivets with the Object Selection tool and go to Objects > Align > Vertical Center.

6. Repeat this process with the two lower rivets.

7. Select the two left rivets and go to Objects > Align > Horizontal Center. **Repeat** this process for the two rivets on the right.

8. Now it's time to add a text label. Deselect all objects (CTRL+D), set the foreground to null, and set the background to solid black in the Materials palette. Activate the Text tool and set the following tool options:

- ★ Create as: Vector
- ★ Font: Arial
- ★ Size: 24
- ★ Stroke: 0
- ★ Alignment: Centered

9. While holding down the ALT key to prevent text on a path, click at the horizontal center of the rectangle about one-third up from the bottom, and type in a text label. Choose a label that's likely to be the longest text entry you expect to make for any button on your web page. If you find that your text is too long, decrease the font size or extend the rectangle. (If you do the latter, you'll have to reposition the rivets.) Center your text on the button using Objects > Align.

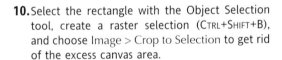

10. Select the rectangle with the Object Selection tool, create a raster selection (CTRL+SHIFT+B), and choose Image > Crop to Selection to get rid of the excess canvas area.

11. Resize the image so that it's more of a typical button size. (We've made it 160 pixels wide and locked the aspect ratio to give 42 pixels in height.)

12. Now save your image as Button template.PspImage so that you can use it as a template for more buttons later. Save this file to a new folder in your My PSP8 Files folder. This will be a vector template for all your web buttons; therefore, you can resize and edit it in the future for updating your web page with new links.

251

Adding extra effects to the button

Now you'll add some raster effects to the button.

1. Select the rectangle with the Object Selection tool and go to Selections > From Vector Object. Now choose Selections > Float to move the selection off the vector layer and make it available for raster effects.

2. Select Effects > 3D Effects > Inner Bevel. Here you may want to experiment with your own settings (ours are shown here). Once you've decided on your bevel settings, click the floppy disk icon to save them as a preset and name it Web Button. This will make the same bevel available for when you make extra buttons. Apply the bevel settings.

3. Finally, go to Layers > Merge > Merge All (Flatten). This turns your image into a background layer. Save the completed button as a .PspImage file in your My PSP8 Files > My Webpage Files folder. We've saved ours as Button Rons Homepage.PspImage. Prefacing the file name with Button makes it easier to organize your My Webpage Files folder.

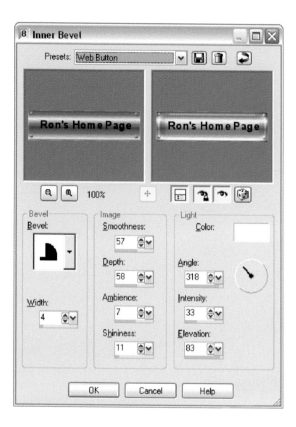

Creating buttons from the template

Now you need some more buttons to add to the home page button you've already made.

1. Open the Button template.PspImage file you saved earlier and use Window > Duplicate to open another copy of the button template. Duplicate this template to create the total number of buttons you need for your planned web page.

2. On one of the new duplicated buttons, expand the vector layer and double-click the text object to bring up the Text Entry palette.

3. Add a new button label to the button.

4. Select the rectangle with the Object Selection tool.

5. At this point you'll record a script to speed things up. In the Script toolbar, click the Start Script Recording button and work through the following steps:

   ★ Press CTRL+SHIFT+B to make a raster selection from the vector object, and then use CTRL+SHIFT+F to float it.

   ★ Select Effects > 3D Effects > Inner Bevel and apply the Web Button preset you made earlier.

   ★ Select Layers > Merge > Merge All (Flatten).

   ★ Click the Save Script Recording button on the Script toolbar and call it Web button script.

   ★ Save the button in your web page files folder using the button naming convention.

6. Now apply a new text label to the next button, select the rectangle, and run the Web button script. Repeat this process for each button you need, saving each one to the My Webpage Files folder.

Designing a banner

Now you'll create an element for a web page banner.

1. Open a new 760x470 image with a black raster background. In the Materials palette, set the background to null and make sure you still have the Metal brass gradient selected for the background. Select a sunburst style and enter 3 in the Repeats field. Make sure the gradient is centered by entering 50 in both Center Point fields.

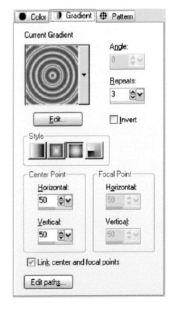

2. With the Preset Shape tool set to Ellipse, Retain style unchecked, and a line width of 20, lay down an ellipse that's 125 pixels in diameter (let the height and width info in the Overview palette guide you) by SHIFT+dragging. This gives you a 3D-looking doughnut.

3. Set that aside by dragging it over to the upper-left corner of the canvas.

4. Click the foreground swatch, set the gradient to Linear, and enter 0 in the Angle and Repeats fields. In the Preset Shape tool options, set the line width back to 1.00.

5. SHIFT+drag an ellipse out that's 105 pixels in diameter.

6. Now you want to make 14 copies of the ellipse to make a total of 15 identical ellipses. Making sure the ellipse is still selected, use CTRL+C to copy and CTRL+G to paste as a vector selection, dropping the copy beside the original. Keep pressing CTRL+G until you have three rows, each containing five ellipses, as shown here:

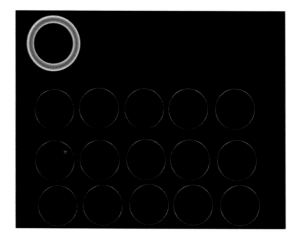

7. Select the second circle on the top row, switch to the Pen tool, and choose Edit > Select All from the right-click context menu.

8. In the Pen tool options, choose Edit mode and select Contract from the Transformation Type drop-down menu.

9. Enter a value of 7.00 in the X field and 0.00 in the Y field. Click the Apply icon.

10. Select the next circle and repeat steps 7 through 9, but this time enter a value of 14.00 in the X field.

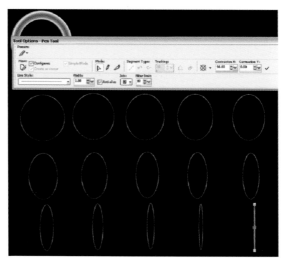

11. Perform these steps for each circle in turn, increasing the X value by 7 each time until you get to the last one, where the value will be 98.00.

12. Now go back to the Object Selection tool, select all 15 ellipses, and click the Center on canvas button in the tool options. With all the objects still selected, copy them and paste as a vector selection (Ctrl+G). Drop the new vector beside the original.

13. Shift+drag the rotate handle by 90°, using the Overview palette as a guide.

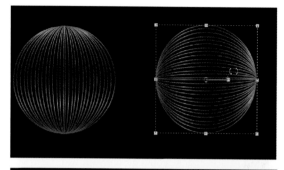

14. Drag-select both the original and the rotated copy, and click the Center on canvas button again.

15. Right-click the object and select Group.

16. Copy the object and use Ctrl+G to paste it as a vector selection. Drop it beside the original.

17. Select the doughnut shape you made earlier and Shift+select the original object group.

18. Click the Center on canvas button in the tool options.

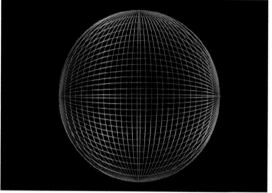

19. Right-click and select Group again.

20. If you expand the vector layer in the Layer palette, you should have Group 1 and Group 2. Right-click each one in turn, renaming Group 1 as Design 1 and Group 2 as Design 2.

Now you're going to export these as preset shapes to make them available for any project.

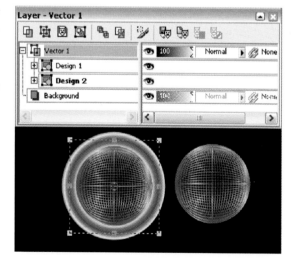

21. Press CTRL+D to deselect everything. Go to File > Export > Shape and give the preset shape file an appropriate name.

These shapes now appear in the Preset Shape tool options, listed by their group names.

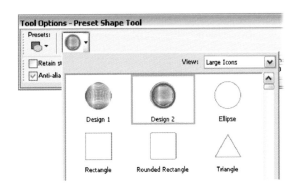

Banner text

Because over 50% of computers use a screen resolution of 800x600, you'll design your web page so that it fits on a maximized browser on this amount of screen real estate.

1. Taking menus, toolbars, and scrollbars into account, a size of 760x470 is appropriate, so open a new image on a black raster background. This will be the base for your web page.

2. Make the foreground null and use the Metal brass gradient for the background, with a Linear style, and Angle and Repeats set to 0 in the Material Picker.

3. Select the Preset Shape tool and choose the Rectangle shape. Check Create as vector, uncheck Retain style, and lay down a rectangle approximately 450x65 close to the top of the canvas. Use the Overview palette as a guide (but absolute accuracy isn't necessary).

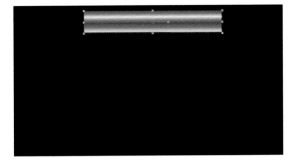

4. Activate the Text tool, change the foreground to null, and make the background solid black. Set the Text tool options as follows:

   ★ Create as: Vector
   ★ Font: Arial Black
   ★ Stroke: 0
   ★ Alignment: Center

5. Holding down the ALT key to prevent text on a path, click at the horizontal center of the rectangle about a quarter of the way up from the bottom.

6. Enter the title text for your web page. If it doesn't fit, reduce the font size.

Now you'll cut the text out of the rectangle.

7. With the text selected, go to Objects > Convert Text to Curves > As Single Shape.

8. Switch to the Pen tool, right-click, and choose Edit > Reverse Path. Now right-click and choose Edit > Select All. Finally, right-click and choose Edit > Cut.

9. Select the rectangle with the Object Selection tool. Return to the Pen tool, right-click, and choose Edit > Paste.

10. Press CTRL+up arrow and CTRL+left arrow to nudge the text back to its original location.

Your banner won't look any different, but now the text is part of the banner as letter-shaped holes in the rectangle. The reason for this will become apparent soon.

Navigation back panel

Now you're going to lay down a back panel for your link buttons.

1. Set the background to the Metal brass gradient (it should return to the same gradient you used for the banner rectangle). Select the Preset Shape tool with the same previous settings as the banner and lay down a shape approximately 50x350 at the left side of the canvas.

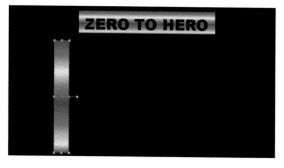

☆ Hero Three

Now you'll apply an inner bevel to both the banner and the back panel.

2. Select both the banner and the back panel rectangles with the Object Selection tool.

3. Go to Selections > From Vector Object.

4. Float the selection with Selections > Float.

5. Go to Effects > 3D Effects > Inner Bevel.

6. You may want to experiment here with bevel settings. Once you've decided on the settings, save them as a preset called Web banner. You can use this along with your button preset to give a consistent look to other pages or elements of pages on your web site. Apply the bevel.

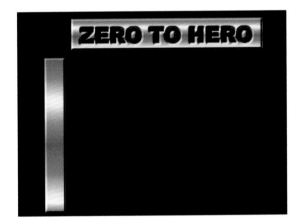

The bevel is the reason you applied the cutout text to the banner rectangle earlier. This way, the text is beveled along with the rectangle shape itself.

Now you'll add the design element shapes you created earlier.

7. Use CTRL+D to deselect. This defloats the selection and promotes it to a layer. In the Layer palette, make sure the Promoted Selection layer is active and click the New Vector Layer icon.

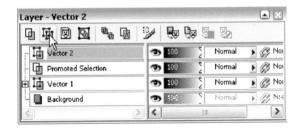

8. Activate the Preset Shape tool and check Retain style. Select the Design 2 shape you made and SHIFT+drag a shape approximately 100 pixels in diameter. Lay it down anywhere on the canvas, and then drag it to slightly overlap the left side of the banner and the top of the back panel.

9. Copy it while it's selected, paste it as a new vector selection (CTRL+G), and drop it overlapping the right side of the banner.

10. Now you'll add the link buttons you made. Open all the button files you made earlier.

11. Use the View menu to turn on Rulers, Guides & Snap to Guides. Drag out a guide so that it just touches the left edge of the Design 2 shape.

12. Copy your first button image and paste it as a new layer (CTRL+L) in the main web page image. Use the Move tool to place the button near the top of the button back panel. When it gets close to the guide it will snap to it. Repeat this with each button, arranging them so that they're equally spaced vertically.

13. Finally, you'll add your other design element. Activate the Preset Shape tool, check Retain style, and choose the Design 1 shape you made. SHIFT+drag out a (approximately) 320-pixel-wide shape and position it in the empty area of the canvas.

14. Save this image to your My Webpage Files folder as webpage.PspImage.

You can use it in the future to make changes and updates to your site using the button templates and presets. As the elements are vectors and layers, you can make selective non-destructive changes by turning off the visibility of specific vector objects and raster layers. If you decide you no longer need a Photography link, you could open the file, turn off the Photography button layer, and re-export it in the Image Slicer. We'll get to that in a minute, but first let's make some rollover buttons.

Rollover buttons

1. Open the `Button template.PspImage` file you made earlier. In the Layer palette, expand the vector layer and double-click the text layer to bring up the Text Entry dialog box. Delete the text and type in Activate.

2. Highlight the text and change the background in the Materials palette to green.

3. Select the rectangle with the Object Selection tool. Now go to the Script toolbar, select the Web button script you made earlier, and run it.

4. Use File > Export > GIF Optimizer to save the button:

★ Under the Transparency tab check None.

★ Under the Colors tab use 256 colors, 100 dithering, and Optimized Octree.

5. Click OK, and when the Save As dialog box comes up, create a new folder off the My PSP Files folder called Webpage to save the file to. You'll use this folder for all the web page files you'll make and upload to the server. Name the file `mouseover.gif`.

6. Close the Button Template file but **don't** save it when prompted.

Building the web page

Now you'll slice the main web page image up so you can apply links and mouse over states to the individual buttons and export it as a web page.

1. Open your main `webpage.PspImage` file and open the Image Slicer (File > Export > Image Slicer). Zoom in very close to the buttons (you can also maximize the Slicer window). Because you'll use a prebuilt mouse over image, you want to be quite accurate when making your slices. Select the Knife tool.

Because you used a guide to line up your buttons vertically, you can make a vertical slice on either side of them and it will match all the buttons.

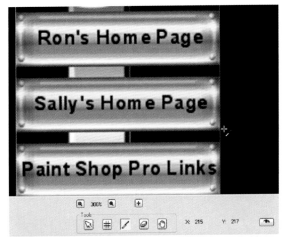

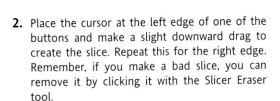

2. Place the cursor at the left edge of one of the buttons and make a slight downward drag to create the slice. Repeat this for the right edge. Remember, if you make a bad slice, you can remove it by clicking it with the Slicer Eraser tool.

3. While the Knife tool is active, you can place the cursor over a slice and drag it. Make horizontal slices at the top and bottom edge of each button by locating the cursor on the edge and making a slight horizontal drag. Once you've done this, each button should be in its own cell.

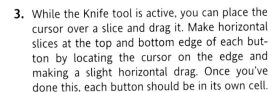

4. Using the Arrow tool, click the first button cell to select it. The slice lines around that cell turn green unless you've changed the Image Slicer preference to another color. Once a particular cell is selected, you can enter the Cell Properties for it. Select each button cell in turn and enter the properties you want.

After you've linked the buttons, you can add the rollovers.

5. Select the first button cell and click the Rollover Creator button. Check the Mouse over box and then click the folder icon to the right to bring up a standard Windows file selector dialog box. Navigate to where you saved the mouseover.gif file and click Open to insert the file into the Mouse over field.

6. Now check the Mouse out box, but don't enter a file in this one—leaving it blank will cause the original button image to appear in the cell once the mouse moves off it. Do the same for each of the remaining button cells. If you want, you can use your button template file to create buttons for all the states available in the Rollover Creator. Click OK when you've finished setting the rollover states.

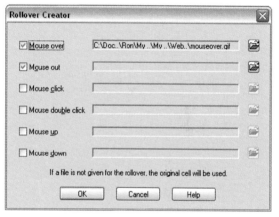

7. This web page contains graphics that will work well as GIFs, so in the Format field choose GIF and check Apply optimization to whole image.

8. Click the Optimize Cell button to bring up the GIF Optimizer. Apply the same settings you did when you saved the mouse over button and click OK.

9. At this point, you might want to save your settings for future editing in the Image Slicer. Click the Save Settings button, navigate to your My Webpage Files folder and give the .jsd file a name. In the future, you can modify webpage.PspImage and load the same slices and links in the Image Slicer. You do this by clicking Load Settings and opening the .jsd file you just saved.

You can preview your web page by clicking the eye icon to make sure everything is working. Once you're happy with it, it's time to export the web page.

10. Click the Save As button in the Image Slicer, navigate to the Webpage folder you saved mouseover.gif to, and give the file a name. If the page is to be the main page on the server, name it index.html.

11. Navigate to the folder where you saved the HTML file and open the file in a browser.

If your computer has a screen resolution greater than 800x600 pixels, there's a lot of screen space that's not black. It may be white, gray, or anything in between, depending on your browser settings. If you're handy with an HTML editor, you can fix this by editing the web page. If not, you can make changes using Notepad.

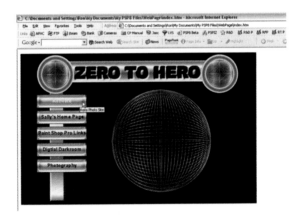

12. Open the HTML file in Notepad and, at the top of the file between the <TITLE> and </HEAD> tags, enter <body bgcolor="#000000"> and save the file. You can also use Notepad to give the page a title. Just enter the text you would like to display as your title between the <TITLE> and </TITLE> tags.

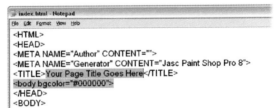

There's a small bug (present in v8.00 and 8.01) in the Slicer that may or may not have been fixed by the time you read this. It creates an image file called blank.gif, which is used as a spacer. It really should be transparent but is actually white. This works fine as long as you leave the HTML page background white, but as you changed the background color, the white spacer might show up at the edge of the table.

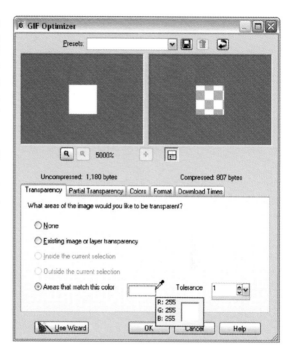

13. You can fix this by opening blank.gif in Paint Shop Pro (you'll find it in the folder in which you saved your image-sliced HTML file). The image is very small (1 pixel square), so you'll need to zoom way in to see it.

14. Once you've loaded the image, open the GIF Optimizer and, under the Transparency tab, check Areas that match this color. Click in the swatch and select white from the palette.

15. Click OK and save your file back to the Webpage folder, giving it the same name, blank.gif, and allowing it to overwrite the original.

Paint Shop Pro 8:

Resources on the Web

Here are some of our favorite web sites and companies offering useful additions to Paint Shop Pro. Also, check www.friendsofed.com for additional resources and future additions to this appendix.

⭐ Appendix

Web sites

www.lvsonline.com
LVS Online is the premier online resource for Paint Shop Pro classes for all skill levels, as well as many other software applications. Ron and Sally teach several classes there, focusing on Paint Shop Pro, digital photography and digital darkroom skills, and Photoshop-compatible plug-in filters. Peggy Taranenko, technical reviewer for *Paint Shop Pro 8 Zero to Hero*, teaches basic-level Paint Shop Pro classes there too.

www.campratty.com
The definitive source for Frequently Asked Questions on Paint Shop Pro.

www.psplinks.com
Comprehensive tutorials listing maintained by Angela Cable, technical reviewer of this book. At the time of this writing, the site has over 10,000 links on all versions of Paint Shop Pro, including Paint Shop Pro 8, and a search facility.

www.digitalartresources.com/PSP/ArtResources.htm
Great tutorials and resources site. You'll also find some of Tracy's resources on this book's download site.

www.freetubes.com
The place for Picture Tubes.

www.dizteq.com
Sally Beacham's site, featuring Paint Shop Pro and plug-in filter resources.

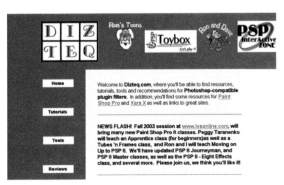

www.state-of-entropy.com
Excellent tutorials for various versions of Paint Shop Pro.

www.ronsfotos.com
Ron Lacey's site for digital photography, photo tutorials for Paint Shop Pro, and Paint Shop Pro links. Includes a photo gallery.

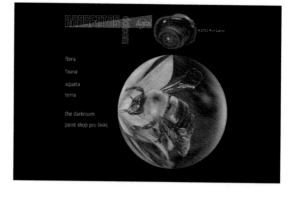

www.loriweb.pair.com/howto.html
One of our favorite sites. See Lori's User Defined Filters tutorials.

www.psptoybox.com
Great site for the Paint Shop Pro novice.

www.home.earthlink.net/~jkabala/tutindex.html
Comprehensive intermediate and advanced tutorials and resources. Find some of site owner JP Kabala's resources on our download page.

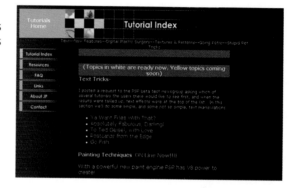

Discussion forums

http://forums.jasc.com
User forums on the Jasc Software site.

www.pspiz.net
The Paint Shop Pro Interactive Zone features tutorials, resources, and forums.

◢ Appendix

Plug-in filters and resources

www.freephotoshop.com
Links for and reviews of hundreds of commercial and
freeware plug-ins.

www.thepluginsite.com
High-quality plug-in filters, including ColorWasher
and HyperTyle, as well as other resources.

http://photoshop.msk.ru
Home of the AmphiSoft filters.

www.namesuppressed.com/design
Good, inexpensive plug-ins.

www.alienskin.com
Versatile commercial plug-ins, excellent interfaces.

www.andromeda.com
Outstanding plug-ins, primarily photographic
enhancement.

www.autofx.com
Commercial plug-ins with superb effects.

www.avbros.com
Puzzle Pro and Page Curl Pro plug-ins.

www.hemera.com
Excellent clip art and royalty-free photo stock.

Index

The index is arranged hierarchically, in alphabetical order, with symbols preceding the letter A. Many second-level entries also occur as first-level entries. This is to ensure that you will find the information you require however you choose to search for it.

friends of ED particularly welcomes feedback on the layout and structure of this index. If you have any comments or criticisms, please contact: feedback@friendsofed.com

Symbols and Numbers

+ (plus sign), meaning of, 31, 64
- (minus sign), meaning of, 32, 64
> (greater than) mark, meaning of, 2
0 to 255 values for histograms, explanation of, 93–95
3D effects
Bevel effects, 116–117
Buttonize effect, 118
Chisel effect, 118–119
Drop Shadow effect, 113–115
overview of, 112
3D gold tube, example of, 162
4x5-inch photos, scanning, 85
8x10 prints, creating with scanners, 85
16.7 Million Colors (24 Bit) image type, selecting with PNG Optimizer, 191
24-bit mode, using filters in, 110
35mm negatives and slides, scanning, 85

A

Add Borders dialog box, displaying for use with masks, 80
Add Mask From Image dialog box, displaying, 81
Add mode, applying with Selection tool, 31–32
adjustment layers
as 8-bit grayscale layers, 99
benefits of, 99
and brightness/contrast, 98
and color balance, 96–97
editing, 99–102
and hue/saturation/lightness, 99
muting effect of, 102
using, 96
Airbrush tool
filling text with, 53–54
painting with, 23–25
aliasing, relationship to selections, 28.
See also anti-aliasing
Alignment icons, using with text, 50
Alpha channel transparency, selecting with PNG Optimizer, 192

alpha channels, saving selections to, 225
Ambience Maximum and Minimum, setting for Balls and Bubbles effect, 129
Ambience settings, using with Bevel effects, 117
AmphiSoft filters web address, 270
angles, changing for patterns, 15
Animal zebra pattern, using with layer blend modes, 68–76
animated tubes, 172
Anti-alias option, using, 137
anti-aliasing. *See also* aliasing
and GIF Optimizer, 188
relationship to selections, 28
using with Drop Shadow effect, 113
areas, defining in Image Mapper, 202
Arrow tool in Image Slicer, using with web pages, 263
Art Media effects
Black Pencil effect, 123
Brush Strokes effect, 120–122
Colored Pencil effect, 123–126
Kaleidoscope and Pencil effects, 124–126
artifacts, 182
artistic effects, creating Balls and Bubbles, 126–130
As Character Shapes option, using with vectors, 145
As Single Shape option, using with vectors, 145
aspect ratio of shapes, preserving, 137, 154, 170, 174
Asymmetric nodes, using with vectors, 147
Auto Action tab, setting preferences for, 220
Auto Human Eye option, removing red-eye with, 103
Auto Proof icon in Effects dialog box, purpose of, 111
automatic color balance, applying to photographs, 86–87
Automatic multiple balls or bubbles option, using, 127
Average size option, setting for Balls and Bubbles effect, 130
Avery business card stocks, sizes of, 244

J

Jasc Software site user forums, web address for, 269
JMD files, saving, 203
JPEG (Joint Photographic Expert Group) format, 182
JPEG Optimizer, exporting web graphics with, 183–186
.jpg files
  advisory about use with layers, 64
  explanation of, 182
JSD format, saving images in, 197, 200

K

Kaleidoscope and Pencil effects, 124–126, 210
Keep transparent option, using with picture frames, 173
Kelvin scale, 86
kerning, 48
Knife tool
  of Drawing mode, 157
  in Image Slicer, 262

L

labels, adding to buttons, 251
Lacey, Ron photography web site, 269
Layer Blend Mode menu, opening, 71
layer groups
  collapsing structure of, 64
  deleting, 64
  working with, 62–64
Layer palette
  displaying, 58, 224
  using with moviefriends.tif example, 224
layer visibility, toggling on and off, 61
layers
  activating, 59, 68, 76
  adding, 58–60, 65
  adding to groups, 63
  adjusting opacity for, 60–61
  advisory about file-format support for, 64
  basics of, 58–62
  blend modes used with, 68–76
  defloating selections in, 59–60
  displaying thumbnails of, 65
  duplicating, 224
  merging, 69, 71, 76
  merging in moviefriends.tif example, 230–231, 235
  moving, 63
  pasting images as, 72
  preserving colors on, 75
  removing shadows from, 235
  turning off, 63
  using with picture tubes, 166
  viewing contents of, 65
  working with, 64–70
Layers palette, location of, 4
leading
  explanation of, 49
  using with vector logos, 239
Learning Center palette, overview of, 4, 215
Legacy notation in blend modes, explanation of, 73
light sources, positioning for Balls and Bubbles effect, 129
Lighten/Darken tool, identifying, 8
Lighten layer blend mode, effect of, 72–73
lightness histogram, use of, 93–94
Lightness setting, using with Brush Strokes effect, 121
lily.jpg file, using Smart Edge mode with, 38–39
Line Before and Line After nodes, using with vectors, 148
Line Segment option in Drawing mode of Pen tool, 156
linear gradients, 12
lines of text, adjusting vertical spacing between, 49
links
  applying to cells using Image Slicer, 195–196
  assigning with Image Mapper, 201–203
  creating for navigation back panel, 257–260**